THE BELIEVING SCIENTIST

The Believing Scientist

Essays on Science and Religion

Stephen M. Barr

WILLIAM B. EERDMANS PUBLISHING COMPANY
GRAND RAPIDS, MICHIGAN

Wm. B. Eerdmans Publishing Co.
Grand Rapids, Michigan
www.eerdmans.com

2018-11

ISBN 978-0-8028-7370-5

Library of Congress Cataloging-in-Publication Data

Names: Barr, Stephen M., 1953- author.Title: The believing scientist :
    essays on science and religion / Stephen M. Barr.
Description: Grand Rapids : Eerdmans Publishing Co., 2016. | Includes
    bibliographical references.
Identifiers: LCCN 2016033602 | ISBN 9780802873705 (pbk. : alk. paper)
Subjects: LCSH: Religion and science.
Classification: LCC BL240.3 .B376 2016 | DDC 201/.65—dc23
    LC record available at https://lccn.loc.gov/2016033602

CONTENTS

SCIENCE VERSUS RELIGION?

RETELLING THE STORY OF SCIENCE

We often hear of a conflict between religion and science. Is there one? Certainly, some religious beliefs are scientifically untenable: for example, that the world is six thousand years old. However, for Jews and Christians not committed to a narrowly literalistic interpretation of Scripture, that kind of direct and clear-cut contradiction between scientific facts and religious doctrines does not exist.

What many take to be a conflict between religion and science is really something else. It is a conflict between religion and materialism. Materialism regards itself as scientific, and indeed is often called "scientific materialism," even by its opponents, but it has no legitimate claim to be part of science. It is, rather, a school of philosophy, one defined by the belief that nothing exists except matter, or, as Democritus put it, "atoms and the void."

However, there is more to materialism than this cold ontological negation. For many, scientific materialism is not a bloodless philosophy but a passionately held ideology. Indeed, it is the ideology of a great part of the scientific world. Its adherents see science as having a mission that goes beyond the mere investigation of nature or the discovery of physical laws. That mission is to free mankind from superstition in all its forms, and especially in the form of religious belief.

There are two grounds for the materialist's indictment of religion as superstition. First, religion is supernaturalist. It teaches that there is a spiritual realm, and supposedly embraces mythological explanations and magical practices. Second, religion is (in the materialist's eyes) irrationalist, because it is based on dogma, faith, and mystery. Science, being based on the natural and the rational, is therefore held to be fundamentally opposed to religion.

In other words, the scientific materialist maintains that there is a conflict between science and religion, and that it is intrinsic and *a priori*, in the sense that it would exist even if science had not yet made any definite discoveries about the world. This supposed opposition flows from what science and religion are in themselves, from their basic views of reality. However, the materialist claims more than this. He also says that many of the particular discoveries of science have demolished the credibility of religion. He claims, in other words, that there is also an *a posteriori* conflict between science and religion. This claim is based on a tendentious reading of scientific history, what I shall call the materialist's "Story of Science." According to this story, the great discoveries since the time of Copernicus and Galileo have disclosed a world that looks ever less like the picture religion painted of it, and have forced religious believers to fight a centuries-long rearguard action against the truth. Science has been the great debunker.

The claims of scientific materialism are hardly new. Indeed, they have not changed substantially in over a hundred years. And yet much else has changed in that time. We know much more than we did about the origins of science; we know vastly more about nature. It is a good time, therefore, to take a fresh look at the materialist ideology of science and its story of science to see how well they have held up in the light of new knowledge.

We begin with the issue of supernaturalism in religion and its supposedly superstitious character. I think we would all agree that most forms of belief in the supernatural are superstitious. However, we must remind ourselves of a vital historical fact, which is that many of these forms of supernaturalism were attacked, and at least partially overthrown, by biblical religion long before the advent of modern science. The Book of Genesis was itself in large part intended, scholars tell us, as a polemic against pagan superstition. For example, whereas the sun and moon were the objects of worship in pagan religion, the Book of Genesis taught that they were nothing but lamps set in the heavens to give light to day and night: not gods, but mere things, creatures of the one true God. Nor were animals and the forces of nature to be bowed down to by man as in pagan religion; rather man, as a rational being made in the image of God, was to exercise dominion over them.

It is true that the Bible is overwhelmingly supernatural in its outlook and literary atmosphere. However, what is critically important is that the Bible's supernaturalism is concentrated in a God who is outside of Nature, and radically distinguished from the world He has made. Therefore the world of nature is no longer seen as populated by capricious supernatural beings, by fates and furies, dryads and naiads, gods of war or goddesses of sex and fertility. The natural world has been "disenchanted." But whereas many give credit to science for this, the distinction belongs in the first instance to the monotheism of the Bible, which by depersonalizing and desacralizing the natural world helped clear the ground for the eventual emergence of modern science.

The Bible taught, then, that whatever reverence it is proper to have for the sun, or the forces of nature, or living things is due not to any divinity or spirituality that they possess, but to the fact that they are the masterworks of God. The universe thus came to be seen as a great work of engineering. We observe this in the Book of Proverbs, where the divine Wisdom is portrayed as a master craftsman directing the work of creation. And according to the rabbis of old the divine craftsman worked from a plan that was none other than the Torah itself. As they put it, "the Holy One, blessed be He, consulted the Torah when He created the world." The Torah, then, was not merely a Law written in a perishable book, or part of a covenant with the people of Israel. It was an eternal Law in the mind of God that He imposed on the cosmos itself. The Lord says through the prophet Jeremiah: "When I have no covenant with day and night, and have given no laws to heaven and earth, then too will I reject the descendants of Jacob and of my servant David" (Jer 33:25-26). Psalm 148 tells of the sun, the moon, the stars, and the heavens obeying a divinely given "law that will not pass away." This emphasis on the lawfulness of the cosmos is found also in the earliest Christian writings. Minucius Felix in the second century wrote:

> If upon entering some home you saw that everything there was well-tended, neat, and decorative, you would believe that some master was in charge of it, and that he was himself much superior to those good things. So too in the home of this world, when you see providence, order, and law in the heavens and on earth, believe that there is a Lord and Author of the universe, more beautiful than the stars themselves and the various parts of the whole world.

Note that these ancient texts do not point to supernatural phenomena or to the miraculous as evidence of God's existence. Neither did St. Paul in the first chapter of Romans, where he discusses the grounds of belief in God. Nor did St. Thomas Aquinas in his famous five-fold proof. Belief in God is not founded upon supernatural manifestations but on the natural order, on the orderliness of things. The role of the miraculous in Judaism and Christianity is quite limited; it is to show God's favor to His people and testify to the authenticity of the oracles of divine revelation, not to ground belief in the Creator.

There is something else that can be observed in these ancient texts, I think, that has some relevance to the long-debated question of Darwin and design. Many seem to have gotten the impression that the old Argument from Design for the existence of God is primarily an argument from biology. Richard Dawkins says, for instance, that it was the discovery by Darwin that biological structure could arise without design that "made it possible to be an intellectually fulfilled atheist." However, most of the ancient Jewish and Christian texts seem to emphasize the structure of the cosmos as a whole more than the structure of living things. Jeremiah speaks of the covenant with day and night, and the laws given to heaven and earth; the Psalmist of the law obeyed by the sun, moon, stars, and heavens; and Minucius Felix of the providence, order, and law in the heavens and on earth.

It was in the heavens that the orderliness of nature was most evident to ancient man. It was this celestial order, perhaps, that first inspired in him feelings of religious awe. And it was the study of this order that gave birth to modern science in the seventeenth century. It is not altogether accidental, then, that it was an argument over the motions of the heavenly bodies that occasioned the fateful collision between science and religious authority that will forever be evoked by the name of Galileo. The case of Galileo raises another important historical point about supernaturalism and biblical religion.

Perhaps I can best introduce it with a personal story. I was asked a few years ago to give the response at a conference of scholars to a talk on the teaching of evolution in high schools. In my presentation I quoted the following piece of antireligious propaganda from a currently used high school biology textbook: "Every so often scientists stir up controversy when they explain part of the world that was considered beyond natural explanation—that is, belonging to the 'supernatural.'" I disputed the idea that such controversies arise "every so often," as the textbook asserted. I said that except for the battle over evolution I could think of no significant controversy that fit this description. At that point, as I had expected might happen, several members of the audience shouted out "Galileo!" But they had no reason to, for (as I went on to observe) the Galileo affair was most certainly not a debate about the supernatural. The geocentric theory that the Church in effect endorsed was no more supernatural than the heliocentric theory that it condemned. This was a clash between two perfectly naturalistic theories of astronomy. It was the veracity of Scripture that the Church authorities (mistakenly) saw themselves as upholding, not supernatural explanations of planetary motion over natural ones. (It is true that the inspiration of Scripture is supernatural, and that Galileo's opponents thus thought they had supernatural warrant for believing what they did. But one may believe a natural fact on supernatural authority. I may believe that figs grow on trees or that Pontius Pilate was procurator in Judea because the Bible says so, without thinking that those facts are in any way supernatural in themselves.)

It was the same in physics: what Galileo and Newton overthrew were the erroneous, but perfectly naturalistic, theories of Aristotle. The Scientific Revolution of the seventeenth century had to overcome the naturalism of Aristotle, not the supernaturalism of Christianity. Christianity had already embraced naturalism in science five hundred years earlier, when Western Christians first encountered Greek science (or as it was called, natural philosophy) through translations from Greek and Arabic texts. Under the aegis of the Church, natural philosophy became a staple of medieval university education and was even a prerequisite for the study of theology. So comfortable were Christians with a naturalistic conception of the cosmos that it was a cliché already in the twelfth century for theologians and other writers to refer to the cosmos as a "machine."

Now, while biblical religion has something to say about the existence of a natural order (which is simply a corollary of its teaching on God and creation), it has for the most part not regarded itself as having much to say about the detailed workings of that natural order. The materialist's notion that religion is about providing mythological explanations of nature in the absence of real scientific understanding—the "God of the gaps" idea—is, as applied to biblical religion at any rate, itself a piece of mythology. It is instructive to look, for instance, at the Roman Catechism, or Catechism of the Council of Trent, published in 1566, exactly fifty years before Galileo's first run-in with the Roman authorities. It contains not a word about botany, zoology, geology, or astronomy. Those were simply not considered part of Christian doctrine. That was the general attitude of the Catholic Church both before and after the Galileo affair, which can now be recognized as an adventitious and unique event in the history of the Church's relationship with science. It was a bump—admittedly, a very bad bump—in what has otherwise been a smooth road.

It is notable in this regard that the Catholic Church never condemned, or even criticized or warned against, the theory of evolution.[1] Its first statement on that subject did not come until 1950, when Pius XII isolated two points concerning evolution as being of doctrinal significance.[2] Both concerned only human evolution. First, he said, the original unity of the human race has to be upheld. And second, whereas the human body might have evolved, the human spiritual soul, not being reducible to matter, cannot be held to have evolved. It was specially created by God in the first human beings as in all subsequent human beings. Here, in this one case, we do see the Church upholding a form of supernaturalism. It is the one great exception to the depersonalizing of nature by Judaism and Christianity. Man himself must not be depersonalized or reduced to the merely natural in the sense of the merely physical. I shall return to this all-important point.

I would like to interject here a comment about what I regard as backsliding from the fundamental Jewish and Christian perspective on nature by some recent theologies. On the one hand, we have some process theologians blurring the distinction between God and the universe, and treating the Godhead itself as part of the cosmic evolutionary process. On the other hand, we have some critics of Darwinism not merely arguing the inadequacy of that theory, but attacking the very idea of naturalism in biology, even when it comes to plants and animals, as inherently unbiblical or irreligious. Although these schools of thought are in some ways opposite, they are equally guilty, it seems to me, of smuggling supernaturalism back where it does not belong, and where neither science nor theology has ever needed it. Some anti-Darwinists need to be reminded that there is a natural order that comes from God, and the process theologians need to understand that God is the author of it, not a part of it.

We turn now to the second reason that the materialist indicts religion as superstitious, namely, its supposed irrationalism. The materialist sees faith and dogma as simply a matter of believing without reason. Religious mystery he imagines to be something dark and off-limits, something we are not meant to understand, and indeed beyond all understanding. All of this adds up, in his eyes, to an obscurantism that sets itself against intellectual freedom and the search for truth.

In responding to these misconceptions, I would like to begin with the notion of intellectual freedom. The great physicist Richard Feynman once observed that the freedom of the scientist is quite different from that of the artist or writer. The artist is free to imagine anything he pleases. The imagination of the scientist, however, is chained to experimental facts. The theories he dreams up must conform to what is already known from observation, and must be abandoned, no matter how rationally coherent, beautiful, or compelling they seem, if they are contradicted by new experimental facts. To put it in religious language, the scientist is answerable to a very stern and peremptory magisterium: the magisterium of Nature herself.

There is a clear analogy between the limitations on the scientist and those on the theologian. The scientist must submit his mind to the data of experiment, the theologian must submit his to the data of revelation. The word "data" means "the things that are given." Both the religious person and the scientist accept givens. The givens may perplex. They may seem difficult to bring into harmony with each other or with what is known on other grounds. They may throw all our theories into confusion. But accepting the data must come before progress in understanding. That is why the words of St. Augustine apply, in a way, to the scientist as much as to the theologian: *credo ut intelligam,* "I believe in order that I may understand."

So we see in science something akin to religious faith. The scientist has confidence in the intelligibility of the world. He has questions about nature. And he expects—no, more than expects, he is absolutely convinced—that these questions have intelligible answers. The fact that he must seek those answers proves that they are not in sight. The fact that he continues to seek them in spite of all difficulties testifies to his unconquerable conviction that those answers, although not presently in sight, do in fact exist. Truly, the scientist too walks by faith and not by sight.

The scientist is convinced that there are certain acts of insight, which he has not yet achieved, and which indeed no human being may ever achieve, that would satisfy a rational mind on the questions he has raised about nature. Faith in God is an extension of this attitude. The believer in God is convinced that reality is intelligible, not merely on this or that point, but through and through. There is some all-embracing act of insight that would satisfy all questioning and leave no further questions to be asked. Such an infinite and perfect act of insight is the state of being of God, indeed for the Christian and Jew it *is* God.[3] In the words of the Jesuit philosopher Bernard Lonergan, God is the "unrestricted act of understanding" that grasps all of reality, all of being.

The materialist imagines that a religious mystery is something too dark to be seen. But, as G. K. Chesterton noted, it is really something too bright to be seen, like the sun. As Scripture tells us, God "dwells in unapproachable light" (1 Tim 6:16). The mystery is not impenetrable to intellect or unintelligible *in itself*; rather, it is not fully intelligible *to us*. And reason itself tells us that there must be such mysteries. For the nature of God is infinite, and therefore not proportionate to our finite minds. The mysteries of the faith primarily concern the nature of God, or they concern man in his relationship to God and as the image of God. They concern, that is, what is infinite or touches upon the infinite. Consequently, religious mystery hardly concerns, if it concerns at all, the matters studied by the physicist, chemist, or botanist. The things they study are quite finite in their natures and therefore quite proportionate to the human intellect. That is why there is nothing in Jewish or Christian belief that implies or suggests any limit to what human beings can understand about the structure of the physical world. Although the writings of scientific materialists are filled with hostility toward religious mystery, in fact religious mystery has never acted as a brake upon scientific progress.

This brings us back to the question of supernaturalism and its proper place. Supernaturalism is out of place in physics, astronomy, chemistry, or botany. However, it is necessary in anything that touches upon the nature of man, for man is made in the image of God. I have noted that biblical religion opposed the supernaturalism of the ancient pagan. In doing so, it clearly served the cause of reason. In our time, biblical religion serves the cause of reason just as much by opposing the absolute naturalism of the modern materialist. Where the ancient pagan went wrong is in seeing the supernatural everywhere in the world around him. Where the modern materialist goes wrong is in failing to see that which goes beyond physical nature in himself. By extending naturalism even to his own mind and soul, the materialist ends up sliding into his own morass of irrationalism and superstition. How so?

In the first place, a purely materialistic conception of man cannot account for the human power of reason itself. If we are just "a pack of neurons," in the words of Sir Francis Crick, if our mental life is nothing but electrical impulses in our nervous system, then one cannot explain the realm of abstract concepts, including those of theoretical science. Nor can one explain the human mind's openness to truth, which is the foundation of all science. As Chesterton observed, the materialist cannot explain "why anything should go right, even observation and deduction.

Why good logic should not be as misleading as bad logic, if they are both movements in the brain of a bewildered ape." Scientific materialism exalts human reason, but cannot account for human reason.

Nor can materialism account for many other aspects of the human mind, such as consciousness, free will, and the very existence of a unitary self. In a purely material world such things cannot exist. Matter cannot be free. Matter cannot have a self. The materialist is thus driven to deny empirical facts—not the facts in front of his eyes, but, as it were, the facts behind his eyes: facts about his own mental life. He calls them illusions, or redefines them to be what they are not. In lowering himself to the level of the animal or the machine, the materialist ultimately denies his own status as a rational being, by reducing all his mental operations to instinct and programming.

Thus, like the pagan of old, the materialist ends up subjecting man to the subhuman. The pagan supernaturalist did so by raising the merely material to the level of spirit or the divine. The materialist does so by lowering what is truly spiritual or in the divine image to the level of matter. The results are much the same. The pagan said that his actions were controlled by the orbits of the planets and stars, the materialist says they are controlled by the orbits of the electrons in his brain. The pagan bowed down to animals or the likenesses of animals in worship, the materialist avers that he himself is no more than an animal. The pagan spoke of fate, the materialist speaks of physical determinism.

Pope John Paul II said that divine revelation reveals not only God to man but man to himself.[4] It reveals to man that he is made in the image of God and therefore endowed with the spiritual powers of rational intellect and free will. Thus the supernaturalism of religion with regard to man is not an attack upon human reason, but ultimately the only basis upon which human reason can be adequately defended.

Up to this point I have been discussing the materialist's claim that religion and science are intrinsically opposed because religion is incompatible with scientific naturalism and rationality. I now turn to the materialist's other claim, that the actual discoveries of science since Copernicus have rendered the religious conception of the world incredible.

This is what I call the materialist's Story of Science. It pervades the atmosphere of the scientific world and of popular writing on science. Let me now briefly outline that story. It has five major themes.

The first theme is the overturning of the religious cosmology—the Copernican theme. We now know that we do not live at the center of a cozy little cosmos, but in what Bertrand Russell called a "backwater" of a vast universe. The earth is a tiny planet, orbiting an insignificant star, near the edge of an ordinary galaxy that contains a hundred billion other stars, in a universe with more than a hundred billion other galaxies.

The second theme is the triumph of mechanism over teleology. The biblical religions did have the concept of a natural order, but they saw that order as embodying purpose. The arrangement of the world and the processes of nature they saw as being directed toward beneficent ends. That is why Christianity had little difficulty in accepting the naturalistic science of Aristotle, which was based on final causes. However, the Scientific Revolution occurred when it was realized that final causes could be dispensed with altogether in physics and that phenomena could be adequately explained in a completely mechanistic way in terms of preceding physical events. Even in biology, apparent purpose is now thought to arise from the undirected mechanism of natural selection acting on random genetic mutations. The materialist argues that the disappearance of purpose from nature undercuts the idea that nature is designed.

These first two themes blend together to give the third theme of the story, what the late Stephen Jay Gould called the "dethronement of man." With the earth but an infinitesimal speck of flotsam in the limitless ocean of space, and the human race but a chemical accident, we can no longer believe ourselves to be the uniquely important beings for whom the universe was created.

The fourth theme, which goes back to Newton, is the discovery of physical determinism. The laws of nature were discovered to form a closed and complete system of cause and effect. Every event could be understood as arising inevitably from the past state of the universe in a way that is precisely determined by the mathematical laws of physics. As Laplace said in the eighteenth century, if the state of the world were completely known at one time, its whole future development could in principle be calculated down to the minutest detail. If this is true, it spells the death of the Jewish and Christian doctrine of free will. For even if we had wills that were free, they could have no effect upon the world of matter, including our bodily organs. They could not affect, in particular, what we say or do.

This leads to the fifth and final theme of the materialist's story, the emergence of a completely mechanistic view of man himself. Already in the seventeenth century the possibility was widely discussed that animals could be understood as machines or automata. The more radical thinkers of the Enlightenment, like La Mettrie and Baron d'Holbach, extended this view to man. Now, with the processes of life understood in terms of chemistry, and the brain understood to be a complex biochemical computer, the triumph of this mechanistic view of man seems virtually complete.

The story that I have just outlined should not be lightly dismissed. There are many people, not all of them hostile to religion, who find this interpretation of scientific history not only plausible but compelling. And it must be admitted that, in part, this is because much in scientific history up through the nineteenth century lent itself to this interpretation, or seemed to. And the startling developments in physics in the twentieth century only reinforced this view of things. People saw dramatic discoveries, like Einstein's theory of relativity and quantum theory, as demonstrating once again that all traditional or familiar or intuitively obvious notions are naïve and fated to be cast aside. Science as debunker, it seemed, was continuing on its relentless course.

However, this view of twentieth-century science is misleading. It is true that science debunked many ideas in the twentieth century, but what it chiefly debunked, I will now argue, was the materialist's old Story of Science. This was not fully appreciated, because people saw what they expected to see. They extrapolated from the past story line. But the discoveries of the twentieth century threw some twists into the plot. Those twists have, in my view, invalidated, or at least called into serious question, every lesson that the materialist wished us to draw from scientific history.

What are those twentieth-century plot twists? There are, it so happens, five of them, which correspond rather closely to the five themes of the materialist's story of science.

We recall that the first theme of that story was the Copernican one, the overthrow of the religious cosmology, and in particular of the supposedly religious idea that man is at the center of the universe. I say supposedly religious idea, because in historical fact the notion that the universe has a center entered Western thought not from the Bible, which knows no such idea, but from Ptolemy and Aristotle. However, there was a question about the structure of the cosmos that historically really did divide Jews and Christians from materialists and pagans. That question was not about space and whether it has a center, it was about time and whether it had a beginning.

The idea that the universe and time itself had a beginning really did enter Western thought from the Bible, and indeed from the opening words of the Bible. Virtually all the pagan philosophers of antiquity, including Aristotle, and, according to most scholars, Plato, held that time had no beginning. Modern materialists and atheists, for obvious reasons, have generally followed the ancient pagan view.

For a very long time, all the indications from science seemed to tell against the idea of a beginning. In Newtonian physics it was natural to assume that both time and space were boundless and infinite in extent. The simplest assumption was that time coordinates, like space coordinates, extended from minus infinity to plus infinity. The discovery of the law of conservation of energy gave further support to the idea of the eternity of the world, for it said that energy could be neither created nor destroyed. And chemists discovered that the quantity of matter, as measured by its mass, is also unchanged in physical processes. Thus almost every scientific indication at the beginning of the twentieth century was that space, time, matter, and energy had always existed and always would. One more nail in the coffin of religion, it would seem. But then came the first plot twist.

The first intimation that time could have had a beginning came from Einstein's General Theory of Relativity—that is, his theory of gravity. In the 1920s, the Russian mathematician Alexander Friedmann and the Belgian physicist Georges Lemaître (who was also a Catholic priest) independently proposed mathematical models of the universe, based on Einstein's theory, in which the universe is expanding from some initial explosion, which Lemaître called the "primeval atom," and which is now called the "Big Bang." Observational evidence for this cosmic expansion was announced a few years later, in 1929, by the American astronomers Edwin Hubble and Milton Humason.

The initial reaction of some scientists to the idea of a beginning was extremely negative. The eminent German physicist Walther Nernst declared, "To deny the infinite duration of time would be to betray the very foundations of science." As late as 1959, thirty years after the discovery of the expansion of the universe, a survey of leading American astronomers and physicists showed that most still believed that the universe had no beginning. Not all, but certainly some, of the resistance to the idea of a beginning can be attributed to materialist prejudice.

None of this is to say that the Big Bang proves the biblical doctrine of creation, or even that it proves conclusively that time had a beginning. It is possible that something existed before the Big Bang, even though in the simplest and currently standard model of cosmology nothing did. Nevertheless, it remains true that on the one question of cosmology where Jewish and Christian doctrine really did have something to say that conflicted with the expectations of materialists and atheists—the question of a beginning—the evidence as it now stands seems strongly to favor the religious conception.

The second theme of the materialist's story was the triumph of mechanism over teleology. Instead of seeing purpose in nature, and thus a Person behind the purpose, science came to see only the operation of impersonal laws. There was no need for a cosmic designer, for it was the laws of physics that shaped and sculpted the world in which we live. When Laplace was asked by Napoleon why God was never mentioned in his great treatise on celestial mechanics, Laplace famously answered, "I had no need of that hypothesis." This revealed a shift in perspective. Whereas once the laws of nature had been seen as pointing to a lawgiver, they were now seen by some as constituting in themselves, and by themselves, a sufficient explanation of reality. This brings us to the second plot twist in the story of science. In the twentieth century another shift in perspective took place. One might call it the aesthetic turn. This requires some explanation.

Physics begins with phenomena that can be observed with the senses, perhaps aided by simple instruments, like telescopes. It finds regularities in those phenomena and seeks mathematical rules that accurately describe them. Physicists call such rules empirical formulas or phenomenological laws. At a later stage, these rules are found to follow from some deeper and more general laws, which usually require more abstract and abstruse mathematics to express them. Underlying these, in turn, are found yet more fundamental laws. As this deepening has occurred, two things have happened. First, there has been an increasing unification of physics. Whereas, in the early days of science, nature seemed to be a potpourri of many kinds of phenomena with little apparent relation, such as heat, sound, magnetism, and gravity, it later became clear that there were deep connections. This trend toward unification greatly accelerated throughout the twentieth century, until we now have begun to discern that the laws of physics make up a single harmonious mathematical system.

Second, physicists began to look not only at the surface physical effects, but increasingly at the form of the deep laws that underlie them. They began to notice that those laws exhibit a great richness and profundity of mathematical structure, and that they are, indeed, remarkably beautiful and elegant from the mathematical point of view. As time went on, the search for new theories became guided not only by detailed fitting of experimental data, but by aesthetic criteria. A classic example of this was the discovery of the Dirac Equation in 1928. Paul Dirac was looking for an equation to describe electrons that was consistent with both relativity and quantum theory. He hit upon a piece of mathematics that struck him as "pretty." "[It] was a pretty mathematical result," he said. "I was quite excited over it. It seemed that it must be of some importance." This led him to the discovery that has been justly described as among the highest achievements of twentieth-century science.

The same quest for mathematical beauty dominates the search for fundamental theories today. One of the leading theoretical particle physicists in the world today, Edward Witten, trying to explain to a skeptical science reporter why he believed in superstring theory in spite of the dearth of experimental evidence for it, said, "I don't think I've succeeded in conveying to you its wonder, incredible consistency, remarkable elegance, and beauty."

All of this has changed the context in which we think about design in nature. When the questions physicists asked were simply about particular sensible phenomena, like stars, rainbows, or crystals, it may have seemed out of place to talk about them, however beautiful they were, as being fashioned by the hand of God. They could be accounted for satisfactorily by the laws of physics. But now, when it is the laws of physics themselves that are the object of curiosity and aesthetic appreciation, and when it has been found that they form a single magnificent edifice of great subtlety, harmony, and beauty, the question of a cosmic designer seems no longer irrelevant, but inescapable.

In 1931, Hermann Weyl, one of the great mathematicians and physicists of the twentieth century, gave a lecture at Yale University in which he said the following:

> Many people think that modern science is far removed from God. I find, on the contrary, that it is much more difficult today for the knowing person to approach God from history, from the spiritual side of the world, and from morals; for there we encounter the suffering and evil in the world, which it is difficult to bring into harmony with an all-merciful and almighty God. In this domain we have evidently not yet succeeded in raising the veil with which our human nature covers the essence of things. But in our knowledge of physical nature we have penetrated so far that we can obtain a vision of the flawless harmony which is in conformity with sublime Reason.

The third theme of the materialist's story was the "dethronement of man." A classic statement of this view was given by Steven Weinberg in his book *The First Three Minutes*. He wrote:

It is almost irresistible for humans to believe that we have some special relation to the universe, that human life is not just a farcical outcome of a chain of accidents, . . . but that we were somehow built in from the beginning. . . . It is very hard for us to realize that [the entire earth] is just a tiny part of an overwhelmingly hostile universe. . . . The more the universe seems comprehensible, the more it also seems pointless.

Certainly, given the immensity of the universe and the impact of Darwinian ideas, it is easy to understand why this sentiment is widespread. However, in the last few decades there has been a development that suggests a very different estimate of man's place in the universe. This plot twist was not a single discovery, but the noticing of many facts about the laws of nature that all seem to point in the same direction. These facts are sometimes called "anthropic coincidences."

The term "anthropic coincidence" refers to some feature of the laws of physics that seems to be just what is needed for life to be able to evolve. In other words, it is a feature whose lack or minute alteration would have rendered the universe sterile. Some of these features have been known for a long time. For example, William Paley, already in 1802, in his treatise *Natural Theology*, pointed out that if the law of gravity had not been a so-called "inverse square law" then the earth and the other planets would not be able to remain in stable orbits around the sun. Perhaps the most famous anthropic coincidence was discovered in the 1950s, when it was found that except for a certain very precise relationship satisfied by the energy levels of the Carbon-12 nucleus, most of the chemical elements in nature would have occurred in only very minute quantities, greatly dimming the prospects of life.

Interest in and attention to anthropic coincidences has greatly intensified since the work of the astrophysicist Brandon Carter in the 1970s. Many such coincidences have now been identified. The most natural interpretation of them is that we were indeed "built in from the beginning," in Steven Weinberg's phrase, and that the universe, far from being "overwhelmingly hostile" to us, as he asserted, is actually amazingly, gratuitously hospitable.

Most scientists take a very jaundiced view of the whole subject of anthropic coincidences. They have some respectable reasons, but the major reason, in my experience, is a knee-jerk reaction against anything that smells like religion or teleology. Moreover, those well-known scientists who have shown interest in anthropic coincidences generally see them as having an explanation that does not invoke purpose in nature. They appeal to what is sometimes called the Weak Anthropic Principle.[5] This is the idea that a variety of different laws of physics apply in different regions of the universe, or even in different universes, and that so many possible laws of physics are sampled in this way that there is really no coincidence in the fact that in some places the laws are "just right" for life. This is a very speculative idea, and as an explanation of all the anthropic coincidences it faces formidable difficulties. However, it cautions us that the anthropic coincidences may not point unambiguously to cosmic purpose. Yet these coincidences do completely vitiate the claim that science has shown life and man to be mere accidents. If anything, the prima facie evidence is in favor of the biblical idea that the universe was made with life and man in mind.

The fourth theme of the materialist's story was the determinism of physical law. Everything in the history of physics up until the last century seemed to support this idea. All the laws discovered—those of mechanics, gravity, and electromagnetism—were deterministic in character. If anything seemed securely established it was physical determinism. However, in the 1920s the ground rumbled under the feet of physicists. Determinism was swept away in the quantum revolution. According to the principles of quantum theory, even complete information about the state of a physical system at one time does not determine its future behavior, except in a probabilistic sense.

This was terribly shocking to physicists. Indeed, one of the hallmarks of an exact science is its ability to predict outcomes. So shocking was this twist in the plot that several of the makers of the quantum revolution, including de Broglie and Schrödinger, were reluctant to accept this aspect of it. Einstein was never reconciled to the loss of determinism. "God," he famously said, "does not play dice." There have been many attempts to restore determinism to physics by modifying, reformulating, or reinterpreting quantum theory in some way. So far, however, it seems unlikely that the old classical determinism will be restored.

There are many who argue, nonetheless, that the indeterminacy of quantum theory does not create an opening or a space for free will to operate. They argue that the basic building blocks of the human brain, such as neurons, are too large for quantum indeterminacy to play a significant role. At this point, who can say? So little is known about the brain. What we can say is that there was for a long time a strong argument from the fundamental character of physical law against the possibility of free will, and this argument can no longer be so simply made. To quote Hermann Weyl again, from the same 1931 lecture:

We may say that there exists a world, causally closed and determined by precise laws, but . . . the new insight which modern [quantum] physics affords . . . opens several ways of reconciling personal freedom with natural law. It would be premature, however, to propose a definite and complete solution of the problem. . . . We must await the further development of science, perhaps for centuries, perhaps for thousands of years, before we can design a true and detailed picture of the interwoven texture of Matter, Life, and Soul. But the old classical determinism of Hobbes and Laplace need not oppress us longer.

We return, now, to the final theme of the materialist's story, the mechanistic view of man himself. It is the final theme in more ways than one. Here the scientist debunks himself. Here all the grand intellectual adventure of science ends with the statement that there is no intellectual adventure. For the mind of man has looked into itself and seen nothing there except complex chemistry, nerve impulses, and synapses firing. That, at least, is what the materialist tells us that science has seen. However, the story is really not so simple. Here again the plot has twisted. Two of the greatest discoveries of the twentieth century cast considerable doubt upon, and some would say refute, the contention that the mind of man can be explained as a mere biochemical machine.

The first of these discoveries is quantum theory. In the traditional interpretation of quantum theory—sometimes also called the "Copenhagen," "standard," or "orthodox" interpretation—one must, to avoid paradoxes or absurdities, posit the existence of so-called "observers" who lie, at least in part, outside of the description of the world provided by physics. That is, the mathematical formalism that quantum theory uses to make predictions about the physical world cannot be stretched to cover completely the person who is observing that world. What is it about the "observer" that lies beyond physical description? Careful analysis suggests that it is some aspect of his rational mind.

This has led some eminent physicists to say that quantum theory is inconsistent with a materialistic view of the human mind. Eugene Wigner, a Nobel laureate in physics, stated flatly that materialism is not "logically consistent with present quantum mechanics." Sir Rudolf Peierls, another leading twentieth-century physicist, said, on the basis of quantum theory, "The premise that you can describe in terms of physics the whole function of a human being . . . including its knowledge, and its consciousness, is untenable. There is still something missing."

Admittedly, this is a highly controversial view. That is only to be expected, especially given the materialist prejudice that affects a large part of the scientific community. Moreover, the traditional interpretation of quantum theory has aspects that many find disturbing or implausible. Some even think (wrongly, in my opinion) that the role it assigns to observers leads to subjectivism or philosophical idealism. Dissatisfaction with the traditional interpretation has led to various rival interpretations and to attempts to modify quantum theory. However, these other ideas are equally controversial. The controversy over quantum theory will not be resolved any time soon, or perhaps ever. But, even if it is not, the fact will remain that there is an argument against materialism that comes from physics itself, an argument that has been advanced and defended by some leading physicists and never refuted.

The second discovery that arguably points to something nonmaterial in man is a revolutionary theorem in mathematical logic proved in 1931 by the Austrian Kurt Gödel, one of the greatest mathematicians of modern times. Gödel's Theorem concerns the inherent limitations of what are called "formal systems." Formal systems are essentially systems of symbolic manipulation. Since computers are basically just machines for doing such symbolic manipulations, Gödel's Theorem has great relevance to what computers and computer programs can do. It was recognized fairly quickly that Gödel's Theorem might have something to say about whether the human mind is just a computer—Gödel himself was firmly convinced that it is not. Indeed, he called materialism "a prejudice of our time." However, he never developed, at least in print, the argument against materialism based on his own theorem. That was first done by the Oxford philosopher John R. Lucas. In 1961, Lucas wrote,

> Gödel's theorem seems to me to prove that Mechanism is false, that is, that minds cannot be explained as machines. So has it seemed to many other people: almost every mathematical logician I have put the matter to has confessed similar thoughts, but has felt reluctant to commit himself definitely until he could see the whole argument set out, with all objections fully stated and properly met. This I attempt to do.

Both Gödel's Theorem and Lucas's argument are extremely subtle, but we can state the gist of them as follows. Gödel's Theorem implies that a computer program can be outwitted by someone who understands how it is put together. Lucas observed that if a man were *himself* a computer program, then by knowing how his own program was put together he could outwit himself, which is a contradiction. One may explain the Lucas argument in another way. Gödel's Theorem also showed that it is beyond the power of any computer program that operates by logically consistent rules to tell that it is doing so. However, a human being, Lucas noted, *can* recognize his own consistency—at least at times—and so must be more than a mere computer.

In recent years, the eminent mathematician and mathematical physicist Sir Roger Penrose has taken up the Lucas argument, further refined it, and answered criticisms that had been leveled at it by mathematicians and philosophers. This has not quieted the criticism. However, the Gödelian argument of Lucas and Penrose, though often attacked, has never been refuted.

Where does this all leave us? After all the twists and turns of scientific history we look around and find ourselves in very familiar surroundings. We find ourselves in a universe that seems to have had a beginning. We find it governed by laws that have a grandeur and sublimity that bespeak design. We find many indications in those laws that we were built in from the beginning. We find that physical determinism is wrong. And we find that the deepest discoveries of modern physics and mathematics give hints, if not proof, that the mind of man has something about it that lies beyond the power of either physics or mathematics to describe.

Chesterton told the story of "an English yachtsman who slightly miscalculated his course and discovered England under the impression that it was an island in the South Seas." The explorer, he said, "landed (armed to the teeth and speaking by signs) to plant the British flag on that barbaric temple which turned out to be the pavilion at Brighton." Having braced himself to discover New South Wales, he realized, "with a gush of happy tears, that it was really old South Wales."[6]

Science has taken us on just such an adventure. Armed not with weapons but with telescopes and particle accelerators, and speaking by the signs and symbols of recondite mathematics, it has brought us to many strange shores and shown us alien and fantastic landscapes. But as we scan the horizon, near the end of the voyage, we have begun to recognize first one and then another of the old familiar landmarks and outlines of our ancestral home. The search for truth always leads us, in the end, back to God.

EVOLUTION

02

EVOLUTION WITHOUT TEARS

The last twenty years have seen an intensifying of the evolution wars in the United States. The passion in these conflicts comes mainly from two groups, fundamentalist Christians and scientific atheists, who feed off each other even as they abominate each other. Although poles apart in their world views, they agree on one fundamental premise, namely that biological evolution is incompatible with biblical religion. Polls show that the fundamentalists have much popular support: 45% of Americans believe that God created plants and animals within the last 10,000 years in approximately their present form (a view called Creationism). The scientific atheists are much fewer in number, but are energetic propagandists. Caught in the middle are the rest of the American people, most of whom see no contradiction between God and evolution. It is often overlooked that a large number of American scientists are traditional religious believers. (A recent survey showed that nearly half believe in a personal God who answers prayers.) The great majority of these religious scientists regard evolution as a well-established fact and look upon the public battles over it as pointless and embarrassing.

One casualty of these battles is religious belief itself. The very fact that religious believers are still attacking evolution after so many decades lends credibility to the atheists' claim that religion and science are irreconcilable. Science too is harmed. With so many people convinced that the scientific establishment is mistaken, or even lying, about an issue of fundamental importance, and with militant atheists claiming to speak for science and using science as a weapon against faith, public trust in the scientific community and its institutions is diminished. This is of no small concern to a profession that lives largely off the public purse. Equally worrisome are attempts by Creationists and others to re-draw the boundaries of science in order to justify the teaching of "alternatives" to "mainstream science" in schools. If that were done, there would be no principled grounds for objecting to the teaching of "alternative medicine," astrology, and many other ideas that have a large popular following, or to the teaching of popular "alternatives" in other fields, such as "afro-centric history." A scholarly discipline that is no longer trusted to police its own boundaries is like a body without an immune system.

A third and more subtle threat to the health of the scientific enterprise is intellectual rigidity. In closing ranks against Creationist pseudoscience, as it has been forced to do, the scientific community has grown increasingly intolerant toward even those who raise reasonable questions about evolution. As Creationists have exploited for propaganda purposes the normal debates within biology, the unresolved puzzles of theory, and the inevitable anomalies in data, some biologists have become afraid to admit any shortcomings or uncertainty in their theoretical framework.

Many religious leaders and theologians have attempted to defuse the conflict by pointing out that orthodox Christian faith is no bar to accepting the established facts of biological science. In 1996, Pope John Paul II made an important statement on the subject to the Pontifical Academy of Sciences, and in 2004, the Catholic Church's International Theological Commission issued an impressive study of the theological issues, entitled *Communion and Stewardship*. Religious scientists have also begun to speak up. In 1999, Kenneth R. Miller, a biology professor at Brown University and co-author of a standard biology textbook, came out with *Finding Darwin's God*. In 2006, *The Language of God* appeared, written by Francis S. Collins, a world-renowned geneticist and head of the Human Genome Project. Both books argue for the compatibility of standard neo-Darwinian evolution and traditional Christian faith. Miller is a Catholic and Collins an evangelical Christian.

Even many scientists who are not religious have tried to smooth things over, because they recognize that the conflict is fraught with dangers for science. One notes, for example, the following statement from the National Academy of Sciences: "[It is false] to think that the theory of evolution represents an irreconcilable conflict between religion and science. A great many religious believers accept evolution on scientific grounds without relinquishing their belief in religious principles." The same point has been emphasized by several well-known scientists who are atheists, including the late Stephen Jay Gould. Unfortunately, these efforts have not brought peace.

When the Intelligent Design (or "ID") movement came along in the late 1990s it looked like an attempt to find a middle ground. The movement did not deny[1] that the earth is billions of years old or that the present species of plants and animals evolved from a common ancestor (the idea called "common descent"). They merely argued that natural mechanisms, including natural selection, are inadequate to explain evolution, a position that is not in itself unreasonable or a threat to science. Far from acting as a moderating force, however, the ID movement quickly ended up exacerbating the conflict. This is due to three strategic decisions they made from the very outset. First, they did not clearly dissociate themselves from Creationism, which they could have done by frankly admitting that the evidence for common descent is compelling. Instead, in some of their writings, such as those of Phillip E. Johnson, that evidence is called into question. It seems that the ID movement did not wish to alienate Creationists, whom they appeared to regard as allies against the common enemy of "Darwinism."[2] An obvious advantage to them in this informal alliance is that their potential audience and influence is enormously expanded. The drawback is that they have come to be seen, even by some people initially disposed to be sympathetic to them, as a stalking horse for Creationism. Second, the "ID theorists," as they style themselves, did not merely argue that there were reasonable grounds to doubt the sufficiency of natural explanations; they sometimes argued that it was already provable that natural explanations will never be able account for certain biological facts.[3] This is a highly provocative claim, since the scientific community sees as its business the search for such explanations. And third, the ID movement announced as one of its goals a redefinition of science to include types of explanation that most people see as religious or quasi-religious. As this kind of redefinition has always been one of the main practical threats to science posed by the Creationists, the backlash against the ID movement from the scientific community was predictably harsh.

At the same time as all this has been going on, some scientists have begun to argue for the importance of various non-Darwinian—but completely naturalistic—mechanisms of evolution. There is quite a grab-bag of such proposals, including "complexity theory" and a set of ideas that have come to be called "evo-devo" (short for "evolution-development").

The result is that there are now several evolution controversies going on at the same time instead of just the one we were all familiar with.

The Evolution Controversy, by Thomas B. Fowler and Daniel Kuebler, is an attempt to sort all this out for the general reader. It succeeds in this goal admirably. The authors begin by presenting the history of evolutionary thought from the forerunners of Darwin up to the present time, as well as the history of opposition to evolution. They note that much of the confusion surrounding the subject comes from the fact that the word *evolution* is used by different people to mean different things. Fowler and Kuebler therefore distinguish three "tiers" in the theory of evolution: The first tier is *historical evolution*, which is the idea that living things have undergone a process of development lasting hundreds of millions of years, the stages of which can be read in the fossil record. The second tier is *common descent*. The third tier is what they call *strong Darwinian evolution*, by which they mean the idea that natural selection is by itself sufficient to account for the facts of evolution. They then proceed to classify the main contending positions into four "schools."

First is the Neo-Darwinian School. *Neo-Darwinism* is the standard term among scientists for the synthesis, achieved in the mid-twentieth century, of Darwin's theory of evolution with modern genetics. The mutations that Darwin saw as fueling evolutionary change are now understood to be genetic mutations. Second is the Meta-Darwinian School. This actually comprises two groups: those who think that neo-Darwinism is basically correct, but accept that some non-Darwinian mechanisms may also be significant, and those who think that non-Darwinian mechanisms play the central and even dominant role in evolution.

Third is the Intelligent Design School. Like the Meta-Darwinians, they accept (or, at least, do not explicitly reject) the first two tiers of evolution. Finally there is the Creationist School. This school is far more radical than the others, for it rejects *all three* tiers of evolution. (There are some Creationists who accept that the universe is billions of years old, but most Creationists are of the so-called "Young Earth" type and believe that the universe is only a few thousand years old.)

Fowler and Kuebler succeed very well in explaining, without oversimplification, but in a way that will be understood by ordinary readers, the positions of each school, the principal arguments and counter-arguments, and the most important scientific evidence. Even fairly knowledgeable readers will come away having learned a great deal. For example, it came as a surprise to me that many Creationists not only believe that new species can evolve, but believe that such evolution can happen far *faster* than Darwinian evolution would allow. (They have to suppose this in order to explain how the relatively few types of animals that would have fit on Noah's Ark could have led to the vast number of life forms we see today.)

Fowler and Kuebler's purpose is not merely to explain the evolution controversies; it is to help ordinary people to "decide for themselves" where the scientific truth lies. This is a somewhat peculiar aim, as they themselves appear to recognize. We do not expect ordinary people to decide for themselves where the scientific truth lies with regard to disputed questions in subatomic physics or other highly technical fields. Common sense tells us that such matters are for trained specialists to debate and judge. What we face in the area of evolution, however, is precisely a crisis of trust. When 45% of the general public think that biologists, astrophysicists, cosmologists, and geologists, are all off by a factor of a million (!) in their calculations of the age of the universe, the age of the earth, and the duration of life on earth, we are no longer in a situation where the authority of experts can be invoked. Fowler and Kuebler therefore feel that there is no other way to proceed than to present the scientific evidence as clearly as possible and trust in ordinary people's good sense.

There is reason to suspect that the authors are secretly hoping that open-minded Creationists who read their book will come to the realization that Creationism is scientifically untenable. Fowler and Kuebler cannot say this, however, because any appearance that they are not impartial would undermine their credibility with the very people they are most trying to reach. In consequence, they bend over backwards to emphasize their "neutrality" and to treat all four "schools" as scientifically respectable. This leads them very often to soften their language to an unjustified, and indeed absurd, degree when discussing Creationism. They speak of the "considerable" problems with fitting the history of the universe and the earth into 10,000 years. (The correct word is "insurmountable.") They say that "there is no guarantee" that Creationist research will lead to viable explanations that can withstand rigorous scrutiny. (The correct statement is that there is an iron-clad guarantee that it will *not* produce such explanations, and that in fact Creationism is already unable to withstand even the mildest scrutiny.) They say that "a very good case" exists for common descent, when they must know full well that the evidence they presented for it earlier in their book is utterly conclusive. They say, "if they [the Creationists] can succeed in demonstrating a young age [of the earth and universe], of the order of 10,000 years or so . . ." That is like saying, "If they can succeed in showing that the moon is made of green cheese . . ." They several times explicitly deny that Young Earth Creationism should be treated as a "crackpot theory," when in fact that is exactly what it is.

It is understandable that the authors want to be tactful, but there is a fine line between tact and lack of candor, and they clearly cross it. Some people might say that their attitude is right, since science should maintain an open mind about all possibilities. But that is nonsense; science can reach firm and reliable conclusions, and has on countless questions. The authors know this, and admit that some theories do belong in the crackpot category. Instead of patronizing the Creationists by pretending to take their theories seriously as science (which is not at all the same thing as taking Creationists seriously as people), Fowler and Kuebler might have explained what it is that distinguishes crackpot theories from serious ones. However, the epistemology of science that they develop in the early part of their book is inadequate to the task.

The misconception many people have about science is that experiments and observations provide one directly with statements about the world that can be lined up alongside the statements of theory in order to verify or falsify the latter. What they actually provide is facts—such as fragments of bone in a riverbed, readings on a dial, or tracks in a particle detector—whose significance cannot be grasped without the application of a large body of existing theory. In other words, every conclusion of science rests upon a large number of assumptions. Each of those assumptions can be questioned; and so it might seem that the uncertainty of scientific conclusions would actually increase as one probed the reasoning upon which they are based. The reason that this epistemological unraveling doesn't occur is that while each conclusion rests upon many assumptions, each assumption also provides the basis for many conclusions. In other words, one does not have a fragile chain of logic that snaps if any link is broken, but a highly connected network of interlocking and mutually supporting facts and inferences. Every part of that network is held in place by many links to other known facts, both near and remote.

How then is it ever possible to revise any conclusion of science, let alone have a "scientific revolution" that revises many of them? The answer is that it is not as easy as some people imagine. In the early days of some branch of science, when few facts are known and their connections are not well understood, wholesale revisions of theory are not uncommon. But as a branch of science matures, it becomes more difficult to formulate a viable theory that departs in some fundamental way from the existing theory. Such radical revisions can still occur, but they are rare, and they generally require that the new theory give the same answers as the old one except in extreme and quite unusual conditions. For example, while Einstein's theory of gravity involved major conceptual revisions, it gives the same answers as Newton's theory to extremely high accuracy unless gravitational fields are enormously strong or the gravitating bodies are moving near the speed of light. Even finding a place where the existing theory can be modified in a minor way is not so simple. That is why coming up with a sensible new theory requires a great deal of technical knowledge and skill: the theorist must be able to spot the elements in the existing structure that are not really supporting much weight, and which can be modified or removed without bringing the whole building crashing down.

The same applies outside the natural sciences—for example in history. It is one thing to question some detail in the received account of, say, Julius Caesar's life. It is quite another to propose a radical new account of history according to which the Roman Empire never existed. We simply know too many things, and the things we know are simply too interconnected for a revision of that sort to be possible. It is a revision of that sort that Creationism proposes, and that is why it is a crackpot idea.

G. K. Chesterton, in *Orthodoxy*, describes the futility of trying to debate on his own terms the ideas of a "maniac," by which he meant someone who is trapped in a tiny circle of logic. It is not that the maniac's logic is flawed, but that his world is too small. His system is self-consistent, but it leaves almost everything out. It is not enough to provide him with a few more facts and arguments to consider, he must be made to see the big picture and how much bigger it is than he supposed.

I do not wish to leave a wrong impression. This is in many ways an excellent book. Indeed, I know of no book that is better for someone wanting to understand the scientific aspects of the "Evolution Controversy." It explains very well a great deal of material, including the strongest pieces of evidence against Creationism. If it tries too hard to be kind to Creationism, that is perhaps an excusable fault. Doubtless, Fowler and Kuebler are trying not to "crush the bruised reed." I hope that in future editions they choose to be more frank. But even as it is, this is a book of considerable merits.

03

THE DEVIL'S CHAPLAIN CONFOUNDED

Richard Dawkins is the most truculent exponent of Darwinian theory writing today. It has been said that if T. H. Huxley was "Darwin's bulldog," Dawkins should be called "Darwin's pit-bull." "Red in tooth and claw" well describes his polemical style; and on the subject of religion, in particular, he is rabid. He has his calmer moments, of course. And when he confines himself to zoology, his field of expertise, he is capable of writing in a lucid manner. Unfortunately, he often prefers to play the philosopher, social critic, and moralist. Some of the results are exhibited in this book.

A Devil's Chaplain is a collection of essays, book reviews, forewords, eulogies, and other short pieces that he has written over the last twenty-five years. They deal with a variety of topics, including postmodernism, the jury system, Stephen Jay Gould, New Age superstitions, death, Africa, and quack medicine. As in most of Dawkins's writings, however, the underlying themes are few and simple: science, reason, and the world of hard facts versus religion, superstition, and wishful thinking.

The title is taken from a letter of Charles Darwin. "What a book," Darwin exclaimed, "a Devil's Chaplain might write on the clumsy, wasteful, blundering low and horridly cruel works of nature." Dawkins remarks that Darwin would probably have added "selfish" and "blind" to the list of "melancholy adjectives" had he decided to extend it. This dispiriting view of nature lies at the heart of Dawkins's philosophy. For him, the great and tragic truth is that the universe and the life it has spawned are without any ultimate purpose. The lesson of evolution as taught by the Devil's Chaplain is cosmic futility.

What are the implications of this for human life and morality? Dawkins deals with this question in the title essay, which was written for this book. He cites two "opposite responses" to Darwinism, those of George Bernard Shaw and H. G. Wells. In the Preface of *Back to Methuselah*, Shaw wrote of Darwinian evolution,

> When its whole significance dawns on you, your heart sinks into a heap of sand within you. There is a hideous fatalism about it, a ghastly and damnable reduction of beauty and intelligence, of strength and purpose, of honor and aspiration.

Wells, on the other hand, reveled in the ruthlessness of nature in his scientific utopian fantasy *The New Republic*:

> And how will the New Republic treat the inferior races? How will it deal with the black? . . . the yellow man? . . . the Jew? . . . those swarms of black, and brown, and dirty-white, and yellow people, who do not come into the new needs of efficiency? Well, the world is a world, and not a charitable institution, and I take it they will have to go. . . . And the ethical system of these men of the New Republic, the ethical system which will dominate the world state, will be shaped primarily to favour the procreation of what is fine and efficient and beautiful in humanity—beautiful and strong bodies, clear and powerful minds. . . . And the method that nature has followed hitherto in the shaping of the world, whereby weakness was prevented from propagating weakness . . . is death. . . . The men of the New Republic . . . will have an ideal that will make the killing worth the while.

What is Dawkins's own response to what he several times calls Darwinism's "moral implications"? It is not to embrace them, as Wells did. Nor is it to reject Darwinism itself, as Shaw did. Rather, it is to accept Darwinism as true, but "rebel" against its implications: "[A]t the same time as I support Darwinism as a scientist, I am a passionate anti-Darwinian when it comes to politics and how we should conduct our human affairs." He quotes the resounding final words of his own first book, *The Selfish Gene*: "We, alone on earth, can rebel against the tyranny of the selfish replicators." What enables us to rebel is the fact that nature, though utterly mindless, has accidentally endowed us with intelligence. Our brain can understand the evolutionary process that gave rise to it, and thus transcend it. Our "blessed gift of understanding" enables us to react with "revulsion" to nature's imperatives and to be the "only potential island of refuge from the implications of the Devil's Chaplain."

This is Dawkins the humanist speaking: man is the great exception. And yet, Dawkins the scientist insists that we must come to terms with the "inescapable factual correctness of the Devil's Chaplain" and his view of life, "bleak and cold though it can seem from under the security blanket of ignorance." Endowed with reason, we have no alternative but to acknowledge the truth, however unpalatable. We cannot be content with "cheap comforts, living a warm and comfortable lie." We cannot bask in "comforting delusions" or "suck at the pacifier of faith in immortality." However, we will have compensation for our putting away of childish things. "There is deep refreshment to be had from standing up full-face into the keen wind of understanding." There is "the joy of knowing that you have grown up, [and] faced up to what existence means," or, rather, to its ultimate meaninglessness.

There is a lot of talk of growing up and facing up in Dawkins. Another Darwinian lesson we must face up to is that we are animals with no special status or unique value. To think otherwise is "flagrant speciesism," "human chauvinism," "human speciesist vanity." It is only "the discontinuous mind" that sees a gap between humans and chimpanzees, our closest relatives; and it is only able to do so because the intermediate forms happen to be dead. Dawkins goes so far as to say that successful human-chimp interbreeding, though he doubts its possibility, is "a pleasing thought." It "would provide exactly the come-uppance that 'human dignity' needs." Here Dawkins the Darwinian seems to have elbowed aside Dawkins the "passionate anti-Darwinian" and humanist.

Religion takes a savage beating from Dawkins, in particular Catholicism, for which he seems to have conceived an almost lunatic hatred. Nuns disturb him especially. His theory of religion is spelled out in a section of the book entitled "The Infected Mind." Religion is simply a "virus of the mind," or a "meme" (a term he coined in his first book). A meme is an idea or word passed from mind to mind somewhat as a gene is passed from generation to generation. Religion exploits the fact that small children are preprogrammed by evolution to accept uncritically what adults tell them about the world. There is too much that small children have to learn about culture and life and language for critical filtering to be anything but a hindrance at that stage of life. It is this natural childish gullibility carried into adulthood that is the basis of religion, and of all belief systems based on authority, tradition, and revelation. In an interview Dawkins has expressed the view that "you won't find any intelligent person who feels the need for the supernatural," unless that person was brought up as a child to believe in it.

For Dawkins, the supernaturalism of religion is antiscientific and its doctrines absurd. The doctrine of the Trinity is "obvious nonsense," and "it takes a real, red-blooded Catholic to believe something as daft as transubstantiation." It is, however, the Catholic dogma of the Assumption of Mary that for him is the ne plus ultra of religious silliness, with Mary's body "zooming" off to heaven. He freely avows both "hostility" and "contempt" for religion, and he feels it his moral duty to mock it as much as he can. In an essay provoked by September 11th he writes, "Those of us who have for years politely concealed our contempt of religion need to stand up and speak out."

Dawkins is much given to invective, not all of it against religion. Here is how he treats some of his other favorite targets: "caterwauling shrieks," "low-grade intellectual poodling of pseudo-philosophical poseurs," "footling debates," "boorish tenured confidence," "yahooish complacency," "driveling ephemera of juvenile pamphleteers and the old preaching of spiteful hard-liners." The man, as they say nowadays, "has issues." It appears that Dawkins has acquired a reputation, even among his admirers, for having a rather icy philosophy and nasty literary personality. We are therefore promised that this book will show us Dawkins's "gentler, more contemplative side, which may surprise many readers," "his warm, personal side," and his "sympathetic side." (These promises are made by the book's dust jacket, its publicist, and *Science News*, respectively.) Dawkins seems aware of his image problem, for he writes in the Introduction to the American Edition: "Though I admit to occasional flames of (entirely justified) irritation in my writing, I like to think that the greater part of it is good-humoured, perhaps even humorous."

It is possible that this anthology is meant to humanize Dawkins. The eulogies and laments for dead friends show off his capacity for deep feeling and deep friendships (as well as his facing-up abilities, of course). Dawkins's reviews of the late Stephen Jay Gould's books and the final e-mail correspondence between them display Dawkins's magnanimity toward a sometime intellectual foe. The essays about Africa reveal his poetic nature. His letter to his ten-year-old daughter, which closes the book, shows his fatherly side and the man who does not talk down to children.

Whether all this humanizes him is not for me to say; it is doubtless a spe-ciesist concern in any case.

Of more concern is the quality of his thinking, which is far from im-pressive. To call it low-grade intellectual poodling would perhaps be too harsh; but it is certainly not high-grade. The first thing to note is Daw-kins's carelessness with facts. (This is especially strange in a man who so emphasizes the factuality of science, with its "testability, evidential support, precision, [and] quantifiability.") Here is a small sampler: he says that "on average one [neutrino] passes through you every second."[1] Actually many billions of them do, a fact well known to science buffs. In explaining an evolutionary idea he states that a certain quantity "grows as a power function,"[2] when any mathematically minded person would see that it grows exponentially. He attempts an elementary combinatoric calculation and gets it wrong.[3] He discusses a well-known quantum phe-nomenon in terms that are incorrect.[4] One should be used to this sort of thing from Dawkins, I suppose. In his previous book he showed that he did not know the difference between a cosmic ray and a gamma ray.[5]

It could be urged, in extenuation of such mistakes, that Dawkins is not a physicist or mathematician. Even so, one might have expected better of a man whose title at Oxford University is the Charles Simonyi Professor of the Public Understanding of Science. And he had the option of check-ing his statements with people who know these fields better. However, his problem is not just with the quantitative sciences. He evinces the same indifference to facts in other areas on which he freely expounds, such as Catholicism. He says, for instance, that the Pope's doctrinal pro-nouncements are based on personal "revelations," a notion totally at odds with Catholic teaching. He asserts that "the present Pope has ordered his followers not to limit the number of babies they have." He absurdly uses the doctrine of the Assumption to rebut the claim that "religion has moved on" and no longer teaches that "God has a long white beard." (The idea seems to be that if people have bodies of some sort in heaven, then so must God.) With little effort, Dawkins might have learned that Christianity has never held the position, from which it might "move on," that God is corporeal, an idea that was indeed dismissed by the Church Fathers as "most foolish."

Dawkins's superficiality extends beyond his treatment of facts. What is clear from these essays is that he has not thought very hard, or at any rate very deeply, about many things on which he writes for a living. Had he done so, he would have seen that a number of his ideas are patently inconsistent with each other. This is particularly true of his ideas on the moral implications of Darwinism.

Darwinism as understood by Dawkins[6] necessarily involves a completely naturalistic conception of the world, in which there is no place for God or ultimate purpose. It is plain that this view is incompatible with belief in an objective moral order[7]; and the more clear-thinking atheistic Darwinians have always understood this. One is prevented, in such a philosophy, from speaking of the "purposes" of things in any sense that can give rise to moral obligation. A natural object can have a purpose only in the limited sense of a function to which its structure suits it, as the biological function of an eye is to see. And what is the biological function of an organism? Simply and solely to survive and propagate its own kind. Natural selection gives nothing beyond that. None of this yields moral obligation. It is quite meaningless to ask, for example, whether one "should" build a dam that will cause the snail darter to go extinct. We can only ask whether building it would be conducive to human survival, or to snail darter survival, or to some other arbitrarily chosen end. People do, of course, have feelings of moral obligation; but only the feelings are real, not the obligations. As Edward O. Wilson and Michael Ruse put it, "human beings function better if they are deceived by their genes into thinking that there is a disinterested objective morality binding upon them, which all should obey."

Given all this, it might seem that Dawkins is simply being consistent when he condemns "speciesism." After all, given his premises, there can be no objective basis for what he calls "absolutist valuings of human life above all other life." Humans may be more important to humans, but snail darters are more important to snail darters. In one of his essays, Dawkins seems more tentative. He admits that the question "What's so special about humans?" may have an answer. He just does not know what the answer is, and objects to the "unthinking nature of the speciesist double standard." Why, he asks, should we treat other people "better than, say, cows"? Whatever the reason, he feels that it ought to be a better one than the mere fact of "cousinship." Perhaps Bentham had the right idea, Dawkins suggests, in saying that we count for more than cows because we can suffer more than they. In his other essays, however, Dawkins is unequivocal in his denunciations of speciesism.

All of this may sound like unflinching logical consistency. However, if we think a little more deeply than Dawkins does, we realize that moralizing about speciesism is utterly silly from the standpoint of atheistic

Darwinism. True, there is no absolute reason to prefer men to cows; but then, there is no absolute reason to prefer anything to anything, including nonspeciesism to speciesism. If all moral standards are arbitrary, one might as well go with the speciesist standard. That, at least, has the human organism acting in a way that corresponds to its biological function. "Cousinship," indeed, is the very best of Darwinian reasons for caring. There is certainly no way to make sense, from a Darwinian perspective, of a trans-species Benthamite calculus of suffering. It has nothing to do with any organism's fitness or survival.

But haven't we forgotten something? Dawkins has already told us that he is passionately anti-Darwinian when it comes to how we should conduct our human affairs. Indeed. But why should that be? Do we detect here an unthinking speciesist double standard? Why should bovine affairs be conducted on a Darwinian basis, and not human affairs? Cows do not seek to minimize our suffering, why should we seek to minimize theirs? Is it because we alone have the "blessed gift of understanding"? We do, but so what? What is there to understand when it comes to morality? Are there objective moral standards "out there" somewhere for our understanding to latch on to? Not on Dawkins's premises. Indeed, he explicitly admits that "science has no methods for deciding what is ethical."

We come down to this: our reason enables us to rebel against the implications of Darwinism. But why rebel? Where does the moral standard come from that says we should? Of course, the question is moot. For the fact of the matter is that rebellion against nature is impossible if atheistic Darwinism is true. We are a part of nature and cannot be anything but that. Dawkins thinks he can prove otherwise. He gives the example of contraception as "anti-Darwinian" behavior. But that behavior is no more anti-Darwinian than is a dog chasing a car and getting run over by it. Evolution programs organisms to think and act in ways that most of the time, but not invariably, favor their chances to survive and reproduce. Dawkins should really listen to the Devil's Chaplain again: nature is "clumsy, wasteful, blundering."

Dawkins argues against genetic determinism. Given his materialism, it is hard to see the point of this. Whether or not genes decide anything, atoms decide everything. Whether or not there is genetic determinism, there is physical determinism. One does not liberate anybody by throwing open the gates of a prison and leaving the inmates locked in their cells. It is of little importance what influence genes or the environment have, or what role is played by individual choices, if in the final analysis everything is just matter anyway, including the genes, the environment, and the individuals who choose. To a materialist, we are just congeries of atoms; and atoms must go whithersoever they are driven by the laws of physics and blind chance. Dawkins wonders whether a child can "escape" the indoctrination of nuns. It is silly of him to wonder. He should know that no one can "escape" anything. There is no place for intellectual or moral freedom in a universe that is mere matter in motion. That is why Sir Francis Crick, Edward O. Wilson, and many others who share Dawkins's basic views, call free will an "illusion."

Dawkins contrasts ideas that are just memes, mindlessly and slavishly copied from brain to brain like computer viruses, with scientific ideas, which he likens to useful software that is critically evaluated by potential users and adopted or rejected on rational grounds. Such a distinction is valid, but it is not one that a materialist can make. It is based on there being an essential difference between machines, which can only do as they are told, and intelligent and free users of those machines, who can decide for themselves what to do. However, in the materialist's universe, all "users" are themselves just machines, and are therefore as much driven by physical necessity (or chance) as everything else. As the great mathematician and physicist Hermann Weyl observed,

> There must be freedom in the theoretical acts of affirmation and negation: When I reason that 2+2=4, this actual judgment is not forced upon me through blind natural causality (a view that would eliminate thinking as an act for which we can be held answerable) but something purely spiritual enters in.

The problem with Dawkins and a lot of other shallow, thoughtless materialists is not that they "stand up full-face into the keen wind of understanding," but that they don't. They don't face the implications of their ideas. If they did, they would have to dismiss all talk of morality, rebellion against nature, and intellectual freedom as so much sentimentality.

The same failure to think things through is evident in Dawkins's views on religion. There is nothing in Darwinism, even in its most naturalistic form, that must lead one to despise religion as Dawkins does. There is every indication that religion is natural to man and conducive, on the whole, to his survival. It can give him hope in adversity, strengthen family bonds, and motivate sacrifice for the common good. Dawkins calls it a virus; but if it is, it is one that, according to the latest research, makes us healthier. "Faith sufferers," as Dawkins calls them, seem to suffer less from a wide array of ills. Among other things, they are less given to depression, anxiety, addiction, criminality, suicide, and divorce. To note this is not to preach the prosperity gospel, but to see the weakness of Dawkins's position even on its own naturalistic terms.

Without religion, says Dawkins, we would not have wars of religion or religious persecution. True. And without sex, fathers, families, material possessions, and governments, we would not have sex crimes, abusive fathers, dysfunctional families, greed for material possessions, and oppressive governments. Every natural and necessary thing can be perverted; even reason. Religion has led to hateful ideas, but no Christian writer has ever published ideas as hateful as the social Darwinism of H. G. Wells. Religion has led to persecutions, but none more massive than those produced by militant irreligion. More people were killed by the "scientific atheism" of Communism on an average day than the Spanish Inquisition killed in an average decade.[8] And largely responsible for this fact was a teaching of contempt for religion of exactly the kind that Dawkins propagates.

Dawkins gave an interview to Belief.net recently. He was asked whether he could think of anything, just "one positive, if minor, thing" that religion has done for the good. No, he replied, he really couldn't. What about great religious art? "That's not religion," said Dawkins, "it is just because the church had the money. Great artists like . . . Bach . . . would have done whatever they were told to do." Johann Sebastian Bach was just in it for the money. What this sordid remark reveals, apart from amazing ignorance and philistinism, is the mind of a true fanatic: it is not enough for Dawkins to say that religion is bad on the whole; it must be wholly bad. Doubtless, he thinks that Mother Teresa had mercenary motives too.

Even without his bigotry, we could not expect balanced judgment or logical consistency from Dawkins, because his mind is a muddle. There are in fact at least three Dawkinses: Dawkins the Humanist, Dawkins the Man of Reason, and Dawkins the Darwinist. Each sits on a different branch, sawing away at the other branches. Dawkins the Humanist is passionate about things. He inveighs; he denounces; he bristles with moral indignation. Dawkins the Darwinist tells him, however, that his humanism is speciesist vanity, his moral standards arbitrary, and his indignation empty. Dawkins the Humanist rebels, proclaiming himself (in human affairs) passionately anti-Darwinian. Dawkins the Man of Reason joins the rebellion, declaring that our minds allow us to transcend our genetic inheritance. Dawkins the Darwinist answers with lethal effect that our brains "were only designed to understand the mundane details of how to survive in the stone-age African savannah."

The blame for this muddle lies not with humanism, reason, or even Darwinism. It lies with Dawkins's atheism and materialism, which prevent any coherent viewpoint from emerging because they deny the spiritual soul in man. That soul is indeed a blessed gift. It is precisely "what is so special about humans." It is what enables us to be men of reason, and not just animals programmed to survive on the African savannah. It is what allows us to grasp moral truth, and to have the freedom to follow it rather than the laws of matter or the law of the jungle. It is what makes it possible for us to have that hope and love to which the subtitle of Dawkins's book refers, but which are absent from its pages, and about which he has nothing in the end to say.

04

MISMEASURE OF MAN

S tephen Jay Gould's latest book, *Full House: The Spread of Excellence from Plato to Darwin*, is a grab-bag of miscellany—his successful struggle with cancer, the disappearance of the .400 hitter in baseball, Plato's theory of ideas, the history of life on earth. Somehow, though, he manages to weave all of this together into a grand philosophical synthesis about the meaning of life and the nature of reality.

The root of much evil in the world, according to Gould, lies in the simple statistic called "the average," or at least in the confusions it engenders in the popular mind. One average in particular bothers Gould a great deal, because it leads to an understanding of evolution that he thinks mistaken. The fact that the average complexity of organisms on earth has increased over time suggests to many people that natural selection is a mechanism for producing complexity and, therefore, ultimately, for producing us. Even many who accept what Gould regards as the atheistic implications of Darwinism "cling" to the notion that we are the goal of evolution, the highest rung of a ladder. If one looks closely at the fossil record, however, one finds according to Gould, that evolution has no preference for complexity. A particular lineage is just as likely to evolve toward less complexity as toward more—if it can. However, since life started with one-celled organisms, it had, on average, nowhere to go but up.

Even though the average complexity of organisms has increased over time, one-celled creatures still (and always will) vastly predominate in number. We do not live in the vaunted Age of Mammals or the Age of Man, says Gould, but in the Age of Bacteria. Far from being the goal of evolution, we are, "a tiny twig on life's tree." This "twig" undergoes a kind of evolution itself in the course of Gould's book, reappearing as "a tiny twig on the floridly arborescent bush of life," "a tiny twig, born just yesterday on an enormously arborescent tree of life," and "only a recent twiglet on an ancient and enormous genealogical bush." Only our "parochialism" and "traditional human arrogance" (as opposed, one imagines, to the cosmopolitanism and traditional self-deprecation of bacteria) leads us "to continue our traditional support for our own cosmic importance," and "to continue to view ourselves as better than all others by cosmic design."

What truly matters in evolution, Gould asserts, is not complexity but "success." For him, evolutionary success is a matter of counting, though he does make clear why this is so or whether one should count by species or by individuals. That 80 percent of multicellular species are arthropods leads Gould to conclude that arthropods are more successful than we vertebrates. And even among the mammalian minority of vertebrates, "the greatest successes" are "bats, rats, and antelopes," not primates, who can boast only 200 species. However, to evaluate the success of a single species, such as *Homo sapiens*, the counting must be by individuals; and, on this basis, Gould judges bacteria to be champions and the human race a flop.

There is a problem of consistency here, which Gould does not notice. There are more species of antelopes than of primates, but more human beings than antelopes; more species of fish than of mammals, but more dogs than snail darters. In any case, it is quite doubtful that proliferation of species is a sign of success. Homo sapiens has a flexibility made possible by his complexity, and, in particular, by his intelligence, which allows him to take advantage of a thousand ecological niches without fragmenting into a thousand different species. Nor does the number of individuals seem a more sensible measure of success. Size obviously has a lot to do with bacterial "success." There are more bacteria than people for much the same reason that there are more grains of sand than boulders.

Indeed, it is difficult to understand why Gould should stop at living things. There are vastly more molecules in the atmosphere than bacteria on (or in) the earth. Why is this not the Age of Air? And why should one not count the dust under one's bed and compare it to the population of China? Does not the fact that cosmic evolution has produced more dust particles than Chinese tell us something? One could even apply the same criteria to ideas. Disraeli observed that "Mormon counts more votaries than Bentham." We are worse off now, for more people will buy books on astrology than will buy *Full House*. Indeed, Gould's ideas could be said to be but a twig on the arborescent bush of human opinion.

Gould is overawed by other large numbers. The vast age and size of the universe in comparison to human scales are further evidence to him of human insignificance in the cosmic scheme. But these numbers can be looked at in another way. The universe must be as old as it is for life to have had time to evolve, and as large as it is for such huge times to be possible. (General Relativity relates the size and longevity of the universe.) Size and number are matters of physical requirements not "cosmic importance." There are basic physical reasons why living things must be small compared to the universe and large compared to atoms.

The "plain meaning" of evolution for Gould is that we were not "meant to be here"; we are a cosmic accident. The emergence of complex beings may have been an inevitable consequence of evolution (even if not its "goal"), but that complexity did not have to take the form of high intelligence. Says Gould:

> If we could replay the game of life again and again, . . . the [organisms] of greatest complexity would be wildly and unpredictably different in each rendition—and the vast majority of replays would never produce . . . a creature with self-consciousness. Human beings are here by the luck of the draw, not the inevitability of life's direction or evolution's mechanism.

Nor, he insists, are we here by some "cosmic preference." Gould seems strangely unaware that these considerations cut rather against atheism than against belief in a Creator. Religious believers say that we are here by the preference not of the cosmos but of God. It is atheists who imagine that evolutionary mechanisms, the inevitability of life's direction, or some cosmic necessity are sufficient to explain human existence.

Gould believes that the notion of "the average" has confused our ideas not only about the meaning of life but about the very nature of reality. It has left "a legacy as old as Plato, a tendency to abstract a single ideal or average as the 'essence' of a system, and to devalue or ignore variation among the individuals that constitute the full population." This gives rise to our cultural "hangup" over what is "normal." Opposed to this Platonic error is the Darwinian truth. The world is not "objectively divided into obvious categories. Taxonomies are human decisions." To those who claim that some "fundamental categories [are] invariant across time and culture," he replies, "Not so—not for these or for any subjects. Categories are human impositions upon nature." Even the idea that there are two sexes is, he claims, a recent cultural development.

It is not clear what any of this has to do with Darwin or biological science, but it certainly has nothing to do with Plato. Averages are not "our closest operational approach to essences." An essence is the intelligible form of something and is not at all a statistical concept. If every person in the world were to be blinded, that would not make sightlessness normal for man or a part of his nature or essence. Nor is a blind eye merely an example of variation: it is defective as an eye, because it does not fulfill the biological function that is evident from its form. On these points, Plato, Darwin, and modern geneticists have no disagreement.

That categories are not "imposed upon nature" is, if possible, even clearer in the physical sciences. For instance, an electron and a photon are quite distinct kinds of things. That an electron has charge, and mass, and is a "fermion," while a photon is neutral, massless, and a "boson," involves very fundamental distinctions that are true across time and culture—indeed to the limits of the known universe. The structure of the physical world turns out to be expressible in the forms of mathematics, the very realm of pure essences. It is not an accident that some of this century's greatest mathematicians and mathematical physicists have considered themselves Platonists.

The stated aim of this book is to "complete the Darwinian revolution." But there have been other revolutions since Darwin—in physics, mathematics, cosmology, and molecular biology—and they too have things to teach us about the universe and about man, things that one will not learn from this book. I recommend it, however, for those who take pleasure in fossils.

05

THE DESIGN OF EVOLUTION

C atholic theology has never really had a quarrel with the idea that the present species of plants and animals are the result of a long process of evolution—or with the idea that this process has unfolded according to natural laws. As the 1909 *Catholic Encyclopedia* put it, these ideas seem to be "in perfect agreement with the Christian conception of the universe."

Catholic theologians were more hesitant with respect to the origin of the human race, but even here, the old encyclopedia admitted, evolution of the human body is "*per se* not improbable" and a version of it had "been propounded by St. Augustine." The crucial doctrinal point was that the human soul, being spiritual, could not be the result of any merely material process: biological evolution any more than sexual reproduction. The soul must be conferred on each person by a special creative act of God. And so the Church is required to reject atheistic and materialistic philosophies of evolution, which deny the existence of a Creator or His providential governance of the world. As long as evolutionary theory confined itself to properly biological questions, however, it was considered benign.

This was the view that was taught to generations of children in Catholic schools. The first formal statement on evolution by the magisterium did not come until the encyclical letter *Humani Generis* of Pope Pius XII in 1950. The only point that the pontiff asserted as definitely dogmatic was that the human soul was not the product of evolution. As for the human body, Pius noted, its evolution from those of lower animals could be investigated as a scientific hypothesis, so long as no conclusions were made rashly.

This is how things stood for another half century. Then, in 1996, in a letter[1] to the Pontifical Academy of Sciences, Pope John Paul II acknowledged that the theory of evolution is now recognized as "more than a hypothesis," thanks to impressive and converging evidence coming from a variety of fields. He reiterated what he called the "essential point" made by Pius XII, namely that "if the human body takes its origin from preexistent living matter, [nevertheless] the spiritual soul is immediately[2] created by God."

Some commentators in the scientific and popular press took this statement to mean the Church had once rejected evolution and was now at last throwing in the towel. The truth is that Pius XII, though cautious, was clearly willing to let the scientific chips fall where they might; and John Paul II was simply noting the obvious fact that a lot of chips had since fallen. Nevertheless, John Paul's statement was a welcome reminder of the Church's real attitude toward empirical science. It was followed in 2004 by a lengthy document from the International Theological Commission (headed by Cardinal Ratzinger) entitled *Communion and Stewardship: Human Persons Created in the Image of God.* This important document contained, along with much else, a lucid and careful analysis of evolution and its relation to Catholic teaching.

So why did Christoph Schönborn, the cardinal archbishop of Vienna, lash out this summer at neo-Darwinism? In an opinion piece for the *New York Times* on July 7, he reacted indignantly to the suggestion that "the Catholic Church has no problem with the notion of 'evolution' as used by mainstream biologists—that is, synonymous with neo-Darwinism." Brushing off the 1996 statement of John Paul II as "vague and unimportant," he cited other evidence (including statements by the late pope, sentences from *Communion and Stewardship* and the *Catechism of the Catholic Church,* and a line from the new Pope Benedict XVI's installation homily) to make the case that neo-Darwinism is in fact incompatible with Catholic teaching.

In the United States, the harsh questions and mocking comments came fast and furious. Could it really be that the modern Church is condemning a scientific theory? How much doctrinal weight does Schönborn's article have? (After all, if a letter by a pope addressed to scientists can be called "unimportant," how important can a letter by a cardinal to the readers of a newspaper be?) Why did he write it? (It appears that it was done at the urging and with the assistance of his friend Mark Ryland, a philanthropist and ardent champion of the anti-Darwinian Intelligent Design movement.³) And what, precisely, was the cardinal saying?

The Church in recent centuries has avoided taking sides in intramural scientific disputes—which means the form as well as the content of the cardinal's article came as a shock. The issues it treats, having chiefly to do with the relation of chance and randomness to divine providence, are extremely subtle and cannot be dealt with adequately in the space of a newspaper column. It was nearly inevitable, therefore, that distinctions would get lost, terms would be ill-defined, and issues would be conflated.

By saying that "neo-Darwinism" is "synonymous" with "'evolution' as used by mainstream biologists," Schönborn indicates that he means the term as commonly understood among scientists. As so understood, neo-Darwinism is based on the idea that the mainspring of evolution is natural selection acting on random genetic variation. Elsewhere in his article, however, the cardinal gives another definition: "evolution in the neo-Darwinian sense [is] an unguided, unplanned process of random variation and natural selection." This is the central misstep of Cardinal Schönborn's article. He has slipped into the definition of a *scientific* theory, neo-Darwinism, the words "unplanned" and "unguided," which are fraught with *theological* meaning.

The line he quotes from *Communion and Stewardship* may seem to support him: "An unguided evolutionary process—one that falls outside the bounds of divine providence—simply cannot exist." And, since it is a fundamental Christian doctrine that God's providential plan extends to all events in the universe, nothing that happens can be "unplanned" as far as God is concerned.

But *Communion and Stewardship* also explicitly warns that the word "random" as used by biologists, chemists, physicists, and mathematicians in their technical work does not have the same meaning as the words "unguided" and "unplanned" as used in doctrinal statements of the Church. In common speech, "random" is often used to mean "uncaused," "meaningless," "inexplicable," or "pointless." And there is no question that some biologists, when they explain evolution to the public or to hapless students, do argue from the "randomness" of genetic mutations to the philosophical conclusion that the history of life is "unguided" and "unplanned." Some do this because of an anti-religious animus, while others are simply careless.

When scientists are actually doing science, however, they do not use the words "unguided" and "unplanned." The Institute for Scientific Information's well-known *Science Citation Index* reveals that only 48 papers exist in the scientific literature with the word "unguided" in the title, most having to do with missiles. Only 467 have the word "unplanned," almost all referring to pregnancies or medical procedures. By contrast there are 52,633 papers with "random" in the title, from all fields of scientific research. The word "random" is a basic technical term in most branches of science. It is used to discuss the motions of molecules in a gas, the fluctuations of quantum fields, noise in electronic devices, and the statistical errors in a data set, to give but a few examples. So if the word "random" necessarily entails the idea that some events are "unguided" in the sense of falling "outside of the bounds of divine providence," we should have to condemn as incompatible with Christian faith a great deal of modern physics, chemistry, geology, and astronomy, as well as biology.

This is absurd, of course. The word "random" as used in science does not mean uncaused, unplanned, or inexplicable; it means uncorrelated. My children like to observe the license plates of the cars that pass us on the highway, to see which states they are from. The sequence of states exhibits a degree of randomness: a car from Kentucky, then New Jersey, then Florida, and so on—because the cars are uncorrelated: knowing where one car comes from tells us nothing about where the next one comes from. And yet, each car comes to that place at that time for a reason. Each trip is planned, each guided by some map and schedule. Each driver's trip fits into the story of his life in some intelligible way, though the story of these drivers' lives are not usually closely correlated with the other drivers' lives.

Or consider this analogy. Prose, unlike a sonnet, has lines with final syllables that do not rhyme. The sequence those syllables form will therefore exhibit randomness. But this does not mean a prose work is "unguided" or "unplanned." True enough, the writer did not select the words with an eye to rhyming them, imposing on them that particular kind of correlation. But the words are still chosen. So God, though he planned His work with infinite care, may not have chosen to impose certain kinds of correlations on certain kinds of events, and the motions of the different molecules in a gas, for example, may exhibit no statistically verifiable correlation.

We should distinguish between what we may call "statistical randomness," which implies nothing about whether a process was planned or guided, and "randomness" in other senses. Statistical randomness, based on the lack of correlation among things or events, can be exploited to understand and explain phenomena through the use of probability theory. We may wish to determine, for example, whether the incidence of cancer in a certain county is consistent with statistical expectations, or whether there is some as-yet-unknown causal factor at work. By looking at the actuarial statistics, the age profile, and so on, one can compute the expected number of deaths due to cancer and see whether there is a statistically significant deviation from it. Implicit in all such computations are assumptions about randomness. Entire subfields in science (such as "statistical mechanics") are based on these methods: the properties of gases, liquids, and solids, for instance, can be understood and accurately calculated by methods that make assumptions about the randomness of molecular and atomic motions.

The promoters of the anti-Darwinian Intelligent Design movement usually admit that the ideas of statistical randomness, probability, and chance can be part of legitimate explanation of phenomena. They argue instead that to be able to make a scientific inference of "design" in some set of data one must first exclude other explanations, including "chance." The members of the International Theological Commission were clearly referring to the Intelligent Design movement when they wrote in *Communion and Stewardship*: "A growing body of scientific critics of neo-Darwinism point to evidence of design (*e.g.*, biological structures that exhibit specified complexity) that, in their view, cannot be explained in terms of a purely contingent process and that neo-Darwinians have ignored or misinterpreted. The nub of this currently lively disagreement involves scientific observation and generalization concerning whether the available data support inferences of design or chance, and cannot be settled by theology."

If an "inference of chance" as part of the explanation of a phenomenon cannot be ruled out on theological grounds, then the competing claims of neo-Darwinians and their Intelligent Design critics about biological complexity cannot be settled by theology. To their credit, many of the best writers in the Intelligent Design movement, including William Dembski and Michael Behe, also insist the issue is one to be settled scientifically.[4]

We cannot settle the issue of the role of "chance" in evolution theologically, because God is omnipotent and can therefore produce effects in different ways. Suppose a man wants to see a particular poker hand dealt. If he deals from a single shuffled deck, his chance of seeing a royal straight flush is 1 in 649,740. So he might decide to stack the deck, introducing the right correlations into the deck before dealing. Alternatively, he might decide to deal a hand from each of a billion shuffled decks. In that case the desired hand will turn up almost infallibly. (The chances it will not are infinitesimal: 10 to the -669 power.) In which way did God make life? Was the molecular deck "stacked" or "shuffled"?

This poker analogy is weak, of course. We don't know the order of a shuffled deck—that's one reason we shuffle it. But God knows all the details of the universe from all eternity. He knows what's in the cards. The scientist and the poker player do not look at things from God's point of view, however, and so they talk about "probabilities."

People have used the words "random," "probability," "chance," for millennia without anyone imagining that it must always imply a denial of divine providence. "I returned and saw under the sun, that the race is not to the swift, nor the battle to the strong, neither yet bread to the wise, nor yet riches to men of understanding, nor yet favor to men of skill, but time and *chance* happeneth to them all," as Ecclesiastes notes. Or, to make the point in dry technical terms, there is not a perfect correlation between being strong and winning or between having bread and being wise.

Why is there statistical randomness and lack of correlation in our world? It is because events do not march in lockstep, according to some simple formula, but are part of a vastly complex web of contingency. The notion of contingency is important in Catholic theology, and it is intimately connected to what in ordinary speech would be called "chance."

Communion and Stewardship settles this point. "Many neo-Darwinian scientists, as well as some of their critics, have concluded that if evolution is a radically contingent materialistic process driven by natural selection and random genetic variation, then there can be no place in it for divine providential causality," the document observes. "But it is important to note that, according to the Catholic understanding of divine causality, true contingency in the created order is not incompatible with a purposeful divine providence. Divine causality and created causality radically differ in kind and not only in degree. Thus, even the outcome of a purely contingent natural process can nonetheless fall within God's providential plan. According to St. Thomas Aquinas: 'The effect of divine providence is not only that things should happen somehow, but that they should happen either by necessity or by contingency. Therefore, whatsoever divine providence ordains to happen infallibly and of necessity, happens infallibly and of necessity; and that happens from contingency which the divine providence conceives to happen from contingency.' In the Catholic perspective, neo-Darwinians who adduce random genetic variation and natural selection as evidence that the process of evolution is absolutely unguided are straying beyond what can be demonstrated by science."

It is not neo-Darwinists as such that are being criticized here, but only the invalid inference drawn by "many" of them (along with "some of their critics") that the putative "randomness" of genetic variation necessarily implies an "absolutely unguided" process. It is clearly the intention of this passage to distinguish sharply the actual hypotheses of legitimate science from the philosophical errors often mistakenly thought to follow from them.

In his article, Schönborn cites the *Catechism of the Catholic Church*: "We believe that God created the world according to His wisdom. It is not the product of any necessity whatever, nor of blind fate or chance." And yet, it is one thing to say that the whole world is a product of chance and the existence of the universe a fluke, and quite another to say that within the universe there is statistical randomness. The cardinal also quotes the following passage from an address of the late pope: "To all these indications of the existence of God the Creator, some oppose the power of chance or of the proper mechanisms of matter. To speak of chance for a universe which presents such a complex organization in its elements and marvelous finality in its life would be equivalent to giving up the search for an explanation of the world as it appears to us." Indeed. But to employ arguments in science based on statistical randomness and probability is not necessarily to "oppose" the idea of chance to the existence of God the Creator.

Even within the neo-Darwinian framework, there are many ways that one could see evidence of that "finality" (the directedness of the universe and life) to which John Paul II refers. The possibility of an evolutionary process that could produce the marvelously intricate forms we see presupposes the existence of a universe whose structure, matter, processes, and laws are of a special character. This is the lesson of the many "anthropic coincidences" that have been identified by physicists and chemists. It is also quite likely, as suggested by the eminent neo-Darwinian biologist Simon Conway Morris, that certain evolutionary endpoints (or "solutions") are built into the rules of physics and chemistry, so that the "random variations" keep ending up at the same destinations, somewhat as meandering rivers always find the sea. In his book *Life's Solution*, Morris adduces much impressive evidence of such evolutionary tropisms. And, of course, we must never forget that each of us has spiritual powers of intellect, rationality, and freedom that cannot be accounted for by mere biology, whether as conceived by neo-Darwinians or their Intelligent Design critics.

I personally am not at all sure that the neo-Darwinian framework is a sufficient one for biology. But if it turns out to be so, it would in no way invalidate what Pope Benedict has said: "We are not some casual and meaningless product of evolution. Each of us is the result of a thought of God. Each of us is willed, each of us is loved, each of us is necessary." In his *New York Times* article, Cardinal Schönborn understandably wanted to counter those neo-Darwinian advocates who claim that the theory of evolution precludes a Creator's providential guidance of creation. Regrettably, he ended up giving credibility to their claim and obscuring the clear teaching of the Church that no truth of science can contradict the truth of revelation.

06

CHANCE, BY DESIGN

Christians who accept Darwinian evolution are, it is sometimes said, trying to have it both ways. If evolution was driven by random mutations, we cannot have been part of a divine plan. How, the critics ask, can we possibly exist by chance and by design, by accident and by intention?

The question of how to reconcile chance with divine providence long predated Darwin. People didn't need science to tell them that chance had something to do with their being here. Each of us is the product of a long and tenuous chain of improbable events. We wouldn't have been born if our parents hadn't happened to meet or if some ancestor hadn't escaped disaster by a hair's breadth. Nor is the role of chance in the world news to theologians. "If the nose of Cleopatra had been shorter," wrote Pascal in the seventeenth century, "the whole face of the earth would have been changed." "No one in this life can escape being tossed about at the mercy of chance and accident," observed St. Augustine in the fourth.[1] "Time and chance happeneth to them all," lamented Qoholeth much earlier than that. (Eccles 9:11)

But in the opinion of some contemporary anti-Darwinians, there cannot really be chance or randomness in the world if God is in charge, and for them that is reason enough to reject Darwinism out of hand. Such rejection, however, doesn't really dispose of the issue, for it arises even more dramatically in other branches of science. It is now thought, for example, that not only did this or that species of plant or animal arise as a result of random processes, but so did our entire galaxy, and thus our sun and earth as well. About 300,000 years[2] after the Big Bang, matter was spread uniformly throughout the universe, but not perfectly so. Some regions were slightly denser than average; and these served as the seeds from which galaxies grew. These "density perturbations" were randomly distributed as far as statistical analyses can tell, and there is reason to believe that they came from quantum fluctuations that occurred moments after the Big Bang.

But for some reason it is Darwinism that provokes the greatest controversy and concern. This controversy flared up in July of 2005, when Cardinal Christoph Schönborn (editor and chief author of the *Catechism of the Catholic Church*) wrote a memorable piece in the *New York Times* suggesting that neo-Darwinism is not "compatible with Christian faith." He defined neo-Darwinism as the view that evolution is an "unguided, unplanned process of random variation and natural selection." The cardinal's concern was precisely whether the randomness posited by neo-Darwinian theory could be squared with a divine plan that guides all things.

I responded a few months later within an article in these pages entitled "The Design of Evolution." My chief point was that the word "random" as used in science does not mean unguided and unplanned, but has a narrow technical meaning having to do with the statistical correlations among things. I gave examples showing that something could be guided and planned and yet exhibit such "statistical randomness," as it is often called. Words like "unguided" and "unplanned" when used in discussions of evolution are philosophical glosses, I said, not technical scientific terms.

Some anti-Darwinists claim that I was simply wrong about what "random" means in evolutionary biology. They assert that it does mean unguided and unplanned and that we have this on the authority of the scientific community itself.

In 1995, for example, the National Association of Biology Teachers stated that "the development of life on earth is the outcome of evolution, an unsupervised, impersonal, unpredictable, and natural process of temporal descent." In their textbook *Biology*, Kenneth Miller and Joseph Levine explain, "Of course, there has never been any kind of plan to evolution, because evolution works without either plan or purpose .... Evolution is random and undirected." Just two months after Cardinal Schönborn's piece appeared, an open letter to the Kansas State Board of Education signed by thirty-eight Nobel laureates in science[3] affirmed that "evolution is understood to be the result of an unguided and unplanned process of random variation and natural selection." (That they used the cardinal's very formulation was doubtless intended as a poke in the ecclesiastical eye.)

Recently, Jay W. Richards of the Discovery Institute averred that "The problem is that Barr is not using these words as they are almost universally used when scientists talk about biological evolution. He's committing what we might call the 'fallacy of private definition.'" Michael Behe, in a debate with me at Wheaton College last year, quipped, "Most scientists—with the exception of maybe one or two in Delaware—understand Darwinian evolution to mean" unguided and unplanned.

My answer is that one must distinguish between words used by scientists and words used scientifically—or, as I put it in "The Design of Evolution," "as used by [scientists] in their technical work." That is what counts philosophically and theologically, not the popular or polemical uses one finds in manifestos or even at times in textbooks.

When biologists start making statements about processes being unsupervised, undirected, unguided, and unplanned, they are not speaking scientifically. No measurement, observation, or mathematical analysis can test whether or not God planned a development like a genetic mutation. What apparatus would one employ? Being "unplanned by God" is simply not a concept that fits within empirical science. Being "statistically random," on the other hand, is, because it can be tested for.

And suppose we did define neo-Darwinism to include the belief that the world is "unguided and unplanned" by God. Then neo-Darwinism would be atheistic simply by definition. Only if neo-Darwinism is defined in terms of its *strictly scientific content* does how well it comports with a religious view of the world become an interesting and debatable question. This is the question I shall now examine, particularly how the kind of randomness posited by neo-Darwinian theory can be consistent with divine providence. But first we must understand what providence and randomness are.

Most traditional forms of biblical religion agree what providence is. They may dispute how providence relates to human freedom, but their differences don't affect their understanding of merely physical processes such as evolution. The traditional doctrine is that God, the transcendent source of being, wills by one timeless act that all things exist, wherever in space and time they do exist. He is the creator of all finite beings in every aspect of their being, and hence he creates them with all their natural potentialities, powers, and relationships, including their causal relationships to each other. A helpful analogy compares God to the author of a play. The playwright is the cause of the entire play in all its aspects—he pens its every character, event, and word. Call this "vertical causality." But it is also true that *within* the play, one thing causes another. Call this "horizontal causality." The two causalities are not in competition.

Consider this question: In the play *Hamlet*, did Polonius die because he was stabbed through a curtain or because Shakespeare wrote the play that way? The question is silly, of course, for the answer is *both*. The stabbing is the cause *within* the play, while Shakespeare is the cause *of* the play and all that happens in it. Similarly, there are causes *within* nature, which are studied by scientists and others, while God is the cause *of* nature. Theology traditionally refers to "primary" and "secondary" causality rather than vertical and horizontal causality. We see, then, how idle it is to ask whether some species of beetle exists because it evolved or because God created it. The species of beetle evolved because God wrote the script that way. And, indeed, each individual beetle only exists because God wrote it in as one of the *dramatis personae*.

The Book of Wisdom declares that God "reaches mightily from one end of the earth to the other and orders all things." His providence is not just some general oversight of the world, leaving the details to be worked out by someone else. Rather, he is the direct cause of every detail of the universe, just as Shakespeare wrote every syllable of *Hamlet*. God orders "all" things, whether the falling of a sparrow or the hairs of your head, which are numbered. This is the doctrine of "particular providence," taught by both Catholic and Calvinist.

Theologians distinguish between "mediate" and "immediate" providence. The former is exercised through natural secondary causes and the latter directly. God does indeed "make the little green apples," as the song says, but he does so by making an entire process of natural growth and development occur, whereas no natural causes were at work when he turned water into wine at Cana of Galilee. Therefore, saying that something arose through natural processes in no way denies particular providence. Indeed, traditional teaching tells us that God's providence *ordinarily* works through natural causes. As the great scholastic theologian Francisco Suarez put it, "God does not intervene directly in the natural order where secondary causes are sufficient to produce the intended effect."

Now we come to the troublesome word "random." It is used throughout modern science. The word appears in the titles of over 70,000 research papers from every branch of science. Here are a few examples: "Domain growth in random magnets," "Random vibration of bridges under vehicles with variable speed," and "Spatial coherence of random laser emission." The concept of "randomness" is useful in science because it allows us to calculate probabilities. If a deck of cards has been randomized by shuffling, one is able to compute the odds of getting dealt various hands. Similarly, assumptions about the randomness of molecular motions allow one to compute the relative probabilities of air molecules moving at different speeds.

Although widely used in science, the concepts of randomness and probability are notoriously slippery for philosophers and mathematicians. There exist, in fact, different and inequivalent definitions of them: "statistical randomness" versus "information-theoretic randomness" and "frequentist probability" versus "Beyesian probability." Fortunately, we need only consider these concepts as they are used in the everyday practice of natural science. It is best to consider a simple example rather than trying to lay down a definition.

Consider a series of coin tosses. The crucial fact is that the coin tosses are causally independent of each other. In other words, there is no mechanism by which one coin toss significantly affects the others. Because of this, there is no reason to expect their results to be correlated with each other in any particular way, that is, to exhibit any particular pattern. Therefore, the results of such tosses would form what mathematicians call a "random sequence." Strong correlations might occur—for example, a series of tosses alternating heads and tails,—but they would be regarded as accidental. In a long random sequence, such striking patterns will be rare, and probability theory can tell us how rare. The odds of 100 coin tosses giving alternating heads and tails is only about 1 in 500 billion billion billion. With a large sample, therefore, it is possible to test statistically for randomness.

But such tests can never be conclusive. Not only can a sequence exhibit an obvious pattern despite actually being produced by a random process, but the opposite can happen. The digits of the number pi, for instance, pass all statistical tests of randomness, but are not really independent of each other.

If statistical tests can never be absolutely conclusive, how do we know that there really is randomness in nature? Ultimately, it is a *postulate* on the same footing as the assumption that nature obeys "universal laws." No number of experimental tests could ever rigorously prove either of those postulates to be true. They are simply part of how we—not just scientists, but people generally—understand the "natural order" of the world. Just as something violating a universal law, such as water flowing uphill, would be regarded as contrary to nature, so would something that was wildly improbable given what one might call "natural randomness," such as all the leaves in your windy tree-lined street landing in your neighbors' yards and none in yours. Every day, in countless contexts, people take natural randomness for granted. Only superstitious people expect to find patterns in tea leaves.

The fact that one cannot rigorously prove randomness or non-randomness by statistical tests doesn't make these concepts useless at the practical level. One can use such tests to look for suspicious correlations in cancer deaths, in election results, in poker hands, and in all sorts of other things. So it is in science. The key point is that randomness in empirical science boils down *in practice* to the absence of significant statistical correlations.

This brings us to our first question. Does "statistical randomness" in a process mean that it is "unguided and unplanned?" Let's start with an analogy used in "The Design of Evolution." Observing the license plates of the cars that pass by on the highway, one will generally find that they are statistically random in the sense that knowing where one car is from provides no information about where another is from. This in no way implies that the cars' movements and locations are "undirected," "unguided," and "unplanned." In fact, the cars are directed by the wills of their drivers, who are guided by maps and pursuing plans. It is just that the lives of the various drivers, and thus their plans, are (generally speaking) causally independent of each other.

This example helps explain why statistical randomness and "chance" events occur in our world. It is not because events are uncaused or because we cannot trace their causes. It is because so many independent causal chains intersect and impinge on each other that sequences or juxtapositions arise that exhibit the lack of correlation we call "statistical randomness."

The intersection of independent chains of causality can give rise to chance events that disrupt the normal course of development in one of them. A dramatic example, which has directly to do with evolution, is the asteroid that struck the earth near the Yucatan peninsula 65 million years ago and (in the view of most experts) was the primary cause of the extinction of the dinosaurs. Here were two systems, each going its own merry way, almost completely independently of each other: life on earth and the bodies orbiting the sun. When these two systems crossed paths, one had what from the point of view of evolutionary history was a "chance" event.

St. Thomas Aquinas had a similar understanding of chance. It is found in Book 3, chapter 74 of his *Summa Contra Gentiles*, which is titled "Divine providence does not exclude fortune and chance." The fourth reason St. Thomas gives is that "the large number and variety of causes [in the world] stem from divine providence and control." But given the large variety of causes,

> one of them must at times run into another cause and be impeded, or assisted, by it in the production of its effect. Now from the concurrence of two causes it is possible for some chance event to occur, and thus some unintended event occurs because of this causal concurrence. For example, the discovery of a debtor, by a man who has gone to market to sell something, happens because the creditor also went to market.

The debtor and creditor happening to be at the market at the same time is like the cars in the license-plate example happening to be at the same place on the highway, or the asteroid happening to be at the same place as the Yucatan Peninsula.

One cause sometimes "run[ning] into another and be[ing] impeded or assisted in the production of its effect" is connected to the distinction St. Thomas makes between "necessary causes," which unfailingly produce their natural effects, and "contingent causes," which can be impeded by the action of other causes. Mass causing space-time to curve due to a universal law is an example of the first, the propagation of dinosaur species being impeded by asteroids is an example of the second. Contingent causes are subject to the vagaries of chance, while necessary causes are not. Aquinas thus sometimes says that things happen "by contingency," where we would say "by processes involving chance."

This is all very well, one might object, but perhaps evolutionary biologists mean something different and more radical when they speak of "random genetic mutations." Well, let's see.

In their college-level textbook *Modern Genetics*, F. J. Ayala and J. A. Kiger explain three senses in which mutations are said to be random: 1) as "rare exceptions to the regularity of the process of DNA replication"; 2) because "there is no way of knowing whether a given gene will mutate in a particular cell or in a particular generation"; and 3) because "[these mutations] are unoriented with respect to adaptation." They note that this last meaning "is very important for evolution. . . . Mutations occur *independently* of whether or not they are adaptive in the environments where the organisms live" (emphasis mine). Mutations are produced by various causes, such as natural radiation or genetic copying errors. The adaptive needs of organisms arise from quite different—and independent—causes, such as changes in climate or food supply. This produces a lack of systematic correlation between when mutations happen and when they are needed, so the former are "unoriented" with respect to the latter.

Or consider the definition given by Ernst Mayr, one of the twentieth century's leading evolutionary biologists: "When it is said that mutation or variation is random, the statement *simply* means that there is no *correlation* between the production of new genotypes and the adaptational needs of an organism in a given environment" (emphasis mine).

We now come to the critical issue. While the example of the license-plates showed that a process may exhibit statistical randomness despite being guided and planned, the randomness occurred in an aspect of the process that was irrelevant to the purposes of those directing it. The motorists were not trying to arrange their license plates in an interesting sequence. This suggests that if certain effects arise through chance—if, for example, a series of cars passed by from states in alphabetical order—the effects were not intended in themselves but were at most accidental byproducts of something else that was intended.

To put it another way, in St. Thomas's example, we call the discovery of the debtor a chance event precisely because the debtor and the creditor independently decided to go to the market. But what if they had the same master, who sent them separately to the market so that they should meet, only seemingly by accident? If God has written the cosmic play so that the human race and each specific human being would come to exist, it would seem that there is no causal independence. Everything in the universe would be rigged and not random. This is the very heart of the problem, and why many people, both religious and nonreligious, do not believe that randomness in evolutionary processes and God's having intended man to exist can both be true.

The problem arises, as do so many other false problems, from a confusion of horizontal and vertical causality. When people speak of randomness, whether in science, in other professions, or in everyday life, they are not speaking of how things in this world relate to God, but how they are related to each other; that is, they are referring to the horizontal level of causality. What is involved is the independence of various *natural* causes from each other, which leads to what I called "natural randomness" earlier.

If you toss a coin ten times, there is no *natural mechanism* by which any toss significantly affects the others. And if you need nine of them to come up heads to win a game, there is no natural mechanism by which your need can cause them to come up heads. The outcomes of the tosses are uncorrelated with your competitive needs, just as genetic mutations are uncorrelated with organisms' adaptive needs. Someone might object that if you get nine heads in ten tosses and actually win the game that proves that the tosses *were* in fact correlated with your needs. But that's an empty statement that misses the point. Obviously, the tosses will turn out to have been correlated with the winner's needs. The point, however, is that no mechanism in the process of tossing a coin takes account of any particular player's needs. And so, in a sense that is objectively meaningful and everyone understands, the coin tosses are random and the game is fair.

In evolutionary biology, too, it is only natural causes and mechanisms that are being talked about. In the words of Elliott Sober, a leading philosopher of science, the "randomness" of genetic mutations in evolutionary theory means that "there is no *physical mechanism* (either inside organisms or outside of them) that detects which mutations would be beneficial and causes those mutations to occur" (emphasis mine). Whenever anyone—whether an actuary, an investor, a weather forecaster, or a physicist—computes probabilities, the assumptions being made have solely to do with *natural* causes being independent of each other.

A comparison of "natural randomness" and "natural laws" may be helpful here. The fundamental laws of nature also have to do with horizontal causal relationships. Ordinarily, God causes things to happen in accordance with those laws, as when water runs downhill, and on much rarer occasions he causes things to happen that contravene those laws, as when water once turned into wine. In all cases, however, whether the kinds of horizontal relationships we call natural laws hold or fail to hold, it is God who, in the vertical sense, is causing things to happen, and to happen just as they do.

Similarly, most things happen in accordance with natural randomness and therefore with natural probabilities, such as coin tosses coming out heads 50 percent of the time, or a certain kind of subatomic particle called the K-short decaying 69.3 percent of the time into electrically charged particles and 30.7 percent of the time into neutral ones. On some occasions, however, things may happen that are so grossly contrary to natural probabilities as to be clearly miraculous. (As in the legend of the seventy-two translators of the Septuagint, who, working independently, arrived at exactly the same Greek translation of the Hebrew Bible.)

In either case, whether or not things unfold in accordance with natural randomness and natural probabilities, it is God who in the vertical sense is causing them to happen that way. As St. Thomas put it, "The effect of divine providence is not only that things should happen somehow, but that they should happen either by necessity or by contingency. Therefore, whatsoever divine providence ordains should happen infallibly and of necessity, happens infallibly and of necessity; [whereas those things] that divine providence conceives should happen from contingency, happen by contingency."

By itself, the doctrine of divine providence only tells us that everything unfolds in accordance with God's plan. It does not tell us what that plan is, either in its general features or in its particular details. It does not tell us the mix of law and chance, or of necessity and contingency, that God chose to use in his plan. Evolutionary history may have unfolded entirely in accordance with natural laws, natural randomness, and natural probabilities, as the great majority of biologists believe or there may have been some extraordinary events along the way that contravened those laws and probabilities. In either case, evolution unfolded exactly as known and willed by God from all eternity.

07

DEBATING DARWIN

O f the many proofs of the existence of God, perhaps the one that
makes the most direct appeal to our intuition and common sense is
the Argument from Design. Writing in 1840, Macaulay observed:

A philosopher of the present day . . . has before him the same evidences of
design in the structure of the universe which the early Greeks had, . . . for
the discoveries of modern astronomers and anatomists have really added
nothing to the force of that argument which a reflective mind finds in every
beast, bird, insect, fish, leaf, flower, and shell.

But if from the time of the early Greeks until Macaulay's day things
were quiet in this particular branch of natural theology, they have heated
up since then. For, just 19 years after Macaulay wrote those words, Darwin published *The Origin of Species*. Now, not only the discoveries of astronomers and anatomists but those of researchers in every field, from
information theory to molecular biology, are marshaled to attack (and to
defend) the Argument from Design.

Many people suppose that Darwin destroyed the Argument from
Design once and for all—at least in biology. But this is not so, as Michael J. Behe convincingly argues in his important new book *Darwin's
Black Box: The Biochemical Challenge to Evolution*. As a molecular biologist[1]
at Lehigh University, Behe writes with authority about such things as
ribosomes and polypeptides. But he writes for the layman, managing

to make the arcana of his field not only very clear but also lively and entertaining. And, from his redoubt in the inhospitable terrain of biochemistry, he has issued a formidable challenge to the current version of evolutionary theory.

There is no denying the brilliance of Darwin's insights. Before he proposed the idea of natural selection, no one had ever found a way to explain the apparent "purpose" of biological structures without invoking Design. In fact, no one seems to have dreamed that there could be some other explanation. Darwin did, even for something as intricate as the human eye. It is obvious that random mutation of the genes that could produce an eye would be absurdly improbable. However, there is an answer in Darwinian theory to the problem of complexity. A large change can be built up through a sequence of "small" (in the sense of probabilistically achievable) steps, each of which need only confer some incremental selective advantage on the organism. This is the idea of Darwinian gradualism. Darwin himself proposed a very plausible sequence of steps that might have led to the human eye.

Behe, significantly, does not reject all of Darwin in his effort to rescue the biological Argument from Design. All that is logically required is to find some—maybe only a few—convincing examples of complex biological systems that cannot be explained by Darwinian gradualism. Darwinism (or neo-Darwinism) does not have to be wrong, just incomplete. As Behe notes, "The production of some improvements in organisms by mutation and natural selection—by evolution —is quite consistent with intelligent design theory."

Thus Behe, unlike many critics of Darwin, is willing to admit a large role for natural selection in evolution—even, it seems, in "macroevolution" (roughly speaking, the production of entirely new species or types). But he finds certain examples in biology—called by him systems of "irreducible complexity" —which he argues natural selection is powerless to explain. These are systems that, in order to function at all, require the coordinated activity of many parts and that consequently can only arise all at once, in an improbable "big" step. The elegant paradox at the heart of Behe's book is that the place to look for these big steps is at the level of the very small.

As Behe emphasizes, the real action of life takes place in the cell, at the molecular level. Until recent decades, the cell was a "black box," which evolutionary biologists could assume would produce the postulated mutations. But to know whether these mutations are really "small" in the required sense, one has to know how they might be produced geneti-cally—and that is a question of molecular biology.

Due to the patient and clever work of generations of scientists, this black box has been opened. And one finds that, as life is examined at smaller and smaller scales, the structures and processes seem not simpler and more elementary, but increasingly complicated. Indeed, what goes on in the simplest cell is of staggering complexity.

Behe focuses on five molecular systems of "irreducible complexity": the cilia of cells, the chemistry of vision in the retina, the blood-clotting system, the system by which new enzymes are manufactured and trans-ported to the sites in the cell where they are needed, and the immune system. It is an important point that all these systems are fundamental and widespread in the animal kingdom and are necessary in particular for the human species.

As anyone who has seen a good magic show knows, sometimes a thing that seems impossible turns out to be rather simple once you know how it is done. Moreover, one can imagine cases where a system that appears, at first sight, to be "irreducibly complex" is not so. An example that occurs to me is a free-standing Roman arch, which would topple if any single stone were removed. Yet one can build up such a structure one stone at a time by using scaffolding in the intermediate stages of construction. Even though I have tried, with thoughts like these, to maintain an attitude of cautious skepticism regarding Behe's claims, I cannot help wondering how on earth such systems as he describes could possibly have evolved in a gradualistic manner.

This is the "challenge" to evolutionary theory to which the subtitle of Behe's book refers. How have biologists responded to it? As biologists, largely by ignoring it.[2] Behe combed the technical literature of his field and found that very little, if any, work has been done that attempts to explain how these systems might have evolved. This is not a reproach to biology. The time is probably not ripe for useful research in this area. Like anyone else, theorists must first "get a handle on a problem" before they can make any progress. That handle, apparently, has not been found.

What is strange, and does deserve reproach, is the insouciance with which many biologists treat these difficulties. In a recent review of Behe's book, a noted biologist takes him to task for "pouncing on a few puz-zles." "Puzzles" is surely not the right word. In my field, particle physics, there are fundamental problems of such long standing and so resistant to solution that they are regarded as "deep," requiring for their solution radical changes in our ways of thinking. What Behe is describing are deep problems in biology.

Of course, the mother of all unsolved problems in biology is the origin of life. This too has resisted gradualistic explanation. Even the simplest self-reproducing organism has to be enormously complicated. Some have estimated that the "protobiont" (the first living thing) must have contained at least 80 different proteins and a DNA (or RNA) molecule about 100,000 nucleotides long (equivalent to 200,000 bits of information). How it could have evolved is still a complete mystery.

But before jumping on Behe's bandwagon, I must sound a cautionary note. Dissenters from the Argument from Design still have a way out of some of these problems, though it relies neither on Darwin nor gradualism. The universe might be infinitely large, strongly implying that there are an infinite number of stars and planets. Then no matter how small the probability of a statistical fluke producing, say, the protobiont—as long as that probability is finite rather than zero—that fluke will happen somewhere and, in fact, in an infinite number of places. Behe is aware of this but perhaps does not take it as seriously as he should. This idea does not rely on bizarre and speculative cosmologies. Even in the simplest standard cosmological model, the universe can be either "closed" and finite or "open" and infinite.

This, I think, will remain a vulnerability of the biological Argument from Design, unless and until the universe is shown to be finite. The Argument from Design, however, goes beyond biology. It can be made at the level of the universe as a whole and its fundamental laws. When it is framed in this way, any attempt to escape from it, whether by appeals to Darwinian mechanisms or to an infinite number of chances, is doomed to circularity. (Did the fundamental laws evolve? According to what laws? Are there an infinite number of "universes"? If unrelated to ours, these universes can explain nothing about ours. If related to ours, by some overarching laws that tell what kinds of universes exist and how many of each, then really they are all parts of one universe.) While some biologists, like Richard Dawkins, think of the universe as being a "blind watchmaker," to a physicist it is more natural to think of it as being a watch.

Behe closes his book with the suggestion that a general theory of intelligent design should be sought and that intelligent design should be introduced into biology and the other sciences along with the usual kinds of scientific hypotheses. A rigorous mathematical theory that would allow one to distinguish designed from accidental patterns would certainly be interesting, if one were possible. It could have applications in many areas, from deciding whether curiously shaped stones were human artifacts to solving crimes.

With regard to introducing the idea of divine intervention into science, however, I must demur, along with many other religious scientists. Such interventions, by definition, take events out of the course of nature that science is trying to understand. Moses' parting the Red Sea tells us nothing about hydrodynamics, and a miraculous cure at Lourdes is not a breakthrough in oncology. The inference that a miracle has occurred can be a legitimate conclusion *from* scientific knowledge, but it is not an addition *to* scientific knowledge.

Behe's book is a major contribution to an important and growing debate. Will he succeed in rousing many materialists from their dogmatic slumbers? That would be a miracle.

08

THE END OF INTELLIGENT DESIGN?

I t is time to take stock: What has the intelligent design movement achieved? As science, nothing. The goal of science is to increase our understanding of the natural world, and there is not a single phenomenon that we understand better today or are likely to understand better in the future through the efforts of ID theorists. If we are to look for ID achievements, then, it must be in the realm of natural theology. And there, I think, the movement must be judged not only a failure, but a debacle.

Very few religious skeptics have been made more open to religious belief because of ID arguments. These arguments not only have failed to persuade, they have done positive harm by convincing many people that the concept of an intelligent designer is bound up with a rejection of mainstream science.

The ID claim is that certain biological phenomena lie outside the ordinary course of nature. Aside from the fact that such a claim is, in practice, impossible to substantiate, it has the effect of pitting natural theology against science by asserting an incompetence of science. To be sure, there are questions that natural science is not competent to address, and too many scientists have lost all sense of the limitations of their disciplines, not to mention their own limitations. But the ID arguments effectively declare natural science incompetent even in what most would regard as its own proper sphere. Nothing could be better calculated to provoke the antagonism of the scientific community. This throwing down of the gauntlet to science explains not a little of the fervor of the scientific backlash against ID.

The older (and wiser) form of the design argument for the existence of God—one found implicitly in Scripture and in many early Christian writings—did not point to the naturally inexplicable or to effects outside the course of nature, but to nature itself and its ordinary operations—operations whose "power and working" were seen as reflecting the power and wisdom of God. The following passage from the Book of Wisdom is essentially a design argument addressed, circa 100 BC, to those impressed by ancient Greek science:

> For all people who were ignorant of God were foolish by nature; and they were unable from the good things that are seen to know the one who exists, nor did they recognize the artisan while paying heed to his works; but they supposed that either fire or wind or swift air, or the circle of the stars, or turbulent water, or the luminaries of heaven were the gods that rule the world. If through delight in the beauty of these things people assumed them to be gods, let them know how much better than these is their Lord, for the author of beauty created them. And if people were amazed at their power and working, let them perceive from them how much more powerful is the one who formed them. For from the greatness and beauty of created things comes a corresponding perception of their Creator. Yet these people are little to be blamed, for perhaps they go astray while seeking God and desiring to find him. For while they live among his works, they keep searching, and they trust in what they see, because the things that are seen are beautiful. Yet again, not even they are to be excused; for if they had the power to know so much that they could investigate the world, how did they fail to find sooner the Lord of these things? (Wisdom 13:1–9)

These words are prophetically relevant to those today who investigate the world but fail to find its author. Note that the evidence of the Creator to which this passage points consists of phenomena that even ID proponents would agree have good scientific explanations: "fire," "wind," "swift air," "the circle of the stars," "turbulent water," and "luminaries of heaven." The Letter of Clement (circa AD 97), one of the oldest surviving Christian documents outside the New Testament, speaks of God's "ordering of His whole creation" by pointing, again, to *natural* phenomena:

> The heavens, as they revolve beneath His government, do so in quiet submission to Him. The day and the night run the course He has laid down for them, and neither of them interferes with the other. Sun, moon, and the

starry choirs roll on in harmony at His command, none swerving from his appointed orbit. Season by season the teeming earth, obedient to His will, causes a wealth of nourishment to spring forth for man and beast and every living thing upon its surface, making no demur and no attempt to alter even the least of His decrees. Laws of the same kind sustain the fathomless deeps of the abyss and the untold regions of the netherworld. Nor does the illimitable basin of the sea, gathered by the operations of His hand into its various different centers, overflow at any time the barriers encircling it, but does as He has bidden it. . . . The impassable Ocean and all the worlds that lie beyond it are themselves ruled by the like ordinances of the Lord. Spring, summer, autumn, and winter succeed one another peaceably; the winds fulfill their punctual duties, each from its own quarter, and give no offence; the ever-flowing streams created for our well-being and enjoyment offer their breasts unfailingly for the life of man; and even the minutest of living creatures mingle together in peaceful accord. Upon all of these the great Architect and Lord of the universe has enjoined peace and harmony.

The emphasis in early Christian writings was not on complexity, irreducible or otherwise, but on the beauty, order, lawfulness, and harmony found in the world that God had made. As science advances, it brings this beautiful order ever more clearly into view. Every photograph from the Hubble Space Telescope, every picture from the ocean's depths, every discovery in subatomic physics, shows it forth. As Calvin wrote in his *Institutes of the Christian Religion*, "God [has] manifested himself in the formation *of every part of the world*, and daily presents himself to public view, in such manner, that they cannot open their eyes without being constrained to behold him." And, "[W]ithersoever you turn your eyes, *there is not an atom of the world* in which you cannot behold some brilliant sparks at least of his glory. . . . You cannot at one view take a survey of this most ample and beautiful machine [the universe] in all its vast extent, without being completely overwhelmed with its infinite splendor" [emphasis mine]. Note that "atoms of the world" are not irreducibly complex, nor is "every part of the world." Irreducible complexity has never been the central principle of traditional natural theology.

But whereas the advance of science continually strengthens the broader and more traditional version of the design argument, the ID movement's version is hostage to every advance in biological science. Science must fail for ID to succeed. In the famous "explanatory filter" of William A. Dembski, one finds "design" by eliminating "law" and "chance" as explanations. This, in effect, makes it a zero-sum game between God and nature. What nature does and science can explain is crossed off the list, and what remains is the evidence for God. This conception of design plays right into the hands of atheists, whose caricature of religion has always been that it is a substitute for the scientific understanding of nature.

The ID movement has also rubbed a very raw wound in the relation between science and religion. For decades scientists have had to fend off the attempts by Young Earth Creationists to promote their ideas as a valid alternative science. The scientific world's exasperation with creationists is understandable. Imagine yourself a serious historian in a country where half the population believed in Afrocentric history, say, or a serious political scientist in a country where half the people believed that the world is run by the Bilderberg Group or the Rockefellers. It would get to you after a while, especially if there were constant attempts to insert these "alternative theories" into textbooks. So, when the ID movement came along and suggested that its ideas be taught in science classrooms, it touched a nerve. This is one reason that the New Atheists attracted such a huge audience.

None of this is to say that the conclusions the ID movement draws about how life came to be and how it evolves are intrinsically unreasonable or necessarily wrong. Nor is it to deny that the ID movement has been treated atrociously and that it has been lied about by many scientists.[1] The question I am raising is whether this quixotic attempt by a small and lightly armed band to overthrow "Darwinism" and bring about a new scientific revolution has accomplished anything good. It has had no effect on scientific thought. Its main consequence has been to strengthen the general perception that science and religion are at war.

Cui bono? Only those people whose religious doctrines entail either Young Earth Creationism or a rejection of common descent. Such people already and necessarily were in a state of war with modern science and have no choice but to fight that war to the bitter end. Many of them see in the ID movement a useful ally in that war (as the Dover trial illustrated), despite the fact that the ID movement does not deny common descent or the age of the earth.[2] Other religious people, however, have nothing to gain and a great deal to lose by the ID movement's frontal assault on well-defended redoubts of modern science—an assault that has come to resemble the Charge of the Light Brigade.

I suspect that some religious people have embraced the ID movement's arguments because they want "scientific" answers to the scientific atheists, and they know of no others. But there are plenty of ways to make a case for the reasonableness of religious belief that can be persuasive to many in the scientific world. Such a case has been made by a growing number of research scientists who are Christian believers, such as John Polkinghorne, Owen Gingerich, Francis Collins, Peter E. Hodgson, Michal Heller, Kenneth R. Miller, and Marco Bersanelli. I have addressed many audiences myself using arguments similar to theirs and have had scientists whom I know to be of firm atheist convictions tell me that they came away with more respect for the religious position. Religion has a significant number of friends (and potential friends) in the scientific world. The ID movement is not creating any new ones.

MIND AND SOUL

09

MORE THAN MACHINES: PHYSICS AND FREE WILL

What is man, that thou art mindful of him? and the son of man, that thou visitest him?" So asked the psalmist three thousand years ago. The question is still with us and as urgent as ever: What are we? The scriptural answer is that we are made in the image of God, but this answer is not as plausible to many people today as it once was. Reductive theories abound that claim that human beings are nothing more than the product of biological and social evolution, of genes and the environment, of instincts and social conditioning, of the wiring of the brain and the chemistry of hormones and neurotransmitters. What gets lost in all of this is free will.

Explaining how man is made in the image of God, the second-century theologian St. Irenaeus of Lyons wrote that "man is rational and therefore like God; he is created with free will and is master over his acts." This freedom is what makes us persons, and it is what allows us to share in the divine life. To share in that life, says St. John the Evangelist, is to abide in love and in truth; and that is only possible for us to do because we are endowed with freedom. If we were entirely controlled by factors of a lower order, by mere material forces, as animals are, we could not be open to realities of a higher order, to goodness, truth, and beauty. According to *The Catechism of the Catholic Church*, in "his openness to truth and beauty, his sense of moral goodness, his freedom and the voice of his conscience," man finds evidence "of his spiritual soul," which is "irreducible to the merely material."

The belief that human beings have spiritual souls and are thereby endowed with free will has been under attack for a long time by philosophers, scientists, and even some theologians. The basis of that attack is a philosophical idea called "physicalism," which maintains that human beings are completely explicable in physical terms: we are, say physicalists, nothing but enormously complicated biochemical machines.

This idea has deep historical roots. The predictable motions of the heavenly bodies led very early to the idea that the astronomical universe is a clocklike mechanism—this was already a commonplace among medieval thinkers. In the seventeenth century, as it became clear that terrestrial phenomena, like celestial ones, are governed by precise mathematical laws, the idea began to emerge that plants, animals, and even the human body can also be understood as machines. This was the view of both Descartes and Pascal, though they drew the line at the human spiritual soul, whose immateriality they continued to affirm. The more radical thinkers of the Enlightenment, including Hobbes, La Mettrie, and Baron D'Holbach, went further. They denied the soul and its freedom and asserted that man in his entirety is mechanical—hence the title of La Mettrie's famous work, *L'Homme machine*.

Such thoroughgoing physicalism was still unusual in the eighteenth century, even among the *philosophes*, but it has gained enormous traction in our own day. As computer technology has advanced, even ordinary people have become accustomed to the idea, popularized by science fiction, that artificial machines might eventually become as conscious and intelligent as we are. This is the natural corollary of the idea that we ourselves are just "machines made of meat," in the famous words of Marvin Minsky, a pioneer in artificial-intelligence research.

Many factors have contributed to this development. The defeat of vitalism in the nineteenth century promised that the same reductionist modes of explanation that had been so successful in physics would unlock the secrets of biology as well—as indeed they have, to a remarkable degree. By showing the continuities that exist between ourselves and the lower animals, Darwin's discoveries weakened belief in human exceptionalism. But a decisive shift had already occurred much earlier, with the discoveries of Isaac Newton, whose laws of gravity and mechanics had two profound features. First, they were *universal*: they governed everything, from the motions of great planets to the minutest constituents of matter. Second, they were *deterministic*: they implied that the state of the physical world at one time completely and uniquely determines its state at all future times. The classic statement of physical determinism was given by the great mathematical physicist Pierre-Simon Laplace in 1819:

> [To] an intelligence which could know all the forces by which nature is animated, and the states at some instant of all the objects that compose it, nothing would be uncertain; and the future, as well as the past, would be present to its eyes.

Every discovery in physics in the century that followed bore out this bold assertion. When, for example, the complete laws of electricity and magnetism were written down by James Clerk Maxwell in the 1860s, they were seen to be as rigidly deterministic as Newton's laws of mechanics and gravity.

The universality and determinism of the laws of physics gave rise to the belief that the entire physical universe is a complete and closed system of cause and effect. This is often called the principle of "causal closure" of the physical world. According to this principle, nonphysical entities (if any exist) can have no effect on anything physical. Whether you have a spiritual soul becomes irrelevant, since it could not affect what you say or do, or what is going on inside your brain. Your brain, as much as the rest of your body, is under the complete control of the laws of physics.

One might say that this was nothing new. There had been thinkers since ancient times who denied the reality of human freedom, claiming that our thoughts and deeds were governed by fate or by the stars. But these ideas were the fruit of mere speculation. What made the Newtonian challenge to free will more pressing was that it came from a powerful scientific synthesis that proved its validity in countless ways over hundreds of years of painstaking research. This doesn't mean that scientists immediately abandoned belief in free will or in a spiritual soul that animates our bodies. In fact, most of the great scientists up through the nineteenth century, including Newton and Maxwell, rejected the causal closure of the physical world and the physicalist picture of human beings it entails. Still, these ideas slowly gained ground. For many thinkers, they are now axiomatic.

It may seem obvious to most of us that we do in fact exercise free will, but it has become customary for philosophers and scientists to dismiss such intuitions or commonsense beliefs about our own minds as mere "folk psychology." Some argue that free will is a natural illusion: we cannot fathom our own behavior, they say, because the true physical causes of it lie below the level of consciousness, and so we posit a mysterious power that we call "the will." The eminent biologist Francis Crick put it this way: "What you're aware of is the decision, but you're not aware of what makes you do the decision. It seems free to you, but it's the result of things you are not aware of." The father of sociobiology, Edward O. Wilson, put it more crisply: "The hidden preparation of mental activity gives the illusion of free will."

Some might object that if free will were illusory then reward, punishment, and even exhortation would be useless. But this objection is easily met. Even animals that no one regards as free can respond to rewards and punishments—as can, in a sense, computer programs that "learn" by feedback. The more serious objection is that without free will there is no such thing as morality. We do not attach moral blame to animals or machines, or to human beings in the grip of a compulsion, precisely because we recognize that they have no power of free choice and are therefore not responsible for what they do. Nor do we attribute moral obligation to them. Without some concept of free will, most of our common moral language loses its meaning.

Many philosophers who are convinced determinists understand this. They have therefore tried to rescue moral language by showing that some notion of free will, even if not the traditional one, is compatible with physical determinism. The more sophisticated versions of "compatibilism" do this by identifying some manner in which human decision-making differs from that of animals and artificial machines and defining that to be free will. To this end, they often focus on the fact that human beings can be self-critical.

One influential version of compatibilism, developed by Harry Frankfurt of Princeton University, analyses freedom in terms of desires. Like animals we have desires, but unlike animals we have desires *about* desires. For example, we may have chaste desires and unchaste desires tugging in contrary directions. But we can also have a general desire *not to have unchaste desires*, or at least not to act on them. This "higher-order" desire could be said to represent our true self. If our lower-order desire wins out over this true desire, we are acting like animals, which are ruled by passion and instinct. To act freely means to be governed by our higher-order desires. According to Frankfurt, what makes us persons—that is, moral agents—is this multi-tiered structure of our wills.

There is obviously a great deal of truth in this analysis. It brings to mind St. Augustine's theory of the "two wills" and St. Paul's discussion of the unfree will in the seventh chapter of Romans: "For I do not do what I want, but I do the very thing I hate." Other compatibilists, such as Susan

Wolf, stress the role of reason in our decision-making. Unlike animals, we can analyze our actions in relation to general principles and abstract standards of right and wrong. This too is clearly a centrally important aspect of what it means to be free.

Compatibilism in its various forms attempts to take seriously the notion of moral agency and moral responsibility, but the moral agency it speaks about is not quite real. Ultimately, the supposed agent has no real choice in anything. If physical determinism is true, as compatibilists believe, then what the "agent" does is in principle computable from a complete knowledge of the state of the physical world long before he made his "decision." Such a computation could be made entirely without reference to the agent's desires, whether higher-order or lower-order.

It is helpful here to consider how physical determinism and causal closure work in the case of animals. Consider a cat whose tail has been stepped on. The cat screeches. What caused this? From the point of view of physics, the screech is simply the result of a chain of measurable and calculable physical events: a nerve is compressed; impulses travel up to the brain, where a complicated set of electrochemical responses is triggered; impulses travel back down certain motor nerves; muscles contract; certain body parts move; and sound waves are produced. This explanation is undoubtedly correct. Nothing important is added if we talk about how the cat felt or what was going on in its mind. A similar analysis can be made of the cat's desire to eat. Molecules wafting from its prey will enter its nostrils and affect some chemical receptors, signals are sent to the brain, and so on—until, finally, some muscle contractions cause the cat's body to lunge. The causal-closure principle says that physical events (such as the screech or the lunge) can only have physical causes. The cat might just as well have no feelings or consciousness at all. (Descartes, a consistent physicalist when it came to animals, saw no reason to believe that animals have feelings.)

The fact is that feelings, desires, sensations, and other subjective experiences are not physical phenomena, in the sense of things that physics explains. Such things do not register in measuring devices, nor do they appear as quantities in the equations of theoretical physics. The paradox, as the Austrian physicist Erwin Schrödinger correctly noted, is that while "all scientific knowledge is based on sense perceptions, the scientific view of natural processes formed in this way lacks all sensual qualities and therefore cannot account for the latter." For example, theoretical physics explains the difference between the light we perceive as red and the light we perceive as blue (they oscillate at different frequencies), but it has nothing to say about the subjective experience of seeing redness and blueness. Physical science can explain to a blind person what goes on in the brain of a seeing person, but not what it is like to see. Subjective experiences may supervene on physical events in the brain, but they are not themselves physical events. And thus, according to a consistent physicalist, they can have no effects on the brain or the body. It is therefore often asserted by philosophers today that subjective experience and consciousness have "no causal efficacy," are purely "passive" or "epiphenomenal."

If one accepts this point of view, what happens to our moral life? Well, to begin with, such things as moral sentiments and feelings of desire, empathy, guilt, shame, or obligation are not actually causes of our behavior. They are just shadows cast on the screen of our consciousness by the unconscious physical processes that are doing all the real work of deciding. Even the "moral reasoning" that goes on in our brains is, in a deterministic world, not essentially different from the computations that go on in a pocket calculator or a chess-playing computer: it is done by material particles unconsciously following the laws of physics. Where is the moral agent in all this? *Who* is actually doing things? The who is really a congeries of particles, not a person.

Notwithstanding the desperately ingenious efforts of compatibilist philosophers, it would seem that physical determinism is fatal to the idea of free will and moral agency, at least as these are usually understood. And most people seem to realize this. Compatibilism is popular among professional philosophers, but it seems that most scientists and ordinary people who end up believing in physical determinism also end up simply concluding that free will is an illusion. They often admit that it is a *useful* illusion—one we need in order to carry on a decent and productive life. Indeed, it may have been necessary for the survival of the whole species for us to have this illusion; and for that reason, presumably, it was bred into us by natural selection.

The irony in all this is that just as many people were concluding that science compels a belief in physical determinism and a rejection of free will, the science itself was beginning to change. Two hundred years after Newton's death, physics underwent a profound transformation with the development of quantum mechanics. Quantum mechanics was not just a theory of some particular class of physical phenomena; it was a new conceptual foundation for all of physics. And this new foundation was radically *non*deterministic. In 1927, the physicist Max Born demonstrated that the formalism of quantum mechanics required a probabilistic interpretation. In particular, its basic principles imply that, *pace* Laplace, even complete information about the state of the physical world at one time would *not* uniquely determine its future state but only the *probabilities* of various future states. In other words, the scientific basis upon which the doctrine of physical determinism had rested for three hundred years disappeared in the 1920s. Why, then, does determinism still have such a strong grip on contemporary philosophy?

The answer usually given is that "quantum indeterminacy" has no relevance to the way the brain functions. The building blocks of the brain are neurons, and neurons, it is claimed, are sufficiently large that a "classical" (i.e., nonquantum) account is perfectly adequate for understanding how they work. But given how rudimentary science's present understanding of the brain is, such a claim looks like an overconfident, not to say arrogant, extrapolation. It suggests we know more than we do. The great mathematician and physicist Hermann Weyl described our situation well in a lecture delivered at Yale University in 1931.

> We may say that there exists a world, causally closed and determined by precise laws, but . . . the new insight which modern [quantum] physics affords . . . opens several ways of reconciling personal freedom with [the laws of physics]. It would be premature, however, to propose a definite and complete solution of the problem. . . . One of the great differences between the scientist and the impatient philosopher is that the scientist bides his time. We must await the further development of science, perhaps for centuries, perhaps for thousands of years, before we can design a true and detailed picture of the interwoven texture of Matter, Life, and Soul. But the old classical determinism of Hobbes and Laplace need not oppress us longer.

Today, though, many scientists are even less patient than the philosophers. Unable to imagine how free will might be interwoven with matter, they adhere to the crudest forms of classical determinism.

In addition to overthrowing determinism, quantum mechanics furnished an unexpected and very powerful argument against the physicalist view of the human mind. In the traditional understanding of quantum mechanics, the "wave functions" that are calculated in it are not simply mathematical representations of "the world as it is," but rather of that which is *known* about the world by various particular "observers" who are part of it. And, according to a classic analysis that goes back to the great mathematician John von Neumann in the 1930s, the minds of these observers (or knowers) cannot themselves be entirely described by quantum mechanical wave functions—that is, by quantum physics. That's why the Nobel prize-winning physicist Eugene Wigner wrote in a famous essay that materialism is "not consistent with present quantum mechanics," and why Sir Rudolf Peierls, another eminent physicist, said, "The premise that you can describe in terms of physics the whole function of a human being, including its knowledge and its consciousness, is untenable. There is still something missing." While the argument against physicalism based on quantum mechanics is very controversial, there are many respected physicists who continue to defend its validity.

Quite aside from physics, there are strong philosophical arguments against physicalism. The theory of causal closure claims to be the truth about the world, and yet if it were true, we could have no access to truth. The closure of the physical world would mean the closure of our minds as well. In other words, physical determinism involves a denial of our intellectual freedom just as much as our moral freedom. In 1932, the famous biologist J. B. S. Haldane wrote, "If materialism is true, it seems to me we cannot know that it is true. If my opinions are the result of the chemical processes going on in my brain, they are determined by chemistry, not the laws of logic."

Interestingly, Haldane eventually reversed his position and came to embrace physicalism. What led him to change his mind was the development of the computer, which demonstrated that a machine, though bound by physical laws, could nonetheless follow the laws of logic. The reason Haldane ended up being misled is that he did not frame the issue in quite the right way to begin with. The real issue is not whether a machine can follow the laws of logic. Certainly it can. If designed and programmed properly, a machine that follows one set of rules (the laws of physics), can by so doing also follow another set of rules (the laws of logic, or arithmetic, or chess). The real question is whether a machine that only follows rules of whatever kind can be *open to the truth*.

The answer seems to be no. Even if we restrict our attention to the realm of mathematics, openness to truth involves more than mere mechanical rule-following. That seems to be the lesson of one of the great discoveries of the twentieth century, Gödel's Theorem. Before Kurt Gödel proved his theorem in 1931, a school of thought called "formalism" was very influential in the world of mathematics. According to the formalists, all of mathematical reasoning could be replaced, in principle, by symbolic manipulations that follow prescribed rules. For a mathematical proposition to be "true" meant simply that it could be derived from prescribed axioms by following prescribed rules. Consequently, the following of mechanical rules could give one access to all of mathematical truth. Gödel stunned mathematicians by showing that no matter how many rules were prescribed, there would remain infinitely many truths of mathematics that could not be reached merely by following them. The power of reason, even in the bloodless realm of mathematics, involves something more than machine-like behavior. It involves understanding of meaning and judgments of truth and falsehood. Hermann Weyl, in the lecture already quoted, made this observation:

> Descartes brings out the decisive point in the problem of free will with particular clarity, when he demonstrates the freedom involved in the theoretical acts of affirmation and negation: When I reason that 2 + 2 = 4, this actual judgment is not forced upon me through blind natural causality (a view which would eliminate thinking as an act for which one can be held answerable), but something purely spiritual enters in.

Weyl went on to explain that the mind, if completely determined by factors that are *below* it, such as chemical reactions in the brain, is not open to those nonmaterial realities that are *above* it, such as truth and meaning. This is indeed the decisive point: our openness to truth not only demonstrates *that* we are intellectually free, but explains what that freedom is for and why it is important. Truth cannot enter a mind that is not first open to it; it cannot move a mind whose movements are already dictated by "blind natural causality." The same is true of moral freedom. The soul cannot be open to the morally good if its movements are determined by the blind natural causality of physics, chemistry, and biology. It is our freedom that makes possible our openness to truth, beauty, goodness. Christians believe that it is primarily in the possession of this freedom that we are made in God's image and likeness. This freedom is not an epiphenomenon of matter or an emergent property of it. Physics cannot explain it or say how it came to be present in the world, but neither does physics contradict it—as it once seemed to. The modern materialism that reduces human beings to the level of machines was a by-product of the science of an earlier age. That science has been overthrown, and the deepest discoveries of the twentieth century have allowed us to see that neither the processes of matter nor the processes of thought are merely mechanical. Or, as Hermann Weyl put it, "the old classical determinism of Hobbes and Laplace need not oppress us longer."

10

DOES QUANTUM MECHANICS
MAKE IT EASIER TO BELIEVE IN GOD?

The question I have been asked to address is whether quantum mechanics makes it easier to believe in God.

My answer is no, not in any direct way. That is, it doesn't provide an argument for the existence of God. But it does so indirectly, by providing an argument against the philosophy called materialism (or "physicalism"), which is the main intellectual opponent of belief in God in today's world.

Materialism is an atheistic philosophy that says that all of reality is reducible to matter and its interactions. It has gained ground because many people think that it's supported by science. They think that physics has shown the material world to be a closed system of cause and effect, sealed off from the influence of any nonphysical realities—if any there be. Since our minds and thoughts obviously do affect the physical world, it would follow that they are themselves merely physical phenomena. No room for a spiritual soul or free will: for materialists we are just "machines made of meat."

Quantum mechanics, however, throws a monkey wrench into this simple mechanical view of things. No less a figure than Eugene Wigner, a Nobel Prize winner in physics, claimed that materialism—at least with regard to the human mind—is not "logically consistent with present quantum mechanics." And on the basis of quantum mechanics, Sir Rudolf Peierls, another great twentieth-century physicist, said, "the premise that you can describe in terms of physics the whole function of a human being . . . including [his] knowledge, and [his] consciousness, is untenable. There is still something missing."

How, one might ask, can quantum mechanics have anything to say about the human mind? Isn't it about things that can be physically measured, such as particles and forces? It is; but while minds cannot be measured, it is ultimately minds that do the measuring. And that, as we shall see, is a fact that cannot be ignored in trying to make sense of quantum mechanics. If one claims that it is possible (in principle) to give a complete physical description of what goes on during a measurement — including the mind of the person who is doing the measuring — one is led into severe difficulties. This was pointed out in the 1930s by the great mathematician John von Neumann. Though I cannot go into technicalities in an essay such as this,[1] I will try to sketch the argument.

It all begins with the fact that quantum mechanics is inherently probabilistic. Of course, even in "classical physics" (i.e., the physics that preceded quantum mechanics and that still is adequate for many purposes) one sometimes uses probabilities; but one wouldn't have to if one had enough information. Quantum mechanics is radically different: it says that even if one had complete information about the state of a physical system, the laws of physics would typically only predict probabilities of future outcomes. These probabilities are encoded in something called the "wave function" of the system.

A familiar example of this is the idea of "half-life." Radioactive nuclei are liable to "decay" into smaller nuclei and other particles. If a certain type of nucleus has a half-life of, say, an hour, it means that a nucleus of that type has a 50% chance of decaying within 1 hour, a 75% chance within two hours, and so on. The quantum mechanical equations do not (and cannot) tell you when a particular nucleus will decay, only the probability of it doing so as a function of time. This is not something peculiar to nuclei. The principles of quantum mechanics apply to all physical systems, and those principles are inherently and inescapably probabilistic.

This is where the problem begins. It is a paradoxical (but entirely logical) fact that a probability only makes sense if it is the probability of something definite. For example, to say that Jane has a 70% chance of passing the French exam only means something if at some point she takes the exam and gets a definite grade. At that point, the probability of her passing no longer remains 70%, but suddenly jumps to 100% (if she passes) or 0% (if she fails). In other words, probabilities of events that lie in between 0 and 100% must at some point jump to 0 or 100% or else they meant nothing in the first place.

This raises a thorny issue for quantum mechanics. The master equation that governs how wave functions change with time (the "Schrödinger equation") does not yield probabilities that suddenly jump to 0 or 100%, but rather ones that vary smoothly and that generally remain greater than 0 and less than 100%. Radioactive nuclei are a good example. The Schrödinger equation says that the "survival probability" of a nucleus (i.e., the probability of its *not* having decayed) starts off at 100%, and then falls continuously, reaching 50% after one half-life, 25% after two half-lives, and so on—but *never reaching zero*. In other words, the Schrödinger equation only gives probabilities of decaying, never an actual decay! (If there were an actual decay, the survival probability should jump to 0 at that point.)

To recap: (a) Probabilities in quantum mechanics must be the probabilities of definite events. (b) When definite events happen, some probabilities should jump to 0 or 100%. However, (c) the mathematics that describes all physical processes (the Schrödinger equation) does not describe such jumps. One begins to see how one might reach the conclusion that not everything that happens is a physical process describable by the equations of physics.

So how do minds enter the picture? The traditional understanding is that the "definite events" whose probabilities one calculates in quantum mechanics are the outcomes of "measurements" or "observations" (the words are used interchangeably). If someone (traditionally called "the observer") checks to see if, say, a nucleus has decayed (perhaps using a Geiger counter), he or she must get a definite answer: yes or no. Obviously, at that point the probability of the nucleus having decayed (or survived) should jump to 0 or 100%, because the observer then *knows* the result with certainty. This is just common sense. The probabilities assigned to events refer to *someone's state of knowledge*: before I know the outcome of Jane's exam I can only say that she has a 70% chance of passing; whereas after I know I must say either 0 or 100%.

Thus, the traditional view is that the probabilities in quantum mechanics—and hence the "wave function" that encodes them—refer to the state of knowledge of some "observer." (In the words of the famous physicist Sir James Jeans, wavefunctions are "knowledge waves.") An observer's knowledge—and hence the wavefunction that encodes it—makes a discontinuous jump when he/she comes to know the outcome of a measurement (the famous "quantum jump," traditionally called the "collapse of the wave function"). But the Schrödinger equations that describe any physical process do not give such jumps! So something must be involved when knowledge changes besides physical processes.

An obvious question is why one needs to talk about knowledge and minds at all. Couldn't an inanimate physical device (say, a Geiger counter) carry out a "measurement"? That would run into the very problem pointed out by von Neumann: if the "observer" were just a purely physical entity, such as a Geiger counter, one could in principle write down a *bigger* wavefunction that described not only the thing being measured but also the observer. And, when calculated with the Schrödinger equation, that bigger wavefunction *would not jump*! Again: as long as only purely physical entities are involved, they are governed by an equation that says that the probabilities don't jump.

That's why, when Peierls was asked whether a machine could be an "observer," he said no, explaining that "the quantum mechanical description is in terms of knowledge, and knowledge requires *somebody* who knows." Not a purely physical thing, but a mind.

But what if one refuses to accept this conclusion, and maintains that only physical entities exist and that all observers and their minds are entirely describable by the equations of physics? Then the quantum probabilities remain in limbo, not 0 and 100% (in general) but hovering somewhere in between. They never get resolved into unique and definite outcomes, but somehow all possibilities remain always in play. One would thus be forced into what is called the "Many Worlds Interpretation" (MWI) of quantum mechanics.

In MWI, reality is divided into many branches corresponding to all the possible outcomes of all physical situations. If a probability was 70% before a measurement, it doesn't jump to 0 or 100%; it stays 70% after the measurement, because in 70% of the branches there's one result and in 30% there's the other result! For example, in some branches of reality a particular nucleus has decayed—and "you" observe that it has, while in other branches it has not decayed—and "you" observe that it has not. (There are versions of "you" in every branch.) In the Many Worlds picture, you exist in a virtually infinite number of versions: in some branches of reality you are reading this essay, in others you are asleep in bed, in others you have never been born. Even proponents of the Many Worlds idea admit that it sounds crazy and strains credulity.

The upshot is this: *if* the mathematics of quantum mechanics is right (as most fundamental physicists believe), and *if* materialism is right, one is forced to accept the Many Worlds Interpretation of quantum mechanics. And that is awfully heavy baggage for materialism to carry.

If, on the other hand, we accept the more traditional understanding of quantum mechanics that goes back to von Neumann, one is led by its logic (as Wigner and Peierls were) to the conclusion that not everything is just matter in motion, and that in particular there is something about the human mind that transcends matter and its laws. It then becomes possible to take seriously certain questions that materialism had ruled out of court: If the human mind transcends matter to some extent, could there not exist minds that transcend the physical universe altogether? And might there not even exist an ultimate Mind?

11

FAITH AND QUANTUM THEORY

Quantum theory is unsettling. Nobel laureate Richard Feynman admitted that it "appears peculiar and mysterious to everyone — both to the novice and to the experienced physicist." Niels Bohr, one of its founders, told a young colleague, "If it does not boggle your mind, you understand nothing." Physicists have been quarreling over its interpretation since the legendary arguments between Bohr and Einstein in the 1920s. So have philosophers, who agree that it has profound implications but cannot agree on what they are. Even the man on the street has heard strange rumors about the Heisenberg Uncertainty Principle, of reality changing when we try to observe it, and of paradoxes where cats are neither alive nor dead till someone looks at them.

Quantum strangeness, as it is sometimes called, has been a boon to New Age quackery. Books such as *The Tao of Physics* (1975) and *The Dancing Wu Li Masters* (1979) popularized the idea that quantum theory has something to do with eastern mysticism. These books seem almost sober today when we hear of "quantum telepathy," "quantum ESP," and, more recently, "quantum healing," a fad spawned by Deepak Chopra's 1990 book of that name. There is a flood of such quantum flapdoodle (as the physicist Murray Gell-Mann called it). What, if anything, does it all mean? Amid all the flapdoodle, what are the serious philosophical ideas? And what of the many authors who claim that quantum theory has implications favorable to religious belief? Are they on to something, or have they been taken in by fuzzy thinking and New Age nonsense?

It all began with a puzzle called wave-particle duality. This puzzle first appeared in the study of light. Light was understood by the end of the nineteenth century to consist of waves in the electromagnetic field that fills all of space. The idea of fields goes back to Michael Faraday, who thought of magnetic and electrical forces as being caused by invisible "lines of force" stretching between objects. He envisioned space as being permeated by such force fields. In 1864, James Clerk Maxwell wrote down the complete set of equations that govern electromagnetic fields and showed that waves propagate in them, just as sound waves propagate in air.

This understanding of light is correct, but it turned out there was more to the story. Strange things began to turn up. In 1900, Max Planck found that a certain theoretical conundrum could be resolved only by assuming that the energy in light waves comes in discrete, indivisible chunks, which he called quanta.[1] In other words, light acts in some ways like it is made up of little particles. Planck's idea seemed absurd, for a wave is something spread out and continuous, while a particle is something pointlike and discrete. How can something be both one and the other?

And yet, in 1905, Einstein found that Planck's idea was needed to explain another puzzling behavior of light, called the photoelectric effect. These developments led Louis de Broglie to make an inspired guess: if waves (such as light) can act like particles, then perhaps particles (such as electrons) can act like waves. And, indeed, this proved to be the case. It took a generation of brilliant physicists (including Bohr, Heisenberg, Schrödinger, Born, Dirac, and Pauli) to develop a mathematically consistent and coherent theory that described and made some sense out of wave-particle duality. Their quantum theory has been spectacularly successful. It has been applied to a vast range of phenomena, and hundreds of thousands of its predictions about all sorts of physical systems have been confirmed with astonishing accuracy.

Great theoretical advances in physics typically result in profound unifications of our understanding of nature. Newton's theories gave a unified account of celestial and terrestrial phenomena; Maxwell's equations unified electricity, magnetism, and optics; and the theory of relativity unified space and time. Among the many beautiful things quantum theory has given us is a unification of particles and forces. Faraday saw that forces arise from fields, and Maxwell saw that fields give rise to waves. Thus, when quantum theory showed that waves are particles (and particles waves), a deep unity of nature came into view: the forces by which matter interacts and the particles of which it is composed are both manifestations of a single kind of thing—"quantum fields."

The puzzle of how the same thing can be both a wave and a particle remains, however. Feynman called it "the only real mystery" in science. And he noted that, while we "can tell how it works," we "cannot make the mystery go away by 'explaining' how it works." Quantum theory has a precise mathematical formalism, one on which everyone agrees and that tells how to calculate right answers to the questions physicists ask. But what really is going on remains obscure, which is why quantum theory has engendered unending debates over the nature of physical reality for the past eighty years.

The problem is this: at first glance, wave-particle duality is not only mysterious but inconsistent in a blatant way. The inconsistency can be understood with a thought experiment. Imagine a burst of light from which a light wave ripples out through an ever-widening sphere in space. As the wave travels, it gets more attenuated, since the energy in it is getting spread over a wider and wider area. (That is why the farther you are from a light bulb, the fainter it appears.) Now suppose a light-collecting device is set up, a box with a shutter—essentially, a camera. The farther away it is placed from the light burst, the less light it will collect. Suppose the light-collecting box is set up at a distance where it will collect exactly a thousandth of the light emitted in the burst. The inconsistency arises if the original burst contained, say, fifty particles of light. For then it appears that the light-collector must have collected 0.05 particles (a thousandth of fifty), which is impossible, since particles of light are indivisible. A wave, being continuous, can be infinitely attenuated or subdivided, whereas a particle cannot.

Quantum theory resolves this by saying that the light-collector, rather than collecting 0.05 particles, has a 0.05 *probability* of collecting *one* particle. More precisely, the *average* number of particles it will collect, if the same experiment is repeated many times, is 0.05. Wave-particle duality, which gave rise to quantum theory in the first place, forces us to accept that quantum physics is inherently probabilistic. Roughly speaking, in pre-quantum, classical physics, one calculated what actually happens, while in quantum physics one calculates the relative probabilities of various things happening.

This hardly resolves the mystery. The probabilistic nature of quantum theory leads to many strange conclusions. A famous example comes from varying the experiment a little. Suppose an opaque wall with two windows is placed between the light-collector and the initial burst of light. Some of the light wave will crash into the wall, and some will pass through the windows, blending together and impinging on the light-collector. If the light-collector collects a particle of light, one might imagine that the particle had to have come through either one window or the other. The rules of the quantum probability calculus, however, compel the weird conclusion that in some unimaginable way the single particle came through both windows at once. Waves, being spread out, can go through two windows at once, and so the wave-particle duality ends up implying that individual particles can also.

Things get even stranger, and it is clear why some people pine for the good old days when waves were waves and particles were particles. One of those people was Albert Einstein. He detested the idea that a fundamental theory should yield only probabilities. "God does not play dice!" he insisted. In Einstein's view, the need for probabilities simply showed that the theory was incomplete. History supported his claim, for in classical physics the use of probabilities always stemmed from incomplete information. For example, if one says that there is a 60 percent chance of a baseball hitting a glass window, it is only because one doesn't know the ball's direction and speed well enough. If one knew them better (and also knew the wind velocity and all other relevant variables), one could definitely say whether the ball would hit the window. For Einstein, the probabilities in quantum theory meant only that there were as-yet-unknown variables: hidden variables, as they are called. If these were known, then in principle everything could be predicted exactly, as in classical physics.

Many years have gone by, and there is still no hint from any experiment of hidden variables that would eliminate the need for probabilities. In fact, the famed Heisenberg Uncertainty Principle says that probabilities are ineradicable from physics. The thought experiment of the light burst and light-collector showed why: if one and the same entity is to behave as both a wave and a particle, then an understanding in terms of probabilities is absolutely required. (For, again, 0.05 of a particle makes no sense, whereas a 0.05 *chance* of a particle does.) The Uncertainty Principle, the bedrock of quantum theory, implies that even if one had all the information there is to be had about a physical system, its future behavior cannot be predicted exactly, only probabilistically.

This last statement, if true, is of tremendous philosophical and theological importance. It would spell the doom of determinism, which for so long had appeared to spell the doom of free will. Classical physics was strictly deterministic, so that (as Laplace famously said) if the state of the physical world were completely specified at one instant, its whole future development would be exactly and uniquely determined. Whether a man lifts his arm or nods his head *now* would (in a world governed by classical physical laws) be an inevitable consequence of the state of the world a billion years ago.

But the death of determinism is not the only deep conclusion that follows from the probabilistic nature of quantum theory. An even deeper conclusion that some have drawn is that materialism, as applied to the human mind, is wrong. Eugene Wigner argued in a famous essay that philosophical materialism is not "logically consistent with present quantum mechanics." And Sir Rudolf Peierls, another leading physicist, maintained that "the premise that you can describe in terms of physics the whole function of a human being . . . including its knowledge, and its consciousness, is untenable."

These are startling claims. Why should a mere theory of matter imply anything about the mind? The train of logic that leads to this conclusion is rather straightforward, if a bit subtle, and can be grasped without knowing any abstruse mathematics or physics.

It starts with the fact that for *any* physical system, however simple or complex, there is a master equation—called the Schrödinger equation—that describes its behavior. And the crucial point on which everything hinges is that the Schrödinger equation yields only probabilities. (Only in special cases are these exactly 0, or 100 percent.) But this immediately leads to a difficulty: there cannot always remain *just* probabilities; eventually there must be definite outcomes, for probabilities must be the probabilities *of* definite outcomes. To say, for example, there is a 60 percent chance that Jane will pass the French exam is meaningless unless at some point there is going to be a French exam on which Jane will receive a definite grade. Any mere probability must eventually stop being a mere probability and become a certainty or it has no meaning even as a probability. In quantum theory, the point at which this happens, the moment of truth, so to speak, is traditionally called the collapse of the wave function.

The big question is when this occurs. Consider the thought experiment again, where there was a 5 percent chance of the box collecting one particle and a 95 percent chance of it collecting none. When does the definite outcome occur in this case? One can imagine putting a mechanism in the box that registers when a particle of light has been collected by making, say, a red indicator light to go on. The answer would then seem plain: the definite outcome happens when the red light goes on (or fails to do so). But this does *not* really produce a definite outcome, for a simple reason: any mechanism one puts into the light-collecting box is just itself a physical system and is therefore described by a Schrödinger equation. And that equation *yields only probabilities*. In particular, it would say there is a 5 percent chance that the box collected a particle and that the red indicator light is on, and a 95 percent chance that it did not collect a particle and that the indicator light is off. No definite outcome has occurred. Both possibilities remain in play.

This is a deep dilemma. A probability must eventually get resolved into a definite outcome if it is to have any meaning at all, and yet the equations of quantum theory when applied to any physical system yield only probabilities and not definite outcomes.

Of course, it seems that when a *person* looks at the red light and comes to the knowledge that it is on or off, the probabilities do give way to a definite outcome, for the person knows the truth of the matter and can affirm it with certainty. And this leads to the remarkable conclusion of this long train of logic: as long as only physical structures and mechanisms are involved, however complex, their behavior is described by equations that yield only probabilities—and once a mind is involved that can make a rational judgment of fact, and thus come to knowledge, there is certainty. Therefore, such a mind cannot be just a physical structure or mechanism completely describable by the equations of physics.

Has there been a sleight-of-hand? How did mind suddenly get into the picture? It goes back to probabilities. A probability is a measure of someone's state of knowledge or lack of it. Since quantum theory is probabilistic, it makes essential reference to someone's state of knowledge. That someone is traditionally called the observer. As Peierls explained, "The quantum mechanical description is in terms of knowledge, and knowledge requires *somebody* who knows."

I have been explaining some of the implications (as Wigner, Peierls, and others saw them) of what is usually called the traditional, Copenhagen, or standard interpretation of quantum theory. The term "Copenhagen interpretation" is unfortunate, since it carries with it the baggage of Niels Bohr's philosophical views, which were at best vague and at worst incoherent. One can accept the essential outlines of the traditional interpretation (first clearly delineated by the great mathematician John von Neumann) without endorsing every opinion of Bohr.

There are many people who do not take seriously the traditional interpretation of quantum theory —precisely because it gives too great an importance to the mind of the human observer. Many arguments have been advanced to show its absurdity, the most famous being the Schrödinger Cat Paradox. In this paradox one imagines that the mechanism in the light-collecting box kills a cat rather than merely making a red light go on. If, as the traditional view has it, there is not a definite outcome until the human observer knows the result, then it would seem that the cat remains in some kind of limbo, not alive or dead, but 95 percent alive and 5 percent dead, until the observer opens the box and looks at the cat—which is absurd. It would mean that our minds create reality or that reality is perhaps only in our minds. Many philosophers attack the traditional interpretation of quantum theory as denying objective reality. Others attack it because they don't like the idea that minds have something special about them not describable by physics.

The traditional interpretation certainly leads to thorny philosophical questions, but many of the common arguments against it are based on a caricature. Most of its seeming absurdities evaporate if it is recognized that what is calculated in quantum theory's wave function is not to be identified simply with what is happening, has happened, or will happen but rather with *what someone is in a position to assert* about what is happening, has happened, or will happen. Again, it is about someone's (the observer's) *knowledge*. Before the observer opens the box and looks at the cat, he is not in a position to assert definitely whether the cat is alive or dead; afterward, he is—but the traditional interpretation does *not* imply that the cat is in some weird limbo until the observer looks. On the contrary, when the observer checks the cat's condition, his observation can include all the tests of forensic pathology that would allow him to pin down the time of the cat's death and say, for instance, that it occurred thirty minutes before he opened the box. This is entirely consistent with the traditional interpretation of quantum theory. Another observer who checked the cat at a different time would have a different "moment of truth" (so the wave function that expresses *his* state of knowledge would collapse when *he* looked), but he would deduce the same time of death for the cat. There is nothing subjective here about the cat's death or when it occurred.

The traditional interpretation implies that just knowing A, B, and C, and applying the laws of quantum theory, does not always answer (except probabilistically) whether D is true. Finding out definitely about D may require another observation. The supposedly absurd role of the observer is really just a concomitant of the failure of determinism.

The trend of opinion among physicists and philosophers who think about such things is away from the old Copenhagen interpretation, which held the field for four decades. There are, however, only a few coherent alternatives. An increasingly popular one is the Many Worlds Interpretation, based on Hugh Everett's 1957 paper, which takes the equations of physics as the whole story. If the Schrödinger equation never gives definite and unique outcomes, but leaves all the possibilities in play, then we ought to accept this, rather than invoking mysterious observers with their minds' moments of truth.

So, for example, if the equations assign the number 0.05 to the situation where a particle has been collected and the red light is on, and the number 0.95 to the situation where no particle has been collected and the red light is off, then we ought to say that *both situations are parts of reality* (though one part is in some sense larger than the other by the ratio 0.95 to 0.05). And if an observer looks at the red light, then, since he is just part of the physical system and subject to the same equations, there will be a part of reality (0.05 of it) in which he sees the red light on and another part of reality (0.95 of it) in which he sees the red light off. So physical reality splits up into many versions or branches, and each human observer splits up with it. In some branches a man will see that the light is on, in some he will see that the light is off, in others he will be dead, in yet others he will never have been born. According to the Many Worlds Interpretation, there are an infinite number of branches of reality in which objects (whether particles, cats, or people) have endlessly ramifying alternative histories, all equally real.

Not surprisingly, the Many Worlds Interpretation is just as controversial as the old Copenhagen interpretation. In the view of some thinkers, the Copenhagen and Many Worlds Interpretation both make the same fundamental mistake. The whole idea of wave-particle duality was a wrong turn, they say. Probabilities are needed in quantum theory because in no other way can one make sense of *the same entity* being both a wave and a particle. But there is an alternative, going back to de Broglie, which says they are *not* the same entity. Waves are waves and particles are particles. The wave guides, or "pilots," the particles and tells them where to go. The particles surf the wave, so to speak. Consequently, there is no contradiction in saying both that a tiny fraction of the wave enters the light collector and that a whole-number of particles enters—or in saying that the wave went through two windows at once and each particle went through just one.

De Broglie's pilot-wave idea was developed much further by David Bohm in the 1950s, but it has only recently attracted a significant following. "Bohmian theory" is not just a different interpretation of quantum theory; it is a different theory. Nevertheless, Bohm and his followers have been able to show that many of the successful predictions of quantum theory can be reproduced in theirs. (It is questionable whether all of them can be.) Bohm's theory can be seen as a realization of Einstein's idea of hidden variables, and its advocates see it as a vindication of Einstein's well-known rejection of standard quantum theory. As Einstein would have wanted, Bohmian theory is completely deterministic. Indeed, it is an extremely clever way of turning quantum theory back into a classical and essentially Newtonian theory.

The advocates of this idea believe that it solves all of the quantum riddles and is the only way to preserve philosophical sanity. However, most physicists, though impressed by its cleverness, regard it as highly artificial. In my view, the most serious objection to it is that it undoes one of the great theoretical triumphs in the history of physics: the unification of particles and forces. It gets rid of the mysteriousness of quantum theory by sacrificing much of its beauty.[2]

What, then, are the philosophical and theological implications of quantum theory? The answer depends on which school of thought—Copenhagen, Many Worlds, or Bohmian—one accepts. Each has its strong points, but each also has features that many experts find implausible or even repugnant.

One can find religious scientists in every camp. Peter E. Hodgson, a well-known nuclear physicist who is Catholic, insists that Bohmian theory is the only metaphysically sound alternative.[3] He is unfazed that it brings back Newtonian determinism and mechanism. Don Page, a well-known theoretical cosmologist who is an evangelical Christian, prefers the Many Worlds Interpretation. He isn't bothered by the consequence that each of us has an infinite number of alter egos.

My own opinion is that the traditional Copenhagen interpretation of quantum theory still makes the most sense. In two respects it seems quite congenial to the worldview of the biblical religions: it abolishes physical determinism, and it gives a special ontological status to the mind of the human observer. By the same token, it seems quite uncongenial to eastern mysticism. As the physicist Heinz Pagels noted in his book *The Cosmic Code*: "Buddhism, with its emphasis on the view that the mind-world distinction is an illusion, is really closer to classical, Newtonian physics and not to quantum theory [as traditionally interpreted], for which the observer-observed distinction is crucial."

If anything is clear, it is that quantum theory is as mysterious as ever. Whether the future will bring more-compelling interpretations of, or even modifications to, the mathematics of the theory itself, we cannot know. Still, as Eugene Wigner rightly observed, "It will remain remarkable, in whatever way our future concepts develop, that the very study of the external world led to the conclusion that the content of the consciousness is an ultimate reality." This conclusion is not popular among those who would reduce the human mind to a mere epiphenomenon of matter. And yet matter itself seems to be telling us that its connection to mind is more subtle than is dreamt of in their philosophy.

12

A MYSTERY WRAPPED IN AN ENIGMA

Physics cannot explain why an apple looks red. This will surprise some people, but it is a fact that can hardly be disputed. Physics does indeed tell us why an apple reflects red light and what red light is—an electromagnetic wave whose wavelength is between 620 and 740 nanometers. Biophysics can explain why different wavelengths of light affect certain retinal cells differently, and thus how the brain can tell one color of light from another.

But what is left to explain is why the apple looks red, the sensual experience of redness. Why is it that when I see light of 650 nanometers I do not experience the sensation of shocking pink or pale yellow, rather than red? Indeed, if mechanical devices can distinguish wavelengths of light without having sensations, then why do I experience any sensation at all?

This is what philosophers nowadays call the problem of "qualia." Physics deals exclusively with quantities: the equations of theoretical physics allow one to calculate only quantities, and the devices of experimental physics measure only quantities. But since one cannot reduce to numbers what it is like to have a toothache or a paper-cut, to taste licorice or smell a lilac, to hear a flute or fingernails on a chalkboard, it is impossible that these subjective experiences, these qualia, can be derived from any equation. As Erwin Schrödinger put it, "[While] all scientific knowledge is based on sense perceptions, the scientific views of natural processes formed in this way lack all sensual qualities and therefore cannot account for the latter."

This problem of qualia is an important part of the larger "problem of consciousness" that is receiving increasing attention from both philosophers and scientists. Most scientific materialists, however, remain unable to admit that there is any problem whatever. Their dogma that all of reality is expressed in physics forces them to declare that anything about subjective experience underivable from physics must be unreal. The attitude of Niels Bohr is typical: "The question of whether [a] machine *really* feels or ponders, or whether it merely looks as though it did, is of course absolutely meaningless."

This view of reality leads to various behavioristic conceptions of the mind. In the "logical behaviorism" of Gilbert Ryle, the mind is analyzed in terms of dispositions to behave in certain ways. In the less crude "functionalism" put forward in the 1960s, internal mental states—though acknowledged to exist—are defined in terms of their role in causing behavior: produced by certain stimuli, they interact with other internal states and tend to lead to certain behavior. There is nothing in all of this that cannot be applied to the internal states of a computer, or indeed of a microwave oven.

To the extent that subjective experience is noticed at all by the modern materialist, it is dealt with—and eliminated—by the "identity theory," according to which mental states and brain states are the same.[1] This is the reigning orthodoxy in modern cognitive science. In the words of the philosopher Hilary Putnam, "It is no longer possible to believe that the mind-body problem is a genuine theoretical problem, or that a 'solution' would shed the slightest light on the world in which we live."

David J. Chalmers, a young Australian-born professor of philosophy at the University of California-Santa Cruz has written a book saying that there really is a problem, that there really is something called consciousness, and that we really do not have even the beginnings of a theoretical understanding of it. His book has attracted considerable attention both within the academic world and in the popular press. That this should be so when he is merely arguing for something transparently obvious may seem odd, but we should be thankful, for we live in an age when the obvious has few partisans.

Chalmers accepts a great deal of the current orthodoxy. He has no doubt that a mechanistic account can be given of all of the behavioral "cognitive mind,"[2] including our capacity to understand and to will. He certainly does not believe in a spiritual component in man. He does believe, however, that missing from the physicalist picture is the "phenomenal mind": the realm of subjective experience and its sensual aspects, the qualia.

Building on the arguments of many philosophers, notably Frank Jackson and Saul Kripke, Chalmers makes the case very powerfully that physical science cannot explain qualia. He is forced, against his own admitted predispositions, to reject materialism and embrace what he dubs a "naturalistic dualism." What makes his dualism naturalistic, he says, is that he posits no "transcendental element" (by which he probably means a soul or spirit). He believes that behavior can be entirely explained physically, and he thinks that consciousness can be naturally, though not physically, explained.

Chalmers makes some advance beyond people like Roger Penrose who suggest merely that consciousness cannot be explained by the presently known laws of physics: *no* physical laws, Chalmers argues, could ever explain qualia. But his own "natural explanation" that consciousness will be explained by "psycho-physical laws" remains unclear. What might such psycho-physical laws look like? They cannot be equations, for then they would no more explain qualia than do the laws of physics. Indeed they would be, in effect, just additional laws of physics. Indeed, there is a question of whether it makes sense even to talk about a "theory" of qualia: If a theory is something by which we understand, and a sensation something we feel, how can a theory ever capture sensation?

Chalmers creates an even greater difficulty for himself by his belief that all of behavior can be understood physically. He has to believe this because he takes it to be a fact that "the physical domain is causally closed" and therefore cannot be influenced by anything that lies outside of physics, such as the "phenomenal mind." For him, consciousness is entirely passive, and he believes he thereby escapes the well-known conundrums of "interactionist dualism."

He ends up, however, in a worse bind, for writing his book was a form of behavior, and there is no way, in his scheme, that his "phenomenal mind"—his experiences of qualia, his consciousness—can have had any influence on what his fingers typed. Indeed, they can have no influence on what he believes about consciousness, since belief for him lies in the behavioral and physically determined "cognitive mind." To put it bluntly, if his noninteractionist dualism is right then he cannot know anything about consciousness and we cannot learn about it by reading his book. He struggles unsuccessfully with this problem:

One might conclude that the *physical* portion of me (my brain, say) is not justified in its belief [that I am conscious]. But the question is whether *I* am justified in my belief, not whether my *brain* is justified in its belief; . . . there is more to me than my brain. I *know* I am conscious, and the knowledge is based solely upon my immediate experience.

He may know more than his brain, but according to Chalmers's own theory it is his brain that wrote the book. Indeed, his brain wrote those sentences, and I wonder how it wrote so knowledgeably about all the things that Chalmers knows and his brain does not.

The truth is that Chalmers need not have gotten into this predicament, for the physical world is not "causally closed." For example, no physical reason can be given why a radioactive nucleus decays at this moment rather than that. Chalmers is fully conversant with the ideas of quantum theory, and so he hedges at one point: "The physical world is more or less causally closed, in that for any given physical event it seems there is a physical explanation ([leaving aside] a small amount of quantum inde-terminacy)." The effects of quantum indeterminacy, however, are not nec-essarily small. In fact, the argument should be turned around, and was in an excellent article by the philosopher and physicist Avshalom Elitzur in 1989. We know from arguments like Chalmers's that consciousness is not explicable entirely by physics. But consciousness clearly affects behavior, and in particular the behavior of people who worry aloud whether their consciousness is explicable entirely by physics! And therefore the phys-ical domain cannot be causally closed. (Though Elitzur himself does not think quantum indeterminacy provides the causal opening.)

The problem of qualia and of consciousness bears out an observation made by Monsignor Ronald Knox in *The Hidden Stream*, where he noted that the supernatural mysteries of faith involve realities about which there is already a mystery at the natural level:

It's not surprising that there is a problem of free will in revealed theology, because there is a problem of free will in common or garden philosophy. The mystery comes in just where you would expect it to come in; where there is a mystery anyhow. The way I have tried to put it . . . is that you may picture human thought as a piece of solid rock, but with a crevice here and there—the places, I mean, where we think and think and it just does not add up. And the Christian mysteries are like tufts of blossom which seem to grow in those particular crevices, there and nowhere else.

Before the mysteries of the Trinity and the Incarnation there is already the mystery of personality. Before the mystery of the Real Presence there is already the mystery of appearance and reality. Before the mystery of spirit, there is the mystery of mind. Chalmers is unaware of supernatural mysteries. Indeed, he is blind even to the natural mysteries of human freedom and rationality. He is concerning himself with things on the much lower level of mere sensation, which we have in common with brutes. Yet even here there is an enigma.

In Knox's words, qualia are something about which we "think and think and it just does not add up." Do the qualia pertain to the level of matter, in which case there is something about matter itself that escapes the laws of physics? Or do they pertain to spirit,[3] in which case we should have to say that animals lack subjective experience? Or is there something between matter and spirit, above the merely physical, but below the rational? None of these ideas is easy to credit.

But whatever qualia are, they are real. And that alone tells us that simple-minded materialism cannot be right.

13

THOMAS NAGEL ON THE HUMAN MIND

S cientific materialism is perhaps the main intellectual rival to religion
today, and one that seems to have grown in popularity. It is therefore
a momentous occasion when a forceful attack on materialism is made
by a leading philosopher who is himself an avowed atheist.

Scientific materialism claims that everything that exists and everything that happens is ultimately reducible to the behavior of particles,
fields, energy, forces, and the other kinds of entities posited by theoretical physics. Those who embrace this view are encouraged to do so by the
enormous explanatory success of modern science. That success has been
based on a form of reductionism that explains physical systems by analyzing them in terms of more fundamental constituents and how those
constituents are organized and interact with each other. Wherever such
analysis has been carried out—at least for inanimate matter—the result-
ing explanations seem complete. Most physicists (myself included) think
it highly implausible that there is anything about a chunk of iron, say, or
a drop of water, or a star, or an atom that is not explicable in this way.
This kind of reductionism has been extended with increasing success to
biology. Molecular biology and related disciplines are giving us an ever
greater and more detailed understanding of the processes of life.

The big question, of course, is whether *minds* can be understood completely in this way. Thomas Nagel contends that they cannot be and that
materialism must therefore be false. His main argument is that materialism cannot account for three aspects of mind: consciousness, cognition

(specifically, certain features of human rationality), and the human capacity to know objective values. He argues, moreover, that even if materialism could explain how minds *can* exist in a purely physical world, it has no plausible account of how and why they did *in fact* come to exist. Darwinian evolution, being a purely physical theory, is not enough. In other words, materialism provides neither a "constitutive" nor a "historical" account of mental phenomena. What is more, materialism leaves unexplained the remarkable fact that the world is intelligible. As Nagel puts it, not only is "nature such as to give rise to conscious beings with minds . . . it is such as to be comprehensible to those minds." On the basis of all these considerations, he concludes that mind must be recognized as a feature of the natural world just as fundamental as matter.

Though I find all of Nagel's anti-materialist arguments cogent, I will confine my comments to the argument that consciousness is not reducible to physics. As a physicist, this conclusion seems to me obvious and to follow directly from the very nature of physical science and the way it explains things.

According to physics, every physical system is completely characterized—indeed, *defined*—by a set of "variables," which mathematically describe what its elementary constituents are doing, and whose evolution though time is governed by a set of mathematical rules and equations. (The transition from classical to quantum physics in the twentieth century did not change this basic framework, it only made the system of rules and equations more subtle.)

Of course, one does not need to keep track of all the variables of a physical system in order to know many interesting and important things about it—otherwise it would be impossible for human beings to do physics. But if one *did* know what all the variables were doing and the laws governing them, one could in principle *derive* everything there was to know about the system's properties and behavior—if the system is just physical. This derivation could be carried out using only the rules of mathematics and logic. That is what physicists generally believe, and for very good reason: in the purely physical realm—for example, the realm of inanimate matter—nothing has ever been found that gives grounds for doubting it.

In any event, whether you believe in this kind of reduction or not, it is the only kind that is done in physics. And so, if the physical sciences provide any warrant for believing in reductionism, it is only *this* kind of reductionism. It is clear, however, that this kind cannot be extended to consciousness. Even if one knew all the variables of a physical system, their values at one time or at all times, and the equations governing them, there would be no way to derive from that information anything about whether the system in question was conscious, was feeling anything, or was having subjective experiences of any sort.

Of course, we sometimes infer from its physically observable behavior that a being has feelings. When my dog begs for a strip of bacon, I am sure it is because he enjoys the taste. But that conclusion is based on an analogy between the dog's reactions and mine, not on a mathematical or logical derivation from physical facts, as is done in physics. Nor could it ever be, for such things as enjoyment or taste are not quantities, and physics deals only with quantities—quantities that appear in equations and quantities that are measured.

While Nagel rejects "psychophysical reductionism," and believes mind to be as fundamental as matter, he rejects any form of mind-matter dualism. "Outright dualism," he says, "would abandon the hope for an integrated explanation . . . and would imply that biology has no responsibility at all for the existence of minds." Instead, matter and mind must be seen as parts of "a single natural order that unifies everything on the basis of a set of common elements and principles." In his view, the evidence "favors some form of neutral monism," i.e., the idea that there is really just one basic stuff in nature, which has both physical and mental aspects.

Nagel may be right to reject dualism, but his reasons for doing so seem weak to me. It is not clear why dualism would preclude an "integrated explanation" of the physical and mental. After all, even *within* the physical realm there can be distinct entities, quite irreducible to each other, that are embraced by a single theory that "unifies [them] on the basis of a set of common elements and principles." Physics provides many instances of this. For example, electromagnetic fields and electrically charged particles are two distinct kinds of entity, whose relationship to each other is explained by an integrated theory called "quantum electrodynamics." Furthermore, in this theory the charged particles have some "responsibility" for the existence of the electromagnetic fields despite being utterly distinct from them. It is not clear why, in an analogous way, matter organized into biological structures couldn't be responsible in some degree for the existence of minds, despite being ontologically distinct from them.

Finally, there is the question of Nagel's atheism. Nagel admits that theism has an advantage over materialism in that it at least "admits the reality of more of what is so evidently the case," in particular the reality of mind, purpose, and value. He also admits that theism has some explanatory power. It might, for instance, be able to explain why the universe is such as to bring forth minds and be intelligible to those minds. (That might be part of God's intention in creating the universe.) But Nagel objects to theism on the grounds that merely positing the existence of God does not provide the kind of explanation he is seeking: an explanation of how matter and mind fit together within a single unified natural order. And, of course, he is right that it doesn't. Knowing that God is the author of the natural order does not, by itself, tell one very much about how the natural order works.

Of course, if one could know completely the mind of God (which is impossible without being God), one would understand what He understands, including everything there is to understand about the natural order. But the theist is not in that position, obviously. To say that God is the ultimate explanation of everything is not to say that *theism* is the explanation of everything. It doesn't have to be, however, in order to be a rational and well-founded belief. It only has to explain more than the alternatives. And a key point, which Nagel at times seems to forget, is that natural explanation and theism are *not* alternatives to each other. The idea that all the various aspects and components of the natural order fit together in some *internally* coherent way and the idea that some mind conceived of the natural order can be seen *themselves* to fit together in a coherent way.

One must be grateful that Nagel has been able to see so much "more of what is so evidently the case" than most contemporary philosophers, even if that does not include the existence of God.

14

MATTER OVER MIND

Th"here was a time when people worried whether God existed. Now, strangely enough, they are beginning to worry whether they exist—whether beneath the flux of their experience there can be found any enduring "self" or "soul" or autonomous person. Not according to some of the prophets of science, and especially of neuroscience, for whom such ideas are mere romantic fictions.

Fifteen years ago, the famous biologist Francis Crick announced in his book *The Astonishing Hypothesis* that

> "you," your joys and your sorrows, your memories and your ambitions, your sense of personal identity and free will, are in fact no more than the behavior of a vast assembly of nerve cells and their associated molecules. As Lewis Carroll's Alice might have phrased it: "You're nothing but a pack of neurons."

Even then, that hypothesis wasn't new. It is exactly what the French physician Pierre Cabanis famously asserted two hundred years ago: "*Les nerfs—voilá tout l'homme!*" ("The nerves: that's all there is to man"). In Cabanis's time this idea could be dismissed as the loosest sort of speculation because hardly anything was known about nerves or the brain. But no more. In our own day, meetings of the Society of Neuroscience draw 30,000 participants, and brain research has at its disposal an array of sophisticated techniques, from functional magnetic resonance imaging (fMRI) and positron emission tomography (PET) to transcranial magnetic stimulation. Could it be that the ideas of Cabanis and Crick, crazy as they sound, will soon be proven right? After all, hasn't science vindicated many other ideas that once seemed absurd?

Among those who look to science for ultimate answers, this is a time of great anticipation. There is a sense that mankind is on the verge of some final, unifying intellectual triumph. Many believe that it will be the privilege of neuroscientists to drive in the golden spike that will link human nature to the rest of the natural world in one all-encompassing, reductive explanatory scheme. In this "physicalist" framework, all the supposedly spiritual dimensions of human life—moral, aesthetic, and religious—will be accounted for as electrochemical processes in the brain.

Malcolm Jeeves and Warren S. Brown are accomplished neuropsychologists and believing Christians. In *Neuroscience, Psychology, and Religion*, they attempt to sort out the human, and in particular the religious, implications of recent discoveries. They provide a readable overview of the history of their field and of what has been learned so far about the structure and functioning of the human brain. They repeatedly emphasize the "rapid growth" and "remarkable advances" of neuroscience. These advances have largely been driven by the development of noninvasive techniques (such as fMRI and PET) for measuring the activity of different parts of the brain while subjects are engaged in particular cognitive tasks or experiencing various mental states.

Here is a small sampling of the things that have been learned so far: Different parts of the language center of the brain are used to understand speech and to formulate speech. Our brains analyze facial expressions differently from all other visual data in a specialized part of the temporal lobe called the "fusiform face area." Different kinds of moral dilemmas (for example, ones that involve accidental versus deliberate harm to others) activate different neural circuitry in our frontal lobes. The parts of the limbic cortex that register the bodily responses associated with social emotions such as empathy and shame are connected by exceptionally long neurons to the regions of the brain where higher mental faculties are based. These special "von Economo neurons" are almost unique to human beings, and it has been suggested that this linkage is what allows us to reflect on and understand our own emotions and those of others and so to be more "deeply social" than other animals.

Much has also been learned from the effects of brain injuries. Most famous is the case of Phineas Gage, a railroad-construction foreman who in 1848 had a metal rod driven through his head by an explosion, damaging his frontal lobes. "From being a reliable, industrious pillar of society," Jeeves and Brown say, "he became dissolute, capricious, and irresponsible." Another curious case occurred in 2000, when a schoolteacher who had begun to collect child pornography and make advances on his stepdaughter had a tumor removed that had been pressing on his right frontal lobe. His lewd behavior ceased. The impulses returned when the tumor began to grow again and ceased again when the regrown tumor was removed.

Such findings show how intimately every aspect of our mental life is tied to neural processes, which often can be precisely located. The principal lesson that Jeeves and Brown draw from this (quite correctly, I think) is that our mental life is "embodied" and that concepts of the mind or soul as "free-floating" and "separate" from the brain and body must be rejected. Frequently throughout their book, Jeeves and Brown disparage the idea of a "separate immaterial part" of the person, a "separate inner agent," a "'self' or 'mind' separate from the body," or a "real 'I' [as] an immaterial 'something' separate from my body."

The authors consider this notion of the soul as a separate entity to be the dominant view throughout most of Christian history and blame this on the influence of Greek metaphysics and Cartesian rationalism. This dualist conception, they say, overlay and distorted the original "biblical" and "Hebrew-Christian" ideas, which were more in accord with modern science and which must now be "recaptured."

This misreading of Christian tradition may have its roots in a common confusion between the idea of "distinction" and the idea of "separation." One can distinguish, but not separate, the three dimensions of space, for instance, or the brightness of light from its color. So, too, the traditionally drawn distinction between spirit and matter in the constitution of a human person need not imply their separation, any more than the infinite and absolute distinction between Creator and creature implies for the orthodox Christian a separation of the two natures of Christ. ("For, as the rational soul and flesh is one man," says the Athanasian Creed, "so God and man is one Christ.")

Apparently unaware of how deeply and pervasively incarnational traditional Christian theology is, Jeeves and Brown imagine that the "embodiment of the mind" supported by neuroscience is something that must be restored to theology and that this requires the abandonment of the concept of a "spiritual soul" distinct from matter. They flee from the dreaded "dualism" they think typified by Descartes into the arms of a materialist monism. For them, the mind is to be identified, without remainder, with the functioning of the neurons of the brain.

Jeeves and Brown are following a well-worn path. It has become the custom to discredit the idea of a soul by trotting out poor old dualist Descartes. The question Descartes notoriously failed to answer was how an immaterial soul could affect a material body. His admittedly unhelpful suggestion that it happened somehow or other in the pineal gland is regarded as the *reductio ad absurdum* of the whole idea. But few who pose this question have stopped to ask themselves how it is that a material body can be affected by anything whatsoever, even by another material body. That is, ultimately, no less mysterious a question.

Material bodies are made up of electrically charged particles that interact with each other through the mediation of electromagnetic fields: the charged particles affect the fields and the fields affect the particles. By what "means" or "mechanism" this happens, physics does not say. It simply says that when electromagnetic fields are present, the charges are, in fact, affected as described by a certain equation; and when charges are present, the fields are, in fact, affected as described by another equation. In other words, physics posits two types of entities and mathematically describes, but does not otherwise explain, their influence on each other.

Fundamentally, we are in the same position today as Newton was: he discovered precise equations describing how mass and gravity affect each other but he famously said, in his *Principia*, "I have not been able to discover the cause of those properties of gravity . . . , and I frame no hypotheses, . . . to us it is enough that gravitational forces really exist, and act according to [these] laws."

It is no less reasonable to accept the existence of both mental and physical aspects of reality and to say that they do in fact affect each other in predictable ways that can be described, without having in hand or even supposing that there exists a "mechanism" for that interaction. Indeed, this is really all that neuroscience itself can do. For instance, it can tell us that a lower than normal concentration in the brain of a molecule called dopamine (a certain arrangement of eight carbons, eleven hydrogens, one nitrogen, and two oxygens) leads to the subjective experience of boredom or apathy. It can find that the electrical stimulation of a certain tiny region of the brain produces mental states ranging from mild amusement to hilarity. It can report, as Jeeves and Brown do, that "damage to a certain small area of the cortex serving vision (called 'V4') can strip color" from one's visual experiences.

But in none of these cases can it explain the connection between motions of material particles and mental experiences any better than Descartes was able to do. For neuroscience, in effect, the entire brain is just Descartes' pineal gland writ large.

But there is one key difference. Neuroscientists, unlike Descartes, tend to see the action as one-way: matter can affect mind but not the other way around. Some justify this by saying that any effect of mind on matter would violate the laws of physics. Nothing that is known about physics, however, compels that conclusion.

In a famous essay on the mind–body question written in 1961, the physicist Eugene Wigner noted that there was a time when "the brilliant successes of . . . physics and chemistry overshadowed the obvious fact that thoughts, desires, and emotions are not made of matter." The successes of contemporary neuroscience are also brilliant; but what was an obvious fact in 1961 remains so today. Science can measure the behavior of "nerve cells and their associated molecules," to recall the words of Francis Crick, but it cannot measure "'you,' your joys and your sorrows, your memories and your ambitions." That we are creatures of flesh and blood and bone—and, yes, nerves—no believing Christian or Jew has ever denied. But that these are "all there is to man" is quite beyond the power of any measurement or computation to demonstrate.

15

THEORIES OF EVERYTHING

Sir John Maddox was for almost a quarter of a century, until 1995, the editor-in-chief of *Nature*, one of the world's premier scientific journals. In this ambitious book he attempts nothing less than an overview of what has been discovered about the natural world in the last three centuries, and what is likely to be discovered in the century ahead.

It is clear that Maddox intended this to be a rebuttal of John Horgan's provocative book, *The End of Science*, published in 1996. Horgan's thesis was that science is entering "an era of diminishing returns." He noted that many fields of research, such as human anatomy or geography, are limited simply by the boundedness of their subject matter. Even chemistry, being based on the periodic table, is bounded. Although the number of compounds that can be built up from these elements is vast, there is a sense in which the problems in chemistry become less and less fundamental as time goes on. In any finite field of inquiry one expects that at some point all the basic principles that are humanly discoverable will be known. There are some who hope—or fear —that we may already be close to that point in fundamental physics. Many leading particle physicists believe that in "superstring theory" they have already hit upon what will turn out to be the ultimate theory of physics—*the* laws of nature.

Even if we are not close to achieving the final theory in physics or other sciences, we may, according to Horgan, be running up against limits to what we can discover. Some of these limits are imposed by nature itself. For example, in astronomy there is a distance beyond which it is impossible to observe because of the finite speed of light. Other limits are practical: a few years ago the U.S. Congress cancelled in mid-construction what was to be the world's largest particle accelerator. Finally, there may be limits imposed by human intellectual capacity. The mathematics of superstring theory, for instance, is of such prodigious depth that after a decade and a half of remarkable progress researchers feel that they are very far from coming to grips with its central principles.

As evidence of his thesis, Horgan argued that there have been no truly revolutionary discoveries in the last several decades. What, he asked, has been done recently that can compare in magnitude to the discovery of evolution, the principles of genetics, and the structure of DNA, or to the discovery of Newton's laws, Einstein's theory of gravity, and quantum mechanics?

Maddox attempts to answer Horgan, although, curiously, he never mentions his name. Maddox makes his purpose clear in the preface: "And [my] message? Despite assertions to the contrary, the lode of discovery is far from worked out. This book provides an agenda for several decades, even centuries, of constructive discovery that will undoubtedly change our view of our place in the world as radically as it has been changed since the time of Copernicus." To answer Horgan, Maddox surveys what is currently known, primarily in cosmology, physics, and biology, indicating along the way which unsolved problems in each field he regards as the major ones.

In biology, Maddox has no trouble coming up with a list of profound issues about which little if anything is known: how life originated from nonliving chemicals four billion years ago; how a single cell is able to assemble itself into a complex multicellular organism; the way in which speciation occurs; how and why sexual reproduction evolved; the way in which the human brain works; and the nature of consciousness. Maddox argues persuasively that great progress is likely to be made in the next century (or at least is achievable) in some of these areas.

His optimism is less plausible, however, when it comes to the deepest questions, such as how the human brain works. He concedes that "progress in this field will not be quick." The complexity of the brain's circuitry is just staggering: "[It] probably contains many times as many neurons as our galaxy contains stars. . . . The complexity of connections between neurons is similarly gargantuan; cells of the cortex may be in a position to signal to as many as ten thousand others, either in the cortex or elsewhere in the head. The combinatorial possibilities are immense."

Moreover, even the most sophisticated means that are presently used to study the living human brain are comparatively crude: "What remains to be seen is whether the detail that can be identified by these means will be fine enough to answer the questions being asked about the function of the brain as a computer." In spite of all this, Maddox asserts that the "circuitry of consciousness" will be understood. "Perhaps new techniques will be required before the goal is truly in sight. But that the goal is attainable seems now to be plain." On what does Maddox base this last confident assertion? As far as I can tell, on nothing at all.

The difficulties that must be faced in understanding the mechanisms of evolution are no less daunting. In discussing one evolutionary puzzle, Maddox admits that "complex questions such as these cannot be tackled with the information now available." In another place he remarks "how little has yet been done to found even rudimentary evolutionary specu-lation on laboratory investigations." He notes that thorny questions such as "the causes of the rapid appearance of novel species at the Cambrian Explosion" will be answerable only at some possibly distant date "when the process of speciation is fully understood in modern genetic language." And yet, in some miraculous manner, Maddox already knows what this far-off research will reveal: "Heritable variation and natural selection, the central tenets of Darwinism, will then be found to account for what is known of the patterns of evolution."

When it comes to particle physics and cosmology, Maddox has some-what less mastery of his material. He makes a disconcerting number of minor technical errors. More seriously, he does not have a very clear picture of what the major unsolved problems in cosmology and particle physics really are. He mentions as puzzles several things that never were or no longer are such, while failing to mention some of the truly great and difficult questions that confront present-day theory. Maddox also has some quirky prejudices, such as a particular dislike of black holes.

More understandable is his hostility to the idea that physics may be close to a "Theory of Everything" in the form of superstring theory. This idea is very controversial even among particle physicists themselves, many of whom complain that there is not a shred of direct experimental evidence for it, and that after years of serious work superstring theorists still cannot make a single testable prediction.

Given these facts, why do so many of the most brilliant people in the field continue to work on superstring theory and regard it as such a prom-ising candidate for *the* ultimate theory of nature? To understand this one has to have some appreciation of the great trends in the history of physics. One trend has been toward an ever more unified picture of nature, beginning when Newton showed that the same laws govern terrestrial and celestial phenomena. As time went on, Newtonian mechanics was able to explain phenomena as diverse as the motion of fluids, the propagation of sound, and the flow of heat. In the nineteenth century the Newtonian framework was extended to describe electrical and magnetic phenomena, as well; and with the equations written down by James Clerk Maxwell in 1865 it was realized that electricity, magnetism, and optics are all different aspects of a single force called "electromagnetism." In 1905, Einstein showed that space and time form a single, four-dimensional whole, and that mass and energy are really the same thing. Quantum theory showed that force fields, wave phenomena, and particles are all manifestations of something called a "quantum field," so that there was no longer any fundamental distinction between matter and the forces that influence matter.

In the 1970s, another enormous unifying step was achieved when it was found that two of the four known forces of nature, electromagnetism and the "weak nuclear force," are really pieces of a single force. Powerful circumstantial evidence also emerged at that time (still not conclusive, however) that a third force, the "strong nuclear force," was unified with these in an analogous way.

Everything that is now known about the physical world[1] can be described by two theoretical structures: Einstein's theory of gravity, and a quantum field theory called "the Standard Model," which incorporates everything *except* gravity. It is clear to almost everyone that these are but two pieces of a grander whole. For decades physicists tried to bring Einstein's theory of gravity under the umbrella of "quantum field theory," but the umbrella was not big enough. All attempts to bring together Einsteinian gravity and quantum theory failed—until superstrings came along. Astonishingly, superstring theory not only could accommodate them both, but actually needed them both for its own completeness and consistency.

The other great trend that has culminated in superstring theory is the increasing role of powerful principles of "symmetry" in our understanding of the laws of physics. Since ancient times people have been impressed by the harmony and order they saw in nature, manifested most clearly in the grand cyclic motions of the heavenly bodies. They pointed to this order as evidence of a cosmic design—and a Designer.

What science has shown is that this order runs far deeper than anyone had imagined. In the phenomena around us we catch mere fragmentary glimpses of order amidst much apparent haphazardness and chaos. But modern physics gives us eyes to see down to the very roots of the world's structure, to the deepest layers of physical law, and what is seen there is an orderliness of the most pristine mathematical purity.

This order is reflected in principles of symmetry of wonderful richness and beauty. It was a new principle of symmetry that led Einstein to his theory of gravity, and a new principle of symmetry that allowed the unification of forces achieved in the 1970s. What scientists have stumbled upon, in superstrings, is a mathematical structure of such towering grandeur that they cannot help but call it "miraculous." It is of a beauty that only a few mathematicians are able to discern, and even the greatest experts feel that they are seeing only a small part of it. Edward Witten, the greatest of all the experts, grew exasperated with John Horgan's lack of appreciation: "I don't think I've succeeded in conveying to you," he said, "its wonder, its incredible consistency, remarkable elegance, and beauty."

If the laws of nature should prove to form a unified and coherent structure of great beauty, that would hardly surprise the religious among us. But would that mathematical structure amount to a "Theory of Everything"? It would certainly be a theory of everything *physical*. But is everything physical? In particular is man, made in the image of God, entirely physical? This brings us out of the realm of particle physics and into the realm of the human mind. It is here that one encounters among certain contemporary scientists an attempt at a unification far bolder than anything ever contemplated by physics.

In this greater unification, all mental phenomena will be explained in physical terms. In the words of Francis Crick, the Nobel-laureate biologist, we humans are "nothing but a pack of neurons." Strangely, Maddox has no qualms in accepting *this* kind of theory of everything. He assures us, with calm confidence, that "an explanation of the mind . . . must ultimately be an explanation in terms of the way neurons function."

What neither Maddox nor the authorities he follows seem to appreciate is how profoundly different this mind-equals-neurons theory is from all scientific theories that have gone before. All scientific theories up till now have been attempts *by the human mind* to grasp the nature of physical reality. The new theory is an attempt to show that the human mind, as such, is a fiction, and that only the physical reality exists. This is the suicide of theory.

Scientific theories are built up of ideas, and ideas exist in the mind. The ideas of modern science are, notoriously, very abstract. Chemistry, for example, uses such concepts as "atomic bond" and "valency" and "activation energy." These concepts rest on yet more abstract concepts in physics, such as "electromagnetic field" and "energy level." These, in turn, entail all of the recondite mathematical ideas of relativistic quantum field theory, which take years of study to comprehend.

We are supposed to believe that these ideas are nothing more than various patterns of neurons "firing" or discharging in human brains. A certain pattern of neurons firing is the concept "energy level." Another pattern of neurons firing is the concept "square root of 2." And so on. Not, mind you, just that a certain pattern of neurons firing accompanies the *concept* "square root of 2," or causes that concept to be present to the mind. That concept is supposed to be *nothing other than* the firing of the neurons. To "understand" the physical world using scientific and mathematical concepts would mean, then, nothing else than that the neurons in one's brain were discharging in particular patterns and sequences.

The concept "neuron" itself, in fact, is on this account nothing other than a certain pattern of neurons firing in the brain. Is there not something here to make us vaguely uneasy? Is not the snake of scientific theory eating its own tail—or rather its own head? Traditionally, we explained the physical world, including the brain, using concepts. Now we are to explain the concepts themselves as being mere physical events in brains. In fact, this whole theory according to which the mind and all conceptual understanding are nothing but electrochemical discharges of nerve cells is *itself*, by its own account, nothing but a discharging of nerve cells. This makes it, as far as I can see, no more significant or interesting than a toothache. We should listen to great scientific minds because they *are* great scientific minds. However, when they begin to tell us that they really have no minds at all, we are entitled to ignore them.

For all that, Maddox has written a most valuable book, and he is certainly right in his main point. There is a long road of scientific adventure ahead of us, and surely many remarkable things await us along that road. The great discoveries, when they come, will commend themselves to us, as they always have, by their "wonder, incredible consistency, remarkable elegance, and beauty," as Witten says. But as for the neuroscientists' "theory of everything," I find no wonder in it.

THE BIG BANG AND CREATION

16

MODERN PHYSICS, THE BEGINNING, AND CREATION

Some religious people look upon the discovery of the Big Bang as a scientific proof that the universe was created by God. Some atheists, on the other hand, point to speculative physics theories in which the universe had no beginning as showing that no Creator is needed. Both of these views are wrong and for the same reason. Both mistakenly equate the idea that the universe was created with the idea that the universe had a beginning some finite time ago. Admittedly, the Book of Genesis itself links creation and beginning when it says, "In the Beginning, God created the heavens and the earth." But even though the two ideas are connected, they are not the same. No less a theologian than St. Thomas Aquinas understood this very well. He believed it possible to prove philosophically that the universe is created, but not possible to prove philosophically that the universe had a beginning rather than having existed for infinite time.

At first, this sounds strange. Isn't it obvious that if something was created, it must have been created a finite time ago? That's certainly true of things that are "created" by human beings. If an artist paints a picture, that picture can be dated to the time when the artist painted it. Because the picture was made, it had a beginning. But the Church tells us that God does not create in the same way that human beings "create"; the comparison between the two is merely an analogy, and in this case somewhat misleading. So let us use a different analogy. Imagine a piece of paper that has been illuminated by a lamp forever, i.e., for time stretching infinitely into the past. Even though the illumination of the paper has always had

a cause—namely the lamp—the illumination of the paper had no beginning. In a similar way, the existence of the universe must have a cause
—namely God—but that does not necessarily imply that the existence of
the universe had a beginning.

Creation has to do with why something exists at all, not with how long
it has existed. One may put it another way: there is a difference between
the *beginning* of a thing and the *origin* of a thing. The beginning of the play
Hamlet is a set of words in act 1, scene 1, whereas the origin of the play
Hamlet is the creative mind of William Shakespeare. Shakespeare is the
origin of the play in the sense that he is the reason that there is a play at
all; he is the cause of its existence as a work of art. Similarly, the beginning of the universe is merely the set of events that happened in its first
moments (about 14 billion years ago, according to present calculations),
whereas the origin of the universe is the mind of God. Just as it would be
silly to answer the question of why there is a work of art called *Hamlet*
by pointing to its opening words, it would be silly to answer the question
of why there is a universe by pointing to its opening events. Indeed, the
opening of a play or the opening of the universe really have nothing to
do with the cause of their existence. One could imagine a play that has
no beginning or end—for example, a play whose plot goes round in a circle—and it would still require an author. Likewise, one could imagine a
universe without beginning or end, and it would still require a Creator.

Now, even though the creation of the universe does not in itself imply that it had a temporal beginning, and even though, according to St.
Thomas, God could have created a universe that had no beginning had he
willed, the Book of Genesis tells us that our world did in fact have a Beginning, and both the Fourth Lateran Council and the First Vatican Council
spoke of God creating the universe "from the beginning of time."

CREATION AND TIME

This brings us to a key point that was first understood by St. Augustine
sixteen hundred years ago and only rediscovered by modern physics in
the twentieth century. This point is that *the beginning of the universe was
also the beginning of time itself*. In antiquity, many pagans mocked the Jewish and Christian teaching that the universe had begun a finite time ago,
and they asked Jews and Christians what their God had been doing for all
that infinite stretch of time before he got around to making the world.

St. Augustine had a profound answer. He started with the idea that time, being a feature of this changing world, is also something created. Therefore, if time is passing, something created—namely, time itself—already exists, and hence creation has already happened. Consequently, it makes no sense to speak about any time passing "before creation." Time itself, as a created thing, began with the beginning of created things. God was not waiting around for infinite time before he created the world, said St. Augustine, for there is no such thing as "a time before creation." As he put it in Book XI of his *Confessions*, "Why do they ask what God was doing 'then' [before creation]? There was no 'then' where there was no time."

Modern physics has reached the same conclusion by a parallel route. Whereas St. Augustine started with the insight that time is something created, modern physics starts with the insight that time is something physical. After Einstein's theory of General Relativity, it became clear that space and time, rather than being something over and above physical events and processes, actually form a physical "space-time manifold" or fabric that is acted upon by other physical entities and acts upon them in turn. Space-time can bend and flex and ripple; and these distortions of space-time carry energy and momentum, just as all physical things do. Indeed, space-time is just as physical as magnetic fields are, or as rocks and trees. It follows therefore, that if the physical universe had a beginning (say, at the Big Bang), then space and time, as features of the physical universe, also began at that point. Before the beginning of the universe, therefore, there was neither time nor space; so that it in fact makes no sense from the viewpoint of modern physics to even use the phrase "before the beginning of the universe." Modern physics has vindicated St. Augustine's profound insight.

It is hard, indeed impossible, for the human mind to imagine time having a beginning. We must therefore again resort to analogies. Let us return to the analogy of a play. The plot of a play has a timeline in which its events can be located. If the play is in book form, we can locate its events by the page and line in which they occur. But the timeline of a book or play only applies to events within that book or play. It makes no sense, for example, to ask where in the timeline of the play *Hamlet*—on which page—the wizard Gandalf fights the Balrog or Sherlock Holmes meets Dr. Watson. Nor can one ask what happens in *Hamlet* after act 5, since the play has only five acts, and its internal time or plot-time simply ceases at the last word that appears at the end of act 5, scene 2. Admittedly, one can, in a certain sense, ask what happens before act 1 of *Hamlet*, because characters in the play recall and refer to prior events—for example the murder of Hamlet's father by Claudius. But strictly speaking, the plot-time *of the play*, measured by page and line, begins with the first line and ends with the last.

In a similar way, in the standard Big Bang theory there is a point (call it $t = 0$) that is the beginning of all physical phenomena, including space and time. As one (mentally) goes back in time toward that "initial singularity," space shrinks faster and faster, until at $t = 0$ it shrinks to nothing. Space and time wink out—or, looking at time in the right direction, they wink *into* existence at that point. In the standard Big Bang theory there are two possible fates for the physical universe: either it will expand forever, growing ever emptier and colder, or it will reach a maximum size and starts to collapse toward what is called the "Big Crunch." (Presently, the evidence favors the former possibility.) If the universe were to end in a Big Crunch, it would mean that space and time wink out at that point, a finite time in the future. That would be "finis" to the universe, and time would stop.

To push the analogy further, we see that the internal time of a play does not even apply to the doings of the play's author. Shakespeare getting married is not an event in *Hamlet* and has no location in *Hamlet*-time. In fact, Shakespeare thinking of ideas for the plot, or inventing characters, or composing soliloquys for *Hamlet* are also not events within the play and have no location in *Hamlet*-time (though they are, of course, the reason why certain things happen when and as they do in the play). Shakespeare is outside of his play and outside of its time. In an analogous way, the traditional Catholic teaching is that the space and time of this universe simply do not apply to God himself, in his divine nature.

Suppose, for example, we think of two physical events A and B that happen in our universe. Event A may come before B in physical time, and may perhaps be the cause of B, or at least influence B. God wills that A happen and that B happen, and he wills that the *occurring of A* come before the *occurring of B* in space-time. But God's *willing of A* does not happen before his *willing of B*. God's willing is not a physical process and therefore (unlike A and B) is not an event in space-time. The *effects* of his willing (namely, the events A and B themselves) do have a location in space and time, but that is not the same thing.

God's causing of A and B is on a different level altogether than A's causing of B. Once again, the analogy of the play makes this clear. One may ask: Did Polonius die because the character Hamlet stabbed him? Or did Polonius die because Shakespeare wrote the play that way? The correct answer, of course, is "both." Hamlet stabbing Polonius is the cause *within the play* of Polonius dying. But Shakespeare is the cause of the whole thing—of the existence of the play *Hamlet*, of all its characters, all its events, and all the relationships among the characters and events, including where they occur within the play and how they fit into the causal structure of its plot. In an analogous way, physical events in this universe have spatio-temporal and causal relationships to each other, but the whole universe and all its events and internal relationships only exist because God conceived of them and willed that they should exist and have these relationships to each other. This is the classical distinction between primary and secondary causality. The causes *within* nature are called "secondary causes," whereas God (the "primary cause") is the cause *of* nature.

This raises the question of whether the beginning of the universe, which may have been the "Big Bang," was a "natural event." There is no reason coming from physics to doubt that it was. To say that an event is natural is to say that it happens in accordance with the laws of nature. It is true that in the classical Big Bang theory the point $t = 0$ is a singular point at which the laws of physics break down, because various physical quantities would be infinite at that point (such as the density of energy and the Riemannian curvature of space-time). But it is known that the classical Big Bang theory cannot be a good description of nature very close to $t = 0$, because quantum mechanical effects should be important there, and present theories are inadequate to describe quantum effects at such high densities and curvatures. It is expected by most physicists that when (and if) the correct theory of "quantum gravity" is known, and the methods needed to apply it to the beginning of the universe are mastered, the singularity at $t = 0$ will melt away, and the laws of physics will be seen to apply at the beginning of the universe just as they do at later times. Nor is this merely a matter of philosophical prejudice. Long experience has taught physicists that when infinite quantities appear in their theories it is always because they have made unrealistic "idealizations."

That the Big Bang was very likely a "natural event," in the sense of obeying the laws of physics, is not a theological problem. It is like saying that the first sentences of *Hamlet* obey the laws of English grammar just as do all the other sentences in the play. One would expect nothing else. It is only a problem if one falls into crude anthropomorphism and imagines creation to be a physical process, like God setting a lighted match to a fuse. But that is not the Christian conception of Creation. Creation is the act by which God gives reality to the universe, and makes it not merely a hypothetical or possible universe, but an actually existing universe. He does not supply energy, as a match does to an explosive, he supplies reality. God supplies this reality equally to every part of the universe—all events at all times and places—just as Shakespeare equally brought forth every word of the play *Hamlet*.

WAS THE BIG BANG THE BEGINNING OF TIME?

Even though the universe being created and the universe having a beginning are two logically distinct ideas, it is a fact that some atheists are discomfited by the idea of a cosmic beginning. For, even though a Beginning does not logically imply creation, it somehow suggests it. This led many in the scientific world to be prejudiced against the Big Bang theory and probably discouraged research on it and delayed its acceptance, as has been admitted by more than one prominent scientist. The Big Bang theory came out of the work of the Russian mathematician Alexander Friedmann and the Belgian physicist (and Catholic priest) George Lemaître in the 1920s. And clear evidence that galaxies are flying apart as from some vast primordial explosion was announced in 1929. Yet even as late as 1959 a survey showed that most American astronomers and physicists still believed the universe to be of infinite age. Nevertheless, evidence in favor of the Big Bang theory accumulated, and became so strong by the 1980s that it was accepted by virtually all scientists. That the Big Bang theory is correct, however, does not necessarily settle the question of whether the universe had a beginning. There remains the possibility that the explosion that occurred 14 billion years ago was only the beginning of a certain part of the universe or a certain phase in its history, rather than the beginning of the universe as a whole. In fact, over the years many scenarios and theories of this type have been proposed. I will briefly discuss three of them, the bouncing universe, the cyclic "ekpyrotic" universe, and "eternal inflation."

I mentioned that in the standard Big Bang theory, the universe has two possible fates; it may expand forever or it may reach a maximum size and collapse toward a Big Crunch. If it does the latter, one may imagine that instead of the universe winking out at the Big Crunch, as usually assumed, it "bounces" and begins to expand again. If this were to happen, the Big Crunch would be the Big Bang of a new cycle of the universe. One can further imagine that such cycles of expansion, contraction, bounce and new expansion have been going on forever and will continue forever in the future. This scenario was proposed by Einstein himself in 1930. Can it be true? Almost certainly not, for several reasons. In the first place, it was shown many decades ago by the theoretical physicist Richard C. Tolman that in such a bouncing universe the cycles grow longer and longer (because of the increase of entropy). This means that they were shorter and shorter the farther one looks back into the past, and in such a way that the total duration of all past cycles added together was finite. That is, even in the bouncing universe scenario the universe had a beginning. Second, the entropy of the universe increases with each cycle, and from the amount of entropy that exists in the present cycle one can conclude that the number of past cycles was finite. Third, it is highly doubtful that a collapsing universe would bounce rather than simply ending in a Crunch. And fourth, it was discovered in 1998 that the expansion of the universe is currently speeding up (the scientists who discovered this were awarded the Nobel Prize in physics for 2011), so that it is doubtful that the expansion will reverse and lead to a collapse at all.

An interesting attempt to revive the idea of a cyclic universe was made about ten years ago by Paul Steinhardt and Neil Turok. In their scenario (called the "ekpyrotic universe"), there are two parallel universes, each having three space dimensions, which move toward each other through a fourth space dimension, collide, bounce, move apart, reach a maximum separation and then move toward each other again, repeating the cycle endlessly. This idea evades several of the problems of the original bouncing universe scenario. In the first place, the three-dimensional space of each parallel universe is always expanding, and the oscillations of contraction and expansion occur only in the fourth space direction (which we cannot experience or directly observe). This allows the scenario to be consistent with the fact that the expansion of our three space dimensions is accelerating and may never reverse. Second, the fact that entropy always increases with time is counterbalanced by the fact that the volume of three-dimensional space is also always increasing. Thus the entropy may always be increasing, whereas the *density* of entropy (i.e., entropy per volume) can be the same in every cycle, and the cycles can all have the same duration. Clever as the ekpyrotic idea is, however, it has been subjected to strong criticism as creating more theoretical problems than it solves. And even if it turns out to be viable as a theory of our universe, there is a powerful theorem proved by the physicists Borde, Guth, and Vilenkin, which implies the oscillations of such an ekpyrotic universe cannot have been going on for infinite past time. There had to be a first cycle.

Another attempt to construct a realistic theory of a universe without a beginning uses the idea of "eternal inflation" developed by Andrei Linde. The idea is that the universe as a whole is perpetually undergoing an "exponential" expansion. (What this basically means is that there is a time scale T, such that whenever a time T passes the universe doubles in size.) Such an exponential expansion is called "inflation." Within this perpetually inflating universe, however, bubbles are continually forming within which space expands in the much slower fashion that characterizes the part of the universe that we can see—i.e., the part of the universe within our "horizon." (We have a horizon since we can only see light that was emitted after the Big Bang, and such light cannot have travelled a distance greater than about 14 billion light-years.) In other words, we are inside one of these bubbles, and it is so vast that it extends far beyond our horizon. In this scenario, the Big Bang that happened 14 billion years ago was not the beginning of the whole universe, but merely the formation of our bubble.

It should be noted that the idea of inflation was not proposed whimsically or arbitrarily, but because it resolves certain very difficult theoretical puzzles in cosmology. Most cosmologists therefore believe that our part of the universe did undergo inflation at some point in the past. And it has been shown that in a wide class of theories, if some region of the universe starts to inflate, inflation tends to take over and lead to eternal inflation. However, almost all theorists agree that "eternal inflation," while it may be "eternal into the future," probably cannot be "eternal into the past." One reason for this conclusion is the theorem of Borde, Guth, and Vilenkin referred to previously.

It seems impossible that we shall ever be able to determine by direct observation whether the universe had a beginning. We cannot see what happened before the Big Bang (if there was a "before"), because the Big Bang would have effaced any evidence of it. And even we could, how could we ever tell by observation whether the past is infinite, since any *particular* past event that we observe must have occurred a finite time ago? Nevertheless, as we have seen, there are very strong *theoretical* grounds for saying that the universe most probably had a temporal beginning.

This is a remarkable vindication of religious ideas. The pagan philosophers of antiquity, including Plato and Aristotle, believed that the universe had always existed. The idea of a beginning of the universe and of time itself entered Western thought from biblical revelation and from the profound reflection upon it of theologians such as St. Augustine. Until the twentieth century, however, modern science pointed the other way.

The idea of a beginning of time seemed to make no scientific sense, and there seemed to be definite evidence that matter, energy, space and time had always existed and always would. For example, physicists discovered the law of conservation of energy, which says that "energy can neither be created nor destroyed." In chemistry it was found that the quantity of matter does not change in chemical reactions. In Newtonian physics, the time coordinate, like the space coordinates, extends from $-\infty$ to $+\infty$. By the beginning of the twentieth century, many scientists looked upon the idea of a beginning of the universe as a relic of outmoded religious or mythological conceptions of the world. One finds, for example, the Nobel Prize winning chemist Svante Arrhenius saying in 1911, "The opinion that something can come from nothing is at variance with the present-day state of science, according to which matter is immutable." And the eminent physicist Walther Nernst (also a Nobel laureate) confidently declared that "to deny the infinite duration of time would be to betray the very foundations of science." When science did begin to see (from Einstein's theory of General Relativity) how time and space could have a beginning, and astronomical observations began to suggest that this might be true, many atheists had a hard time accepting it. And yet, despite all the doubts and misgivings of scientists, it seems to be the case after all that the universe had a beginning.

Faced with this fact, some atheists now pin their hopes on the idea that physics will "explain" this beginning. They believe that if the beginning of the universe can be shown to be natural, then the need for a supernatural cause of the universe would be avoided. We have already seen the mistake involved in such thinking. The beginning of the universe unfolding in accordance with natural laws no more renders a Creator unnecessary than the opening passages of a book unfolding in accordance with the laws of grammar renders an author unnecessary. Nevertheless, scientific theories of the beginning of the universe are interesting in their own right, even if they cannot bear the weight that atheists want to place on them.

QUANTUM CREATION OF UNIVERSES

The most promising approach to "explaining" the beginning of the universe physically is a speculative idea called "quantum creation of universes." This idea is based on an analogy with the unquestionably real effect called the quantum creation of particles. This effect sounds mysterious and profound (and perhaps it is), but it is a fact of everyday life, familiar to all of us. Every time you walk into a dark room and flip on the light switch, you cause a flood of particles to be "created," namely particles of light (called "photons"). Other kinds of particles, even the massy kind that make up what we think of as ordinary matter, such as electrons or protons, can be created, though they have to be created in conjunction with "anti-particles." For example, an electron can be created along with an anti-electron (called a "positron"), and a proton can be created along with an anti-proton. Such "pair creation" can happen in several ways. For example, in an intense electric field, an electron-positron pair can suddenly appear out of the "vacuum," by what is called a "quantum fluctuation" or "quantum tunneling." Pair creation is a well-understood effect, which has been observed countless times in the laboratory, and the probability of its happening in various circumstances can be calculated precisely using the mathematical machinery of "quantum field theory."

When an electron-positron pair is "created," it isn't produced out of nothing. The electron-positron pair has energy (including the mc^2 each particle has from its mass). Since energy is "conserved," that energy must have come from somewhere. For example, when pair creation occurs in an intense electric field, what happens is that some of the energy stored in the electric field is converted into the energy associated with the masses of the electron and positron. One starts with an electric field and ends up with an electron, a positron and a somewhat weaker electric field. This "creation" is really just a transition of matter and energy from one form to another.

In quantum field theory, particles are "excitations" (or, if you will, disturbances) of "fields." So, for example, there is an "electron field" that extends throughout all of space and time. When that field is disturbed, waves develop in it, just as when a pond is disturbed ripples are produced. Quantum mechanics says that waves and particles are two different ways of looking at the same thing. So producing ripples in the electron field is equivalent to producing electron particles (and anti-particles). We can push the pond analogy further. A pond that is still and a pond that has ripples in it are the same physical system in different states of agitation. In the same way, a situation in which there are no electrons or positrons, and a situation where there is an electron-positron pair (or several electron-positron pairs) are really just different states of agitation of the same system, namely the electron field.

Actually, one should not think of the electron field in isolation. It is merely part of a greater system that encompasses many other kinds of fields, including electromagnetic fields, neutrino fields, gravitational fields, quark fields, and so on. When an intense electric field results in electron-positron pair creation, what is happening is that a disturbance of the electromagnetic field is causing a disturbance of the electron field. This is similar to the way that a disturbance of the air (a breeze) might produce a disturbance of the water in a pond (ripples). In other words, the greater system, encompassing all the different kinds of fields that interact with each other, is making a transition from one of its many possible states to another.

In physics, one always considers some definite "system," which has various possible "states," and is governed by dynamical laws (which depend on the nature of the specific system) and by the overarching principles of quantum mechanics (which apply to all systems). The dynamical laws and the principles of quantum mechanics allow one to calculate the probabilities of the system making a transition from one of its states to another. The system might comprise only electrons, positrons, and electromagnetic fields (in which case the dynamical laws are called "quantum electrodynamics"). Or the system could be a simple pendulum, or a hydrogen atom, or the whole universe.

The idea of the quantum creation of universes pushes the mathematics of quantum theory to its logical limit—and maybe even beyond it. Here one contemplates not merely a pair of particles suddenly appearing "in empty space" by a quantum fluctuation or quantum tunneling, but an entire universe—along with its space—appearing in this way. By "universe," in this context, is not meant the "totality of things," but rather a space-time manifold in which there exist fields that interact with each other. Our universe, for example, has one time dimension and at least three space dimensions (there may be more), and many kinds of fields, including electron fields, neutrino fields, quark fields, electromagnetic fields, gravitational fields, and so on. There could be other universes of the same kind. The idea is that one can go (by a quantum fluctuation) from a situation in which there are no universes, to a situation in which there is one universe; or more generally, from a situation with some number of universes to a situation with a different number of universes.

Several apparent difficulties with this idea immediately present themselves. The first of these is that the transition from no universes to one universe would at first sight seem to violate the conservation of energy. Presumably zero universes have zero energy, whereas one universe has a lot of energy, due to all the matter that is contained in it. It turns out, however, that a "closed universe" (one whose space closes in on itself, the way a circle closes in on itself) has zero total energy: the positive energy of the matter is canceled out by the negative gravitational energy. Thus, changing the number of such universes does not violate energy conservation.

A second apparent difficulty has to do with time. In a conventional calculation using the principles of quantum physics, one considers a system making a transition from one "state" at an earlier time (e.g. an intense electric field) to a different "state" at a later time (e.g. a weaker electric field plus an electron-positron pair). However, if we talk about a transition from a "zero-universe state" to a "one-universe state," in what sense is the zero-universe state "earlier"? Indeed, *at what time* was there such a state? We have already seen that time (at least as physicists understand it) is a feature of a universe: if there is no universe, there is no time. If we look at a universe that was produced by a quantum fluctuation, we can talk about time *within* that universe, and even about the beginning of that time, but not about a time "before the universe."

We have to be careful in discussing such scenarios of falling into the verbal trap of saying that "first" there was nothing and "then" there was something. In fact, the same sloppy way of speaking is sometimes found in theological discussions of "creation *ex nihilo.*" When the Church teaches that God created the universe *ex nihilo*, she is not saying that there was once a time when there was no created thing (a contradiction in terms, as St. Augustine pointed out). Rather, she is saying that there never was a time when there was a created thing that preceded the universe and out of which the universe was made. In fact, the meaning of *ex nihilo* is deeper. It is saying not only was the universe not temporally *preceded* by anything, but also that its creation *presupposes* nothing other than the will of God.

If that is what creation *ex nihilo* means, do quantum creation scenarios yield a physical mechanism of "creation ex nihilo," as some seem to believe? One can restate the question in this way: Do quantum creation scenarios presuppose "nothing" in explaining the origin of the universe? They certainly talk about a "state" with no universes. But a state with no universes is not nothing; it is a definite something—a "state." And that state is just one among many states of a complex physical system. That system has states with different numbers of universes. And all of those states are related to each other by precise rules: the dynamical laws and the principles of quantum mechanics that govern the system.

An analogy may be of help here. There is a difference between my having a bank account with zero dollars in it, and my having no bank account at all. As far as my finances go, they may both be said to be "nothing" or "no money"; but there is a big difference. A bank account, even one with zero dollars in it, is something. It presupposes that there is a bank and that I have some contract with that bank. Those facts presuppose, in turn, that a monetary system and a legal system are in place. My bank account is thus a small subsystem of a much larger and more complex system that is governed by precise rules. My account has various "states"; a state with zero dollars, states with a positive numbers of dollars, and even states with negative numbers of dollars (if my account is overdrawn). Transitions are not made between those states willy nilly, but in ways governed by the rules of the bank. For example, if the balance is negative and goes below some threshold, a rule may prevent further withdrawals and transitions to states with more negative balances. A state with a positive balance may periodically make a transition to a state with lower balance, due to service charges. Moreover, the rules may only allow transitions between states containing money of a certain type: dollars, say, rather than rubles, pesos, or Euros. Moreover, I can have several bank accounts with zero balances, perhaps an account in an American bank with zero dollars and an account in a Russian bank with zero rubles. They are different and distinguishable accounts, which obviously shows that each of them is something, rather than nothing.

In the same way, even to talk about a "state with zero universes" presupposes a great deal, as we have seen, namely a rule-governed system with many possible states. In any quantum creation scenario, the rules governing the system allow the "zero universe state" to make transitions to states with one or more universes, but only if those universes have precise characteristics, such as a certain number of space dimensions and certain kinds of fields—just as the rule of my bank may only allow my account to make transitions to states with dollars rather than rubles. I can imagine many different rule-governed systems. In system A, the rules may only allow states whose universes have three space dimensions, whereas in system B the rules may only allow states with universes having ten space dimensions. The "zero-universe state" of system A is not the same entity as the "zero-universe state" of system B: they are subject to different rules that give them different potentialities.

So system A is one where three-dimensional universes come into and out of existence, and system B is one where ten-dimensional universes come into and out of existence. At this point one may ask which, if either, of these systems is *real* as opposed to hypothetical. Are there *actually* three-dimensional universes coming into and out of existence, so that the mathematical laws of system *A* are governing real events? Are there *actually* ten-dimensional universes coming into and out of existence, so that the mathematical laws of system *B* are governing real events? Maybe one or the other is true, or maybe neither, or maybe both. Suppose system *A* is real, whereas system *B* is merely hypothetical. What made system *A* real, but not system *B*? *That* is the question of "creation" in the theological sense of the word: What confers *reality* on system *A* but not system *B*? And *that* is a question that the mathematical rules of system *A* and system *B* cannot possibly answer.

In his 1988 bestseller *A Brief History of Time*, the physicist Stephen Hawking correctly noted that a theory of physics is "just a set of rules and equations," and then went on to ask, "What is it that breathes fire into the equations and makes a universe for them to describe? The usual approach of science of constructing a mathematical model cannot answer the question of why there should be a universe for the model to describe." Strangely enough, it seems that Hawking forgot this key insight by the time he co-authored the book *The Grand Design* in 2010. He now thinks that a mathematical model can answer the question of why there should be a universe for the model to describe. The absurdity of that, which was not lost on the younger Hawking, can be made clear by a simple analogy. A story may be a work of fiction or of history; it may describe actual events or not. A story may tell of Stephen Hawking being born in 1942 and going on to become an acclaimed physicist. Another story may tell of Stephen Hawking being born in 1842 and becoming prime minister of the United Kingdom. Can I determine just by studying the words of the two stories which one describes a real state of affairs? Do the mere *words* of either story have in themselves the power to make real the events they describe? Does the mere fact that the second story purports to tell of something (i.e., Hawking, the future prime minister) coming into being in 1842 mean that the thing described *actually* did come into being? Obviously not. And neither does a mathematical model purporting to describe a universe coming into being by a quantum fluctuation mean that any such thing actually happens.

In sum, the theoretical ideas by which physicists hope one day to describe the beginning of the universe, while being very interesting, and possibly correct, are not alternatives to the Creator in whom Jews and Christians believe. That Creator is not a physical mechanism or phenomenon. He is the giver of reality.

17

PHYSICS, THE NATURE OF TIME, AND THEOLOGY

The title of this symposium is in the form of a question: "Can science inform our understanding of God?" If the question is whether science can directly tell us anything about the divine nature, then of course the answer is no. Natural science studies the natural world, and God is not a part of the natural world. On the other hand, the things that science can tell us are not without relevance to theology, for several reasons.

HOW SCIENCE CAN AFFECT THEOLOGY

One reason is that our theological ideas are shaped, often unconsciously, by nontheological ideas and assumptions. As has been emphasized by the Polish philosopher, physicist, and priest Michal Heller, it is natural for people in every age to form a "World Picture" by integrating whatever they have learned from various sources, including revealed truth, common knowledge, common sense, prevailing scientific ideas, and philosophical speculation. Our World Picture conditions how we think, the kinds of concepts and images we form, and what is regarded by us as reasonable or plausible, both on theological and on nontheological subjects. But World Pictures change over time, and what seemed perfectly plausible at one time may seem quaint or absurd at another. A simple example that illustrates this is the question of the location of hell. Consider this passage from the article on hell in the Catholic Encyclopedia, written in 1910:

As to its locality all kinds of conjectures have been made; it has been suggested that hell is situated on some far island of the sea, or at the two poles of the earth; Swinden, an Englishman of the eighteenth century, fancied it was in the sun; some assigned it to the moon, others to Mars; others placed it beyond the confines of the universe. The Bible seems to indicate that hell is within the earth, for it describes hell as an abyss to which the wicked descend. We even read of the earth opening and of the wicked sinking down into hell (Numbers 16:31; Psalm 54:16; Isaiah 5:14; Ezekiel 26:20; Philippians 2:10; etc.). Is this merely a metaphor to illustrate the state of separation from God? Although God is omnipresent, He is said to dwell in heaven, because the light and grandeur of the stars and the firmament are the brightest manifestations of His infinite splendour. But the damned are utterly estranged from God; hence their abode is said to be as remote as possible from his dwelling, far from heaven above and its light, and consequently hidden away in the dark abysses of the earth. However, no cogent reason has been advanced for accepting a metaphorical interpretation in preference to the most natural meaning of the words of Scripture. Hence theologians generally accept the opinion that hell is really within the earth. The Church has decided nothing on this subject; hence we may say hell is a definite place; but where it is, we do not know.

Why did Catholic theologians for so long "generally accept the opinion that hell is within the earth"? It was not because of some general commitment to biblical literalism. Nor was there any authoritative magisterial teaching on the question. Most likely the reason had to do with what seemed plausible within the context of their World Picture. Some of the biblical imagery of lakes of fire and sulfurous pits was presumably inspired in the first place by volcanoes and their attendant phenomena; and at later times these phenomena would have served to make a literal interpretation more credible, as would widespread notions about the netherworld as the abode of the dead. But our World Picture has changed. In particular, science has learned what the interior of the earth is like, and that the earth will eventually be obliterated when the Sun explodes and becomes a red giant. Very few if any Catholic theologians today would take seriously the idea that hell is inside the earth.

The point is that prevailing ideas about the structure of the physical world and its history have always influenced theological reflection, opinion, and speculation. This is not necessarily a bad thing. Theology attempts to render the truths of faith intelligible and plausible in the context of the knowledge of the day. Nevertheless, there is an obvious danger of the faith becoming adulterated. This can happen in two opposite ways. One is that theology becomes wedded to scientific ideas of an earlier era that turn out to be false, as happened in the Galileo case. The other is that in attempting to stay up-to-date, theologians chase after new ideas in science, without recognizing how speculative and ephemeral these sometimes are. There is no simple formula for steering a middle course; discernment is required, and that in turn requires a certain level of scientific judgment and knowledge.

I did not choose the example of the location of hell at random. One's understanding of eschatological realities will tend to be particularly affected by one's World Picture. How, for instance, are the "clouds of heaven" on which the Lord will return to be understood, or St. Paul's statement that those who are still alive at the parousia will be caught up into the clouds to meet the Lord "in the air"? A question that has been speculated about since the time of the apostles is what our resurrected bodies will be like. A traditional opinion is that our bodies will be similar in structure and composition to those we now have, but perfected and freed from some physical limitations. This view is highly problematic, however, from the viewpoint of any World Picture that incorporates our modern understanding of matter. Bodies made up of the same kinds of matter would have to be subject to very similar physical laws, and that would inevitably entail the corruptibility of those bodies, because of fundamental physical considerations having to do with entropy. One theologian who was aware of this problem was Joseph Ratzinger, who argued in his *Introduction to Christianity* that the resurrection cannot simply be "the return of the 'fleshly body', that is, the biological structure," as that would necessarily mean a perishable body, and "the perishable cannot become imperishable." He noted that St. Paul in 1 Corinthians 15 was "far less naive than later theological erudition with its subtle constructions on the question how there can be eternal physical bodies."

A second reason that science is relevant to theology is that theology cannot do without philosophy, and philosophy is always in conversation with science. It certainly was in the Middle Ages. Aristotelian philosophy gained prestige and a large following in the Middle Ages, even at a time when it was still theologically suspect, in large part because it was thought to give a correct account of natural phenomena. Indeed, long after the Middle Ages, we find Thomistic philosophers passing judgment on scientific theories. (In the 17th century, for instance, many of them reacted quite negatively to the idea that matter is made up of atoms and to ideas about vacuums and air pressure that turned out to be correct.) So, while theology, philosophy, and natural science are distinct disciplines, with their own sources, methods, and competences, they inevitably influence each other.

A contemporary example of this relates, again, to our resurrected bodies. It is *de fide* Catholic teaching that we shall have "the same bodies" that we now have, in some sense that hasn't been defined.[1] In contemporary philosophy there is much discussion of what makes something "the same thing" through time. One school of thought holds that there needs to be some degree of material continuity at the level of the elementary constituents of the things, which we may suppose to be particles. And this continuity is held by some to require not just particles of the same type, but some, at least, of the very same particles. However, this runs up against a basic fact about matter discovered in the twentieth century, which is that elementary particles have no individuality, or what medieval philosophers called *haecceitas* ("thisness"). Given a set of electrons, say, there is no meaning to saying which electron is which—for example, asking whether the electron over here now is the same one as the electron over there later. So we see here a case where a fact of physics has relevance to an issue in philosophy (identity of things through time), which in turn has relevance to a theological question (in what sense our resurrected bodies will be the same).

A KEY ISSUE: THE NATURE OF TIME

The rest of my talk will be about a subject where theology, philosophy, and science quite clearly intersect, namely the nature of time. It is obvious that science has something to say about this question. Two of the major breakthroughs of twentieth-century physics—Einstein's theories of Special Relativity and General Relativity—gave us a much deeper understanding of time. It is also clear that the nature of time is an important subject for theologians, as can be seen from the fact that St. Augustine devoted Book XI of his *Confessions* to a famous analysis of it. Let us begin with that analysis.

Virtually all the ancient pagan philosophers, including Aristotle, believed that the universe had always existed. And it seems that some pagans were given to mocking the Jewish and Christian belief that the universe had a Beginning. They would ask what the God of the Bible was doing for the infinite time before he got around to creating the world. To this St. Augustine gave a profound answer. He started with the fact that time is a feature of the created world and is therefore itself something created. As he put it, "There can be no time without creation." "What times could there be that are not made by you, [O Lord]?" But if time is something created, then the beginning of created things must also be the beginning of time. It is self-contradictory, therefore, to speak of a "time before Creation." To quote St. Augustine once again: "You [O Lord] made that very time, and no time could pass by before you made those times. But if there was no time before heaven and earth, why do they ask what you did 'then'? There was no 'then', where there was no time."

The brilliance of this insight is staggering. It was fifteen centuries ahead of its time. Not until Einstein's theory of General Relativity, which was proposed in 1916, did science catch up to it.

St. Augustine started with the fact that time is something created; modern physics starts with the fact that time is something physical. This fact was not apparent before General Relativity. Up to that point, space and time tended to be thought of by scientists as a kind of mathematical backdrop to physical events. Physical events and processes unfolded in space and time, but space and time themselves took no part in events and underwent no processes. With General Relativity, however, it became clear that space-time is a fabric that bends, flexes, stretches, and ripples in response to the energy and momentum of the matter that fills it. Indeed, these movements of the space-time manifold themselves carry energy and momentum. Space-time, in short, is no less physical than atoms, or magnetic fields, or rocks, or trees. It necessarily follows that if there was a beginning to the physical universe it was also the beginning of space and time. It therefore makes no sense to speak of a time before the universe began. St. Augustine's great insight has triumphed.

Notice that what had seemed a formidable *theological* problem ("What was God doing before he made the universe?") was shown to be a pseudo-problem by St. Augustine's *philosophical* analysis, which was later confirmed or seconded by the insights of modern theoretical *physics*.

St. Augustine's understanding of time has further consequences. It implies that God is "outside of time." "Past," "future," "before," and "after" refer to relationships among created things, and therefore do not apply to God at all. God may cause physical event A to *happen* before physical event B. But God's *willing of A* does not happen before his *willing of B*. Nor does God's *knowing of A* happen before his *knowing of B*. God knows and wills a world in which things happen in temporal succession, but his knowing and willing do not happen in temporal succession. God is atemporal. He dwells, as St. Augustine put it, in the "sublimity of an ever-present eternity," or in St. Thomas's words, in the "nunc stans," the now that stands still. God, one might say, is the still "eye" at the center of the storm of being. In the twentieth century, various theological movements posited temporality in the Godhead. These include "process theology," "kenosis theology," and "open theism." These movements, though mainly Protestant in origin, have had some influence in Catholic circles.

Process theology seems to have been inspired by the facts of biological evolution and cosmic evolution. The idea is that the evolving universe is ever open to "novelty," in the sense of developments that could not have been foreseen. The world is an ongoing "creative" process, and God is seen (at least by some of these theologians) not as the Creator of the universe so much as the immanent creativity of the universe. In their eyes, this allows the universe and especially human beings to have more autonomy and genuine freedom than if God foreknew and forewilled events in accordance with an eternal plan. This is a major concern also of the open theists, who believe that human freedom is incompatible with divine "foreknowledge." God must therefore, they think, be ignorant of the future, either because the future does not exist to be known or because he chooses not to know it. Kenosis theology ("kenosis" means emptying) takes as its point of departure Philippians 2:7, which speaks of Christ emptying himself and taking the form of a slave. There are many strains of kenosis theology, but the more radical ones suggest that the Son divested himself of divinity for a period of time. He did not merely assume a human nature, but shed his divine nature, or at least some of the attributes of divinity. They think it necessary that the Son be able to suffer for our redemption, not only in his human nature, but in his divine nature as well. Some of the advocates of process theology, open theism, and kenosis theology also imagine that by rejecting traditional beliefs about God's omniscience and omnipotence they can resolve or lessen the problems of theodicy. God is less liable to blame for the evil and suffering in the world, they think, if he is less in control.

Whatever else may be said about these theological movements, it is clear that insofar as they deny the immutability, impassibility, omniscience, and omnipotence of God they contradict solemn decrees of Ecumenical Councils and are incompatible with the Catholic faith. For faith, that is all that needs to be said. But faith seeks understanding, and so it is the task of reason enlightened by faith to show how these erroneous opinions fail to accord with the whole structure and pattern of revealed truth and with sound philosophy. This theological and philosophical task I do not propose to undertake here. Rather, since this talk is about the relation of science to our understanding of God, I wish to make a different point, namely that these theological innovations are not only heterodox but also deeply problematic from the perspective of what we have learned about the nature of time from modern physics.

Let us consider the statement, made by many open theists, process theologians, and kenosis theologians, that "God does not know the future." What is problematic about this statement for the orthodox theologian is its concept of God and divine knowledge. What would be problematic for the modern physicist, however, is its concept of "the future." The physicist has no trouble understanding what "future" means. But he has a great deal of trouble with the idea of "the future." So let us take a closer look at the concepts of future and past.

Our experience of time begins with our own stream of consciousness, which has a simple linear ordering of past, present, and future. The past is what we remember, and the future is what we anticipate. (To quote St. Augustine's *Confessions*, "The past is present memory. . . . The future is present anticipation.") Let us call this "psychological time."

When we turn to the physical world, we find that it has a causal structure; and it is this causal structure that gives a temporal ordering to events. From a physics point of view, *event B is in the future of event A if and only if A can physically influence B.* Let us call this ordering "physical time."

Clearly, human psychological time and physical time are connected. We are embodied beings, and as St. Thomas Aquinas noted, whatever exists in our intellects must first exist in our senses. You can only acquire natural knowledge about physical events if they have had an effect upon your sense organs through some chain of physical causation. Consequently, only events that are in your physical past can be naturally known to you, exist in your memory, and thus be in your psychological past. Similarly, your will can only produce outward effects through physical motions of parts of your body; so that what you anticipate doing or intend to do, which belongs to your psychological future, must also lie in your physical future.

Given the close connection between our psychological time and physical time, it is quite natural to assume that the physical universe has the same simple, linear past-present-future ordering that we experience in our mental life. And, indeed, this was the assumption made in Newtonian physics. Einstein's theory of Special Relativity, however, showed that this is wrong. The causal structure, and hence the temporal structure, of the physical universe is more subtle. It consists not of a one-dimensional chain, but a four-dimensional web of causal relationships.

In Newtonian physics, it makes sense to speak of a set of events extending throughout all of space as being "simultaneous," that is, as all happening "now" with respect to each other. Such a universally defined "now" or "present moment" is a slice that divides the universe into "the past" and "the future" with respect to that moment. Any event that is happening "now" anywhere in the universe can physically influence any event that is in "the future" anywhere. Similarly, any event in "the past" anywhere can physically influence any event that is happening "now" anywhere. That is, in Newtonian physics, one has a *universal* definition of past, present, and future with respect to any moment.

Special Relativity has shown, however, that this is not the way the universe works. The reason is that physical influences cannot propagate faster than a certain fundamental speed, called c or "the speed of light in vacuum." Because of this, an event B lies in the physical future of event A if and only if influence could travel from A to B going at the speed of light or slower. (That is, in physics jargon, the future of event A consists of all events that lie within or on the "future light cone" of A.) Similarly, the events that lie in the physical past of A are those from which influence traveling at the speed of light or slower would be able to reach event A (in the jargon, those that lie within or on the "past light cone" of A). What this means is that there is a *third* class of events, namely those that are too far away from event A either to physically influence it or to be influenced by it. These events lie neither in the past nor in the future of A, but are said to have a "space-like separation from A."

Note that one is no longer speaking about the past and the future in a *universal* sense, but about the past and future *of particular events*: "the past of event A," for example, or "the future of event A." (And as far as the "present" goes, one no longer speaks about it at all, since according to Relativity no two events in the universe are simultaneous with each other in any absolute sense.) The reason that there is no such thing as simply "the future" unanchored to particular events is that Relativity tells us no two events have the same futures or pasts. That is, given two events, X and Y, there will always be some events that are in the future of X but not of Y, and others that are in the future of Y but not of X.

To sum up, in Newtonian physics one had only two regions, past and future, divided by a slice called the present. In Relativity, however, each event has *three* regions of space-time associated with it: past, future, and "space-like separated," which are divided from each other by *two* slices called the "past light cone" and the "future light cone." The technical details do not matter for the purposes of the present discussion. What does matter is that such a dividing up of space-time can only be done with respect to some specific event. Given some event *A* that happens at some particular time and place, one can talk about events that lie in its future or in its past. For example, it is perfectly meaningful for me to speak of something happening in *my* future. If I say, "*B* will happen in the future," what I am really saying is that *B* lies in the future *of this utterance*, which is being made here and now, i.e., an event located at a specific place and time. On the other hand, it does not make sense to speak about God's future, unless God is localized in space. Another way to understand this is that Relativity ties time and space together in a way that wasn't true in Newtonian physics, which is why one speaks of "space-time." To make God dwell in time, therefore, is also to make him dwell in space.

Newtonian physics made a naïve mistake in projecting onto the physical universe temporal concepts based on our own psychological time. In most practical situations, this mistake makes no difference. One can ask without any significant ambiguity what people are doing "now" in the next room. (It only takes light a few nanoseconds to propagate to the next room, so the ambiguity in the concept "now" is negligible.) And it should be emphasized that the Newtonian mistake was not harmful for physics, but on the contrary Newtonian concepts were a necessary stage in the progress of physics.

If it was a naïve mistake to project our one-dimensional psychological time onto the four-dimensional physical universe, how much more naïve is it to project it onto God himself as those do who say that "God does not know 'the future'"?

I should note that there is one theologian who argues that God does not know the future and who cannot be accused of naïveté about physics, and that is John Polkinghorne. Polkinghorne is a theoretical particle physicist, as I am. He knows very well what Special and General Relativity say about the nature of time, and is well aware of the problem that they pose in making sense of the notion of "the future." He proposed a technical answer in his book *Science and the Trinity*. He notes that if the universe is "homogeneous and isotropic" (to use the technical jargon), there is a natural way to define a "cosmic time" or age of the universe. This cosmic time is defined as the time that has elapsed since the Big Bang as measured in the reference frame in which the radiation filling the universe is at rest. Polkinghorne suggests that this cosmic time could be used to define "the future" of which God is supposedly ignorant. At any cosmic time, Polkinghorne suggests, God might know only the events that happen at that cosmic time or earlier.

It is true that a cosmic time can be defined in a reasonably (but not entirely) unambiguous way for the part of the universe that we can see. There are strong reasons to suspect, however, that on larger scales of distance the universe is not "homogeneous and isotropic," in which case cosmic time becomes an ill-defined concept. But aside from this technical objection, I think Polkinghorne is losing sight of the basic lesson that the physics is teaching us.

To reiterate the crucial point, *physical time is rooted in physical causality*. Event *A* is physically prior to event *B* if and only if it can physically influence *B*. Thus it is really only sensible to apply the categories of physical time to entities that are involved in physical cause and effect. We human beings are physical as well as spiritual, and so are subject to physical time. Even our intellects, though not physical, are tied (at least in this life) to the space and time of this universe, because we acquire knowledge through our physical senses. God's knowledge, however, is not of this sort. Polkinghorne himself would reject the notion that God makes use of physical processes to learn about what is going on in the world. God's mind is therefore not subject to physical time as our minds are. (It is true that the Son of God assumed a human nature, and so in his human nature was subject to physical time, but no one has ever denied this.)

I should emphasize that physics cannot prove that open theism is wrong or that God is immutable. Polkinghorne's version of open theism, for example, is not logically inconsistent with physics. Nor does Catholic theology need to make use of physics to show that open theism is wrong. Nevertheless, what physics teaches us about time casts a helpful light on the issue. Anything that gives us a deeper understanding of time is surely relevant to the question of God's relation to time.

THE RELEVANCE OF THESE ISSUES TO THE "SCIENCE-RELIGION" QUESTION

So far I have been talking about open theism, process theology, and kenosis theology, which are, admittedly, somewhat esoteric ideas chiefly popular among non-Catholic academic theologians. So why does any of this matter? If the kinds of errors I have been discussing were confined to those narrow circles, they would not matter very much, to be sure. But I think that similar confusion about God's relation to time are very widespread and contribute a great deal to popular and even scholarly confusion about the relation between science and religion and to the perception that they are at odds with each other or at least in tension.

Time-bound creatures that we are, it is impossible for us to imagine eternity, and very difficult to think clearly about it. Almost inevitably we tend to imagine God as a temporal being. But in thinking of him this way, we unwittingly drag him down to the level of a creature, and not just a creature but a physical creature. He becomes in our thought just one thing among things in our universe, one physical cause among other physical causes. One can see the symptoms of this thinking in many places.

One symptom is the tendency of people to think of God's role in Creation as that of some physical force that acted 14 billion years ago (or more recently, for biblical literalists). Many times I have been asked by religious people, "What caused the universe to start expanding in the first place?" I think that in many cases they expect to hear, or hope to hear, that it is beyond the possibility of scientific explanation, because they think this would create a job opening for God to act as the "force" that started things off, as though he were the explosive that produced the Big Bang or the match that lit it. Atheists too think this way, including Hawking, who has recently suggested that certain speculative ideas in cosmology show that "[I]t is not necessary to invoke God to light the blue touch paper and set the universe going."

Another symptom is the notion, held by most atheists and many Christians, that God as an explanation of things is in competition with natural explanations, so that the more science explains the less there is for God to do. Several years ago, in an article in the journal *First Things*, I asked why the evolution of species should be a disturbing thought to Christians, since, "If one is happy with natural explanations of the formation of stars and planetary systems, why not of plants and animals?" This provoked an angry letter from a well-known evangelical Protestant gentleman,[2] who asked,

> Is it possible that a man of Barr's education really wonders *why* some of us would not accept a natural explanation for the formation of stars and planets in light of discoveries made possible by the Hubble telescope? A Big

Bang presupposes a force that brought all this into being (that is, God). People who believe there is a natural explanation for the formation of stars, the
planetary system, plants, and animals are, by any definition, naturalists.
Neo-Darwinists have made it clear that they presuppose a natural beginning of the universe (that is, no God).

We see here again the idea that God is a "force" needed to set off the
Big Bang. But we also see the idea that "natural explanations" mean "no
God." It may seem strange that someone who sees in natural explanations
a threat to God's role in the world would use such naturalistic language
of God ("a force"), but actually the two ideas are logically linked. It is precisely to the extent that God is seen as being like a natural force himself
that he is seen as competing with other, ordinary natural forces—they
have been put on the same playing field.

A third symptom is the idea that if there is chance or randomness or
accident in nature, then God is not in control, or doesn't know where
things are headed. A related idea that if one attributes blindness or aim-
lessness to natural processes one is necessarily denying God. The point is
that if God is being thought of as though he were another part of nature,
then saying that nature is stumbling along blindly, as it were, is tanta-
mount to saying that God is too. I think this is what may underlie some
of the opposition aroused by the idea that "random" genetic mutations
drive evolution.

The disease underlying all these symptoms, I believe, is an inadequate
idea of how God relates to time, which leads to an inadequate theology of
Creation and of divine action in the world. The cure is to go back to the
profound insights of St. Augustine.

To see how these issues are all related, it is helpful to use an old analogy
that compares God as the Author of the universe to a human author of
a book. Let us consider, then, a novel. The events in a novel are causally
related to each other. This causal structure gives the novel an internal
time, which we may call "plot-time." For simplicity, let us suppose that
the story unfolds in a simple sequence—no flashbacks, for example—so
that events that occur on one page only affect events on later pages or
later on the same page. This allows us to "measure" the plot-time by page
and line. Plot-time starts on the first page of the text and ends on the last
page—both past and future are finite in extent.

Note that the doings of the author—his getting married, or deciding
what to have for dinner—are not events of the novel's plot (assuming it

is not autobiographical), and thus have no page and line number. They are completely outside of the novel's plot-time. This is true even of the author's activities related to the writing of the book. The author's deciding to write the book, outlining the plot, inventing characters, and composing dialogue are not themselves events in the novel and have no plot-time, even though they do determine what events happen in the novel and when in plot-time they happen.

At this point one sees that two levels of causality are involved in the novel. There is the causality whereby one event in the novel causes another event in the novel, which one could call "horizontal causality." And there is the causality whereby the author conceives of the novel and brings it into being as a work of art, which does not take place in plot-time. One could call this "vertical causality." These two kinds of causality are obviously not in competition. For example, in talking about the novel *Crime and Punishment* is it silly to ask whether the old pawn broker woman died because Raskolnikov struck her with an ax or because Dostoevsky wrote the book that way. The answer is *both!* Raskolnikov's murderous act is the cause *within* the novel of the pawnbroker's death, while Dostoevsky is the cause *of* the novel and of all its plot, including the death of the pawnbroker.

The analogy universe and its Creator to a novel and its author is obviously not perfect, but it does illuminate the key insights of St. Augustine. First, we see that time is something created. The author of the novel is the one who gave its plot whatever internal causal and temporal structure it has. He could have written a book with no internal causality or time, that is, just disjointed and chaotic events. Or he could have had the plot-time go around in a circle (or, equivalently, repeat endlessly). Or he could have devised very intricate causal and temporal structures as in some science fiction books involving time travel. Second, we see that the author of the universe is outside the time of the universe. Third, we see that time can have a beginning and an end, as the pages and lines of a book do. And, fourth, we see two noncompeting levels of causality, which I have called vertical and horizontal, but which with regard to the universe and God are traditionally called "primary" and "secondary" causality.

But the analogy takes us further and allows us to understand how time relates to Creation. The *creation* of the book is not the same thing as the *beginning* of the book, in the sense of its first words or the first events of its plot. That is confusing the two levels of causality. The first events in the novel's plot are causes *within* the novel of later events in the plot; but they do not cause the novel itself, that is, they do not explain why there is a novel. The cause of the novel is its author. In the same way, the temporal beginning of the universe (whether it was the Big Bang, as in the standard cosmological model, or some other event) is not the same thing as the cause of the universe. By the same token, Creation is not just something that happened at the temporal beginning of the universe. God equally creates all times, places, and events in the universe, just as the author of a novel is equally the author of every word of it, the last word as much as the first. (In theology, there is a distinction made between God's Creating at the beginning of time, and his Conservation of the universe in being; but St. Thomas and other scholastic theologians taught that this distinction is only notional; there is no real distinction between God's act of Creating and Conserving, they are one timeless act.)

From the fact that there are two levels of causality, one sees that thinking of God as the "force" that made the universe expand is a simple blunder. Physical "forces" that push matter around are like the causes that operate within the plot of a book. Creation, on the other hand, is the "thinking up" of the universe, like the author's thinking up the whole book, its whole plot, and all the causes that act within it.

And there is no reason whatever to think that the "beginning of the universe," in the sense of its opening events, must have violated the laws of physics any more than the first sentence of a novel should violate the rules of good grammar. In that sense, the beginning of the universe may have been a perfectly "natural event."

We also see how absurd it is to imagine that natural causality is in competition with divine causality. It makes no more sense to ask whether horses evolved or were created by God than to ask whether the old pawnbroker was murdered by Raskolnikov or died because that was what Dostoevsky wrote. Of course, it is possible for the author to write events into the plot that are miraculous, in the sense that they are exceptions to the rules that govern the internal causality of the rest of the plot. But the author is equally the author of the nonmiraculous and the miraculous events.

And finally, the idea that randomness and chance in nature mean that God is not in control, or doesn't know where things are headed, is to confuse the point of view of the characters in the novel with that of its author. The characters may be taken by surprise or be stumbling along in the dark, but the author knows very well what lies in store. As the eminent geneticist Francis S. Collins wrote in his book *The Language of God,*

But how could God take such chances? If evolution is random, how could He really be in charge, and how could He be certain of an outcome that included intelligent beings at all?

The solution is actually readily at hand, once one ceases to apply human limitations to God. If God is outside of nature, then He is outside of space and time. In that context, God could in the moment of the creation of the universe also know every detail of the future. That could include the formation of the stars, planets, and galaxies, all of the chemistry, physics, geology, and biology that led to the formation of life on earth, and the evolution of humans, right to the moment of your reading this book—and beyond. In that context, evolution could appear to us to be driven by chance, but from God's perspective the outcome would be entirely specified.

It does not require a knowledge of physics, of course, to understand these things. St. Augustine and St. Thomas understood them long before anything much was known about the laws of nature. But modern physics is actually quite helpful in reinforcing a correct way of thinking about time. The training of those who do fundamental physics makes them more aware than most people that time is merely a feature of our physical universe; that time could have had a different structure (after all, they know at least two such structures, Newtonian and Einsteinian); and that there can be realities that lie outside of our time and space (for example, other spatial dimensions of our universe, or other universes). The traditional Augustinian conception of time, which is so central to a sound understanding of Creation, may come more naturally to the modern physicist (even if he is an atheist) than to the scientific layman (even if he is religious).

This is another example of how science can enlarge our imaginations and free us from naïve misconceptions about the physical world that can lead theology into errors. Perhaps this what Pope John Paul II meant when he said, "Science could purify religion from error and superstition." Science can play this role by correcting the mistakes of older science that may have distorted the thinking of theologians and philosophers. It is a limited and ancillary role, to be sure, but an important one.

18

MUCH ADO ABOUT "NOTHING": STEPHEN HAWKING AND THE SELF-CREATING UNIVERSE

Has physics done away with God? A newly released book by Stephen Hawking and Leonard Mlodinow says, "Yes."

What is a Jewish or Christian believer to make of this? Is the Creator now out of a job? The short answer is (unsurprisingly) *no*: the ideas propounded in Hawking's book constitute no threat whatever to the Jewish and Christian doctrine of Creation.

The idea that Hawking is now touting is not new—in fact, within the fast-moving world of modern physics it is fairly old. My first introduction to it was reading a very elegant theoretical paper entitled "Creation of Universes from Nothing," written in 1982 by the noted cosmologist Alexander Vilenkin, who argued that our universe might have arisen by a "quantum fluctuation." This idea is sometimes referred to as the quantum creation of the universe. There are different variants, but the basic idea is well known among particle physicists and cosmologists.

Right up front, it must be noted that this idea is extremely speculative, has not yet been formulated in a mathematically rigorous way, and is unable at this point to make any testable predictions. Indeed, it is very hard to imagine how it could ever be tested. It would be more accurate to call these "scenarios" than theories. It would be a mistake, however, for religious believers to dismiss these scenarios as mere fanciful conjecture or as motivated merely by atheist ideology. Based on a plausible analogy with the experimentally observed and well-understood phenomenon of the quantum creation of particles, the idea of quantum creation of universes is not without merit.

The salient point has to do with how quantum mechanics works. In quantum mechanics one always considers some physical "system," which has various possible "quantum states," and which is governed by certain well-defined "dynamical laws." The dynamical laws that govern the particular system and the fundamental principles of quantum mechanics allow one to calculate the probability that the system will make a transition from one of its states to another. To take a simple example, the system might be an atom of hydrogen, and its states would be the different "energy levels" of the atom.

The highly speculative idea is that these ways of thinking can be applied to entire universes, which is what Hawking (and many others) have tried to do. For physicists (as opposed to theologians and metaphysicians) the concept of the universe does not refer to "all there is" or the "totality of things." It refers to a single, self-contained physical structure, comprising a "spacetime manifold" and particles and other things moving around in that spacetime.

If one thinks of a universe as a particular structure, then one can imagine a multiplicity of universes, with universes coming into and going out of existence in various ways. For example, a new universe might split off from an already existing universe in a manner analogous to the way a small balloon can be "pinched off" from a larger balloon. Or one can imagine a universe starting off as a point of zero size (which is, in effect, no universe at all) and then growing continuously to some finite size.

By such processes, the number of universes can change. However, we need to keep in mind the special way in which physicists use the concept of "universe," for these various universes are really features of a *single* overarching physical system—call it a "system of universes."[1] When the number of universes changes, it is because that single overarching system has undergone a transition from one of its "quantum states" to another. Such transitions are precisely governed by dynamical laws (assumed to include the laws of quantum mechanics). These laws would govern not only how many universes there were, but the characteristics of these universes, such as how many dimensions of space they could have and what kinds of matter and forces they could contain.

Some states of the system of universes would correspond to just one universe being in existence; others to two universes, and so on. And there would also be a state with no universe in existence. The dramatic possibility Hawking is considering (and many others before him) is that such a system might make a transition from its "no-universe state" to a state with one or more universes.

Would this be "creation" in the sense that theologians mean it? And in particular, would it be creation *ex nihilo*, creation from nothing?

The answer is no. First of all, one isn't starting from "nothing." The "no-universe state" as meant in these speculative scenarios is not nothing, it is a very definite something: it is one particular quantum state among many of an intricate rule-governed system. This no-universe state has specific properties and potentialities defined by a system of mathematical laws.

An analogy may help here. A checking account is a system that has many possible states: the zero-dollar state, the thousand-dollar state, the negative-thousand-dollar state (if one is overdrawn), the million-dollar state, etc. And this system can make transitions from one state to another; for instance, by a finance charge or by accruing interest. Even if your checking account happens to be in the zero-dollar state one day, the checking account is nevertheless still something definite and real—not "nothing." It presupposes a bank, a monetary system, a contract between you and that bank—all being governed by various systems of rules.

Imagine the day on which your bank account balance is zero. Then imagine a deposit the next day that raises it to one thousand dollars. A quantum theory of the creation of a universe (in Hawking's version, or Vilenkin's, or anyone else's) is akin to this transition from an empty account to one full of money. Obviously, therefore, the "nothing" that Hawking makes part of his theory of the creation of our universe is not nothing in a metaphysical sense. The "no-universe" of his speculations is like the "no-dollars" in my account. It exists within the framework of a complex overarching system with specific rules. So we can see that, if true, the way of thinking put forward by Hawking does not threaten the classical doctrine of creation out of nothing.

Perhaps my explanations are not really necessary. Even the most casual readers recognize that the cosmological theories put forward by Hawking do not bear upon larger questions that motivate classical views of creation out of nothing. Nonscientists are quick to ask the obvious questions. Why a system obeying quantum mechanics, M-theory, superstring theory, or whatever laws of physics that make scientific speculations possible in the first place? Why not no system at all, with no laws at all, no anything, just blank nonbeing?

Physics, by its very nature, cannot answer these questions. And the funny thing is that Hawking himself is perfectly aware of this. Indeed, he said it himself in a previous book! In *A Brief History of Time*, Hawking observed—quite correctly—that any theory of physics is "just a set of rules and equations." And he asked, "What is it that breathes fire into the equations and makes a universe for them to describe? The usual approach of science of constructing a mathematical model cannot answer the question of why there should be a universe for the model to describe." (Here he was using the word "universe" to mean what I called the "system of universes": the entirety of physical reality described by the laws of physics.)

Physics scenarios and theories are merely mathematical stories. They may be fictional or describe some reality. And just as the words of a book by themselves can't tell you whether it's fact or fiction—let alone have the power to make the world they describe real—so with the equations of a physics scenario. As Hawking once understood, equations may turn out to be an accurate description of some reality, but cannot *confer* reality on the things they describe.

What Hawking called in his previous book the "usual approach of science" is in fact the *only* genuinely scientific approach in physics. From the time Hawking wrote that earlier book until now, nothing has changed in this regard: theories of physics are still "just sets of rules and equations."

There are two answers to the question: "Why does anything exist rather than nothing at all?" The atheist answers, "There is no explanation." The theist replies, God. An intelligent case can be made for either answer. But to say that the laws of physics alone answer it is the purest nonsense—as Hawking himself once realized.

REDUCTIONISM

19

FEARFUL SYMMETRIES

Since the time of Newton, science has advanced by a strategy rightly called "reductionism." This method, which explains things by analyzing them into smaller and simpler parts, has yielded a rich harvest of discoveries about the natural world. As a means of analysis, then, reductionism has certainly proven its value. But many wonder whether science is reductive in a more radical and disturbing way—by flattening, collapsing, and trivializing the world. For all its intellectual accomplishments, does science end up taking our sense of reality down several notches? One could well get that impression from perusing the writings of certain scientists. Francis Crick famously asserted that human life is "no more than the behavior of . . . nerve cells and their associated molecules." Marvin Minsky, a pioneer in the field of artificial intelligence, once described people as "machines made of meat." Neuroscientist Giulio Giorelli announced that "we have a soul, but it is made up of many tiny robots." And biologist Charles Zuker has concluded that "in essence, we are nothing but a big fly."

This tendency to downgrade and diminish reflects a metaphysical prejudice that equates explanatory reduction with a grim slide down the ladder of being. Powerful explanatory schemes reveal things to be simpler than they appear. What *simpler* means in science is much discussed among philosophers—it is not at all a simple question. But to many materialists it seems to mean lower, cruder, and more trivial. By this way of thinking, the further we push toward a more basic understanding of things, the more we are immersed in meaningless, brutish bits of matter.

The philosopher Georges Rey has written, for example, that "any ultimate explanation of mental phenomena will have to be in *non*-mental [i.e., *sub*-mental or material] terms or else it won't be an *explanation* of it." Of course, the logic of this could be turned around. One could just as well say that any ultimate explanation of the material world must be in nonmaterial terms. But for materialists the lower explains the higher; and *lower* does not just mean *more fundamental* but instead suggests a diminished ontological status. The presumption is that explanations move from evolved complexity to primitive *stuff*.

At first glance, the history of the cosmos seems to bear this out. Early on, the universe was filled with nearly featureless gas and dust, which eventually condensed to form galaxies, stars, and planets. In stars and supernovas, the simplest elements, hydrogen and helium, fused to make heavier ones, gradually building up the whole periodic table. In some primordial soup, or slime, or ooze on the early earth, atoms agglomerated into larger and more intricate molecules until self-replicating ones appeared and life began. From one-celled organisms, ever more complicated living things evolved, until sensation and thought appeared. In cosmic evolution the arrow apparently moves from chaos to order, formlessness to form, triviality to complexity, and matter to mind.

And that is why, according to philosopher Daniel Dennett, religion has it exactly upside down. Believers think that God reached down to bring order and create, whereas in reality the world was built—or rather built itself—from the ground up. In Dennett's metaphor, the world was constructed not by "skyhooks" reaching down from the heavens but by "cranes" supported by, and reaching up from, the solid ground.

The history to which the atheist points—of matter self-organizing and physical structures growing in complexity—is correct as far as it goes, but it is only part of the story. The lessons the atheist draws are naïve. Yes, the world we experience is the result of processes that move upward. But Dennett and others overlook the hidden forces and principles that govern those processes. In short, they are not true reductionists because they don't go all the way down to the most basic explanations of reality.

As we turn to the fundamental principles of physics, we discover that order does not really emerge from chaos, as we might naïvely assume; it always emerges from greater and more impressive order already present at a deeper level. It turns out that things are not more coarse or crude or unformed as one goes down into the foundations of the physical world but more subtle, sophisticated, and intricate the deeper one goes.

Let's start with a simple but instructive example of how order can appear to emerge spontaneously from mere chaos through the operation of natural forces. Imagine a large number of identical marbles rolling around randomly in a shoe box. If the box is tilted, all the marbles will roll down into a corner and arrange themselves into what is called the "hexagonal closest packing" pattern. (This is the same pattern one sees in oranges stacked on a fruit stand or in cells in a beehive.) This orderly structure emerges as the result of blind physical forces and mathematical laws. There is no hand arranging it. Physics requires the marbles to lower their gravitational potential energy as much as possible by squeezing down into the corner, which leads to the geometry of hexagonal packing.

At this point it seems as though order has indeed sprung from mere chaos. To see why this is wrong, however, consider a genuinely chaotic situation: a typical teenager's bedroom. Imagine a huge jack tilting the bedroom so that everything in it slides into a corner. The result would not be an orderly pattern but instead a jumbled heap of lamps, furniture, books, clothing, and what have you.

Why the difference? Part of the answer is that, unlike the objects in the bedroom, the marbles in the box all have the same size and shape. But there's more to it. Put a number of spoons of the same size and shape into a box and tilt it, and the result will be a jumbled heap. Marbles differ from spoons because their shape is spherical. When spoons tumble into a corner, they end up pointing every which way, but marbles don't point every which way, because no matter which way a sphere is turned it looks exactly the same.

These two crucial features of the marbles—having the same shape and having a spherical shape—should be understood as *principles of order* that are already present in the supposedly chaotic situation before the box was tilted. In fact, the more we reduce to deeper explanations, the higher we go. This is because, in a sense that can be made mathematically precise, the preexisting order inherent in the marbles is *greater* than the order that emerges after the marbles arrange themselves. This requires some explanation.

Both the preexisting order and the order that emerges involve symmetry, a concept of central importance in modern physics, as we'll see. Mathematicians and physicists have a peculiar way of thinking about symmetry: a symmetry is something that is *done*. For example, if one rotates a square by 90 degrees, it looks the same, so rotating by 90 degrees is said to be a symmetry of the square. So is rotating by 180 degrees, 270 degrees, or a full 360 degrees. A square thus has exactly four symmetries.

Not surprisingly, the hexagonal pattern the marbles form has six symmetries (rotating by any multiple of 60 degrees: 60, 120, 180, 240, 300, and 360 degrees). A sphere, on the other hand, has an infinite number of symmetries—doubly infinite, in fact, since rotating a sphere by *any* angle about *any* axis leaves it looking the same. And, what's more, the symmetries of a sphere *include* all the symmetries of a hexagon.

If we think this way about symmetry, careful analysis shows that, when marbles arrange themselves into the hexagonal pattern, just six of the infinite number of symmetries in the shape of the marbles are expressed or manifested in their final arrangement. The rest of the symmetries are said, in the jargon of physics, to be *spontaneously broken*. So, in the simple example of marbles in a tilted box, we can see that symmetry isn't popping out of nowhere. It is being distilled out of a greater symmetry already present within the spherical shape of the marbles.

The idea of *spontaneous symmetry breaking* is important in fundamental physics. The equations of electromagnetism have a mathematical structure that is dictated by a set of so-called gauge symmetries, discovered by the mathematician and physicist Hermann Weyl almost a century ago. For a long time it seemed that two other basic forces of nature, the weak force and the strong force, were not based on symmetries. But about forty years ago it was found that the weak force is actually based on an even larger set of gauge symmetries than those of electromagnetism. Because the symmetries of the weak force are spontaneously broken, however, they do not manifest or express themselves in an obvious way, which is why it took so long to discover them. (The strong force is based on a yet larger set of gauge symmetries, but this fact was obscured by a quite different effect and also was not discovered for a long time.)

This history illustrates a general trend in modern physics: the more deeply it has probed the structure of matter, the greater the mathematical order it has found. The order we see in nature does not come from chaos; it is distilled out of a more fundamental order.

Symmetry is just one kind of order. In the case of the marbles in the box, other principles of order were also at work, such as the principle that caused the marbles to seek out the configuration of lowest energy. This is an aspect of a beautiful mathematical principle, called the principle of least action, that underlies all of classical physics. When physicists investigated the subatomic realm, however, they discovered that the principle of least action is just a limiting case of the much more subtle and sophisticated path integral principle, which is the basis of quantum mechanics, as Richard Feynman showed in the 1940s. The lesson is the same: the deeper one looks, the more remarkable the mathematical structure one sees.

The mathematical order underlying physical phenomena is most easily observed in the motions of the heavenly bodies. Even primitive societies were aware of it, and it inspired not only feelings of religious awe (many expressions of which are found in the Bible itself) but also the earliest attempts at mathematical science. And when scientists began to study the solar system with more precision, they discovered unsuspected patterns even more beautiful than those known to the ancients.

Four hundred years ago, for example, Johannes Kepler discovered three marvelous geometrical laws that describe planetary motion. So impressed was he by the beauty of these laws that he wrote this prayer in his treatise *Harmonices Mundi* (The harmonies of the world): "I thank thee, Lord God our Creator, that thou hast allowed me to see the beauty in thy work of creation." Decades later, Newton succeeded in explaining Kepler's laws—but he did not explain them *down*, if by down we mean reducing what we observe and experience to something more trivial or brutish. On the contrary, he explained them by deriving them from an underlying order that is more general and impressive, which we now call Newton's laws of mechanics and gravity. Newton's law of gravity was later explained, in turn, by Einstein, who showed that it followed from a more profound theory of gravity called General Relativity. And it is now generally believed that Einstein's theory is but the manifestation of a yet more fundamental theory, which many suspect to be superstring theory. Superstring theory has a mathematical structure so sophisticated that, after a quarter of a century of study by hundreds of the world's most brilliant physicists and mathematicians, it is still not fully understood.

It is true that science seeks to simplify our picture of the world. An explanation should in some sense be simpler than the thing it explains. And, indeed, there is a sense in which Einstein's theory of gravity is simpler than Newton's, and Newton's theory of planetary motion simpler than Kepler's.

As physics Nobel laureate Frank Wilczek notes, however, Einstein's theory is "not 'simple' in the usual sense of the word." Whereas Kepler's laws can be explained in a few minutes to a junior-high-school student, Newton's laws cannot be fully explained without using calculus. And to explain Einstein's theory requires four-dimensional, curved, non-Euclidean space-time and much else besides. And yet, once we know enough, Einstein's theory does have a compelling simplicity greater than Newton's theory. The simplicity to which scientific reductionism leads us, then, is of a very paradoxical kind. It is a simplicity that is by no means simpleminded. It is not at all jejune, but deeply interesting and intellectually rich.

The same paradox can be found in many fields. The chess world champion Capablanca was admired for the purity and simplicity of his style. But to understand his moves one must have an understanding of the game that can be acquired only by years of experience and study. A later world champion, Mikhail Botvinnik, wrote of him, "In this simplicity there was a unique beauty of genuine depth." Another world champion, Emanuel Lasker, observed that "[in Capablanca's games] there is nothing hidden, artificial, or labored. Although they are transparent, they are never banal and are often deep." Wilczek had just the right term for this kind of simplicity, which is also found in the fundamental laws of physics: *profound simplicity.*

Profound simplicity always impresses with its elegance, economy of means, harmony, and perfection. This perfection, as Wilczek notes, is such that one feels that the slightest alteration would be disastrous. He quotes Salieri's envious description of Mozart's music in the film *Amadeus*: "Displace one note and there would be diminishment. Displace one phrase and the structure would fall." Applying this to physics, Wilczek says, "A theory begins to be perfect if any change makes it worse. . . . A theory becomes perfectly perfect if it's impossible to change it without ruining it entirely."

Symmetry is one of the factors that contribute to profound simplicity, both in the laws of physics and in works of art. Paint over one petal of the rose window of a cathedral, remove one column from a colonnade, and the symmetry is destroyed. Each part is necessary for the completion of the pattern.

The symmetries that characterize the deepest laws of physics are mathematically richer and stranger than the ones we encounter in everyday life. The gauge symmetries of the strong and weak forces, for example, involve rotations in abstract mathematical spaces with complex dimensions. In other words, the coordinates in those peculiar spaces are not ordinary numbers, as they are for the space in which we live, but complex numbers, which are numbers that contain the square root of minus one. Grand unified theories—which combine the strong, weak, and electromagnetic forces into a single mathematical structure—posit symmetries that involve rotations in abstract spaces of five or more complex dimensions.

Stranger and more profoundly simple are supersymmetries. There is much reason to think that supersymmetries are built into the laws of physics, and finding evidence of that is one of the main goals of the Large Hadron Collider outside Geneva, Switzerland, which has recently begun to take data. Supersymmetries involve so-called Grassmann numbers, which are utterly different from the ordinary numbers we use to count and measure things. Whereas ordinary numbers (and even complex numbers) have the common-sense property that $a \times b = b \times a$, Grassmann numbers have the bizarre property that $a \times b = - b \times a$. A simple enough formula, but hard indeed for the human mind to fathom.

Esoteric symmetries also lie at the heart of Einstein's theory of relativity. These Lorentz symmetries involve rotations not just in three-dimensional space but in four-dimensional space-time. We can all visualize the symmetries of a sphere or a hexagonal pattern, but Lorentz symmetries, supersymmetries, and the gauge symmetries of the weak, strong, and grand unified forces lie far outside our experience and intuition. They can be grasped only with the tools of advanced mathematics.

Physicists have found beauty in the mathematical principles animating the physical world, from Kepler, who praised God for the elegant geometry of the planets' orbits, to Hermann Weyl, for whom mathematical physics revealed a "flawless harmony that is in conformity with sublime Reason."

Some might suspect that this beauty is in the eye of the beholder, or that scientists think their own theories beautiful simply out of vanity. But there is a remarkable fact that suggests otherwise. Again and again throughout history, what started as pure mathematics—ideas developed solely for the sake of their intrinsic interest and elegance—turned out later to be needed to express fundamental laws of physics.

For example, complex numbers were invented and the theory of them deeply investigated by the early nineteenth century, a mathematical development that seemed to have no relevance to physical reality. Only in the 1920s was it discovered that complex numbers were needed to write the equations of quantum mechanics. Or, in another instance, when the mathematician William Rowan Hamilton invented quaternions in the mid-nineteenth century, they were regarded as an ingenious but totally useless construct. Hamilton himself held this view. When asked by an aristocratic lady whether quaternions were useful for anything, Hamilton joked, "Aye, madam, quaternions are *very* useful—for solving problems involving quaternions." And yet, many decades later, quaternions were put to use to describe properties of subatomic particles such as the spin of electrons as well as the relation between neutrons and protons. Or again, Riemannian geometry was developed long before it was found to be needed for Einstein's theory of gravity. And a branch of mathematics called the theory of Lie groups was developed before it was found to describe the gauge symmetries of the fundamental forces.

Indeed, mathematical beauty has become a guiding principle in the search for better theories in fundamental physics. Werner Heisenberg wrote, "In exact science, no less than in the arts, beauty is the most important source of illumination and clarity." Paul Dirac, one of the giants of twentieth-century physics, went so far as to say that it was more important to have "beauty in one's equations" than to have them fit the experimental data.

At the roots of the physical world, therefore, one does not find mere inchoate slime or dust but instead a richness and perfection of form based on profound, subtle, and beautiful mathematical *ideas*. This is what the famous astrophysicist Sir James Jeans meant when he said many decades ago that "the universe begins to look more like a great thought than a great machine." Benedict XVI expressed the same basic insight when in his Regensburg lecture he referred to "the mathematical structure of matter, its intrinsic rationality, . . . the Platonic element in the modern understanding of nature."

Modern science does not directly imply or require any particular metaphysical theory of reality, but it does suggest to us that the picture presented by Daniel Dennett and Richard Dawkins is false because the picture is only partial. In the terms of Dennett's metaphor of cranes constructing complexity, one sees what is built from the ground up; but delving beneath the surface, one finds an astonishing, hidden world—the underground mechanisms of the cranes, as it were.

It is true that the cosmos was at one point a swirling mass of gas and dust out of which has come the extraordinary complexity of life as we experience it. Yet, at every moment in this process of development, a greater and more impressive order operates within—an order that did not develop but was there from the beginning. In the upper world, mind, thought, and ideas make their appearance as fruit on the topmost branches of an evolutionary tree. Below the surface, we see the taproots of reality, the fundamental laws of physics that shimmer with ideas of profound simplicity.

To describe people as machines made of meat is as scientifically un-sophisticated as to think of the sun as a heat-emitting machine made of swirling gas. It ignores the reasons why the machines function as they do—reasons that the explanations of modern physics reduce to simplic-ities as elegant as they are elusive. Peering into the hidden depths, we see that matter itself is the expression of "a great thought," of ideas that are, as Weyl said, "in conformity with sublime Reason." And we begin to discover that matter, although mindless itself, is the product of a Mind of infinite profundity and infinite simplicity.

20

THE HUMAN GENOME IN HUMAN CONTEXT

O n June 26, 2000, two teams of scientists announced jointly that they had virtually completed the task of mapping the human genome. The announcement was made at a White House ceremony featuring the president of the United States, the prime minister of England, and the heads of the two teams. The following day, the banner headline in the *New York Times* read, "Genetic Code of Human Life Is Cracked by Scientists." The *Times* devoted ten full pages to the subject. *Time* magazine made it the cover story. The *Wall Street Journal* opined, "This is truly big stuff."

Though big stuff, it was really not a big discovery or even big news. That there is such a thing as a human genome and what it does have been known for several decades; and the project to map it, which is now all but complete, was initiated ten years ago. The mapping of the human genome is a milestone, not a breakthrough.

In spite of the hoopla and hype attending the announcement, much of the media commentary and analysis was reasonably sober and matter of fact. It focused chiefly on the anticipated benefits to biology and medicine, which are indeed potentially immense. These include a much greater understanding of the processes of life, and the prediction, treatment, and cure of many diseases. Amidst all the justified celebration, however, some darker notes were sounded. President Clinton warned that in using future discoveries "we must . . . not retreat from our oldest and most cherished human values." Francis Fukuyama, writing in the *Wall Street Journal*, expected that "we probably won't like the answers" that genome research will give to age-old questions. The editors of that paper agreed and suggested that future findings may "stand many of our beliefs on their heads." Articles in the *New York Times*, while mostly optimistic, also warned of the "risks" and "temptations" that would come with progress.

What are those risks, temptations, and frightening answers? The perceived dangers of genetic research fall into several categories, ranging from the practical to the apocalyptic. At the practical end are issues relating to medical privacy, the insurability of people with genetically identifiable risks for disease, and the use of genetic information "to stigmatize or discriminate against individuals or groups," as President Clinton put it.

Still at the practical level, but reaching much deeper, are a host of fears surrounding the "genetic engineering" of human beings. Here there are at least three dangers. First, there is the possibility that social imbalances may arise as the result of parents "improving," "enhancing," or even designing their own offspring. Lee Silver, professor of biology at Princeton University and author of *Remaking Eden*, has warned that the technology of inserting genes into fertilized eggs—which he calls "reprogenetics"— will lead to a two-tier society: the "GenRich," who can afford to genetically enrich their children, and the "Naturals," who can't and will be left behind. Aside from such egalitarian concerns, there is the possibility that human genetic engineering will simply skew the human gene pool. As some traits are selected for, other traits that are less obviously desirable, or less understood, or more subtle, but nevertheless needed by society, may inadvertently be selected against.

A second danger of the engineering of humans is that it will profoundly change the relationship between parent and child. The child who is designed by his parents is in some measure made, not begotten, and becomes no longer a given to be accepted, but an invention, a technical artifact.

The third and most fearsome danger is that this kind of genetic control will eventually lead to the radical transformation of the human species itself. In the words of Fukuyama, "The way is then open to superseding the human race with something different." Indeed, the prophecy of Prof. Silver is that the GenRich and the Naturals will form not two social classes, but two distinct human *species*. As the scientist and futurist Freeman Dyson observes in *The Sun, the Genome, and the Internet*, "When we have mastered the technology of reprogenetics, we shall be creating our own genetic barriers, not in opposition to nature, but enabling the natural processes of human evolution to continue." In *Imagined Worlds*, Dyson develops this scenario further: "The process of speciation, the division of our species into many varieties . . . , will then be under way. . . . The most serious conflicts of the next thousand years will probably be biological battles, fought between different conceptions of what a human being ought to be."

Aside from what it will allow mankind to do to itself, genetic research may also alter the way humanity thinks about itself. Philosophers will certainly be tempted to demystify man, seeing people as mere sequences of digits that can be stored in a database rather than as beings made in the image of God with immortal souls. (The old fear of "becoming a statistic," a number in a file, would then be realized in a way more awful and profound than anyone expected.) This view will feed belief in genetic determinism, already a common response to the news of June 26. One of the cherished beliefs that the *Wall Street Journal* foresees being stood on its head is "the idea that man can choose between right and wrong." The "answer" that Fukuyama says "we probably won't like" is that "we are much less free to choose our destinies" than we thought. Even more radically, the knowledge of the human genome may further the already pronounced trend toward a materialistic view of man, the view that we are at bottom naught but "a fortuitous concourse of atoms."

In the face of all these threats to humanity should we panic? I do not think so. Or at least, if we do panic, it should not be because of knowing the genome.

First, we should keep in mind that in a certain sense the remaking of man has been going on since the Stone Age. Genetic engineering might be used, say, to increase our powers of sight. But we have done that already with the invention of eyeglasses, telescopes, binoculars, magnifying glasses, microscopes, infrared scopes, and countless other devices. Genetic engineering may or may not lead to supermen, but we already have X-ray vision; we just don't carry it around with us.

It might be objected that I have given examples of mere sensory enhancements, not improvements in mental abilities. But memory is a key mental ability, and many inventions have enhanced that power: writing, books, printing, photography, tape recorders, and moving pictures, to name but a few. This shows why remodeling human beings—even if possible—is unlikely in itself to radically change our lives. Enhancements in human abilities that may come through genetic engineering will in most cases be negligible compared to those already achieved, or achievable in the future, through tools.

Suppose we can make the average man able to run a three-minute mile. What is that when he can go much faster with a bicycle or car? Or suppose we can give each man the strength of Samson? What is that compared to what he can do with a forklift truck? It is true that genetic engineering can make the changes directly into the human body. But that too has been done, albeit by cruder methods. Will men want bigger biceps, abs, and lats? There are exercise machines and creatine. Will women want bigger breasts? There are silicone implants.

As far as fears that human beings will end up evolving themselves into shapes unrecognizable, this ignores the human hunger for normality. Breast implants, for example, have not led to breasts of ever increasing size. Contrary to Mae West's famous dictum, too much of a good thing is *not* necessarily wonderful, or perceived as such. To pursue the example of body shape further, there are biological factors that condition what we want. Cross-cultural studies have shown, for instance, that the ideal female waist-to-hip ratio in the eyes of men is 0.7, and the ideal male waist-to-hip ratio in the eyes of women is 0.9. Biologists believe that there are evolutionary reasons for these inborn preferences. What this suggests, rather than a danger of going to extremes, is a danger of too much normality. It is not just inborn preference that favors the mean, but practicality. Being seven feet tall is an asset in the NBA, but a dis-advantage almost everywhere else. Most parents will not want that for their children.

Of course, there are some things of which more is always better, such as talent or intelligence. And it is precisely the mental remaking of man that provokes the greatest worry. Will man, in attempting to improve him-self mentally, turn himself into a creature altogether different psycho-logically, emotionally, aesthetically, morally, and spiritually—a creature no longer human?

There is reason to doubt the possibility of such a hideous outcome. What militates against it is the sheer difficulty of achieving a radical transformation of human nature. It should be appreciated to begin with that we have *not* come anywhere near to "cracking" the human genetic code, the headline in the *Times* notwithstanding. To "crack" the genetic code would involve three levels of understanding: of the human organ-ism and its mechanisms down to the cellular level; of the developmental processes by which the structures of the body and brain are built up; and of the way in which these developmental processes are guided by the in-formation encoded in the genome.

Suppose, for instance, one wanted to engineer into a person some radically new mental power, such as the ability to visualize five-dimensional shapes and diagrams. This would be very useful in many kinds of mathematical, scientific, and technical work. First, one would have to understand the neural paths involved in our present powers of visualization. Then one would have to invent new circuitry for the brain and find the developmental steps by which it could actually produce such circuitry. And finally, one would have to figure out genetic instructions to get those steps to take place. To state the task is to see its impossibility.

What we might really be able to do is either imitate what nature already knows how to do, or use trial and error, as nature did, to learn to do new things. By comparing the genomes of people with different athletic abilities, for instance, we can perhaps learn how to enhance athletic ability. Or we can learn tricks from the genomes of other species. But imitation of existing models will not bring great improvements in, say, human intellectual powers, since there are no models of higher intellect in nature to imitate. We might try to use geniuses as models, but it is foolish to suppose that by rooting around in the genome we will ever find out why Mozart wrote greater music than Salieri, or why Aquinas had more profound ideas than A. J. Ayer.

Nor will we make supermen by trial and error. The trouble is that almost all the trials will be errors, given the immense complexity of human beings. The problem is compounded by the fact that the relation of genes to traits is not one-to-one. Some traits are influenced by many genes, and some genes influence many traits. The law of unintended consequences is therefore bound to operate with a vengeance. The full results of some genetic "improvements" may only become evident a generation or two later, when it will be much too late. People will not long tolerate the succession of mental freaks and failures that will result from trying to engineer the human mind.

The bad news here is also, in a way, good news: man lacks not only the wisdom to play God, but also the intelligence. It is blasphemous and wicked to try to outdo God's work in creating man, but it will also prove to be futile, since we are no more up to the job technically than we are morally. In *Rerum Novarum*, Pope Leo XIII observed, in regard to socialism's utopian schemes, that "all striving against Nature is vain." That is still true. Socialism failed to create the promised New Man, and the new eugenics will fail just as surely. We can only pray that the toll of suffering brought on by human arrogance and folly will be less horrible this time around.

In the meantime we should recognize that many of the evils that are discussed hypothetically in connection with genetic engineering are already upon us. Children are already being manufactured using in vitro fertilization, surrogate mothers, and sperm banks. Fertilized human eggs are put into cold storage or disposed of as waste products of the child-manufacturing process. People right now are designing their offspring by means of donated eggs or sperm. True, the present methods are technically crude, but the technically most sophisticated methods aren't always the most widely employed. In the half century in which we have had nuclear weapons, they have killed fewer people than were slaughtered in Rwanda over a few months with machetes and clubs.

Genetic engineering will indeed skew the human gene pool, but we have been doing that for thirty years by means of contraception with hardly anyone raising a cry of protest. In every developed country today, the most talented and the most intelligent are having far fewer children than average. This is an unprecedented genetic experiment on a massive scale, whose dysgenic effects will surely swamp any "positive" results that eugenicists could hope to achieve.

Finally, it seems safe to say that just as in the long run the utopian fantasy of genetic engineering will wither in the light of scientific reality, so will the philosophical fantasy of genetic determinism. In fact, there is already quite conclusive evidence that human behavior, though strongly conditioned by genetics, is not completely determined by it. The identical twins of homosexuals, for instance, have only a 50 percent chance of being homosexual themselves. And even statistical correlations as high as 50 percent do not imply causation. Certain genes may be correlated with a kind of sensitivity that makes one more susceptible to environmental influences in favor of being an artist, say, or a hairdresser, or a homosexual. That would not be the same as a "gay gene," or a "hairdresser gene," or an "art gene." And even if genes do control certain of our *inclinations*, it does not follow that they therefore control our *behavior*.

Valid or not, the philosophical conclusions that are drawn from science often depend on what people want to believe. Some, for instance, will point, as President Clinton did, to the fact that all human beings genetically overlap by 99.9 percent as proof that we all have equal human dignity. Others, with as much or as little logic, will argue from the 98 percent genetic overlap of humans and chimpanzees that we have no special dignity at all. In short, the genome can tell us much about ourselves, but not the most important things. Genetics will not answer philosophical questions, nor will genetic engineering make us better philosophers. There is no wisdom gene. One safe prediction, therefore, is this: after all eugenic efforts have been made, the amount of human folly, and the suffering it brings, will be as great as ever.

SCIENCE AS A
SUBSTITUTE FOR RELIGION

21

THE IDOL OF SCIENCE

I f there is a single word that sums up the life and work of Edward O. Wilson, it is *naturalist.* The dictionary defines a naturalist to be either "an expert in natural history; a person who makes a special study of plants or animals" or "a person who believes that only natural laws and forces operate in the world; a believer in philosophical naturalism," and Wilson is the perfect embodiment of both. He has studied plants and animals for sixty-five years, making himself the world's leading authority on ants. He is also the father of sociobiology, championing an uncompromising metaphysical naturalism in many of his writings. More than a mere scientist, Wilson is a devotee of the natural—which has led him in recent years to become an eloquent defender of "Living Nature" against the encroachments of man and technological spoliation.

At one level, his new book, *The Creation,* is simply a conservationist tract, a passionate plea that we wake up to the rapid and accelerating loss of "biodiversity." Much of the book is filled with descriptions of the astonishing variety of living things (900,000 classified species, with perhaps ten times as many remaining to be discovered) and accounts of the myriad ways in which we benefit from even the humblest of these creatures. Wilson spices up his account with many fascinating examples:

> [People] forget, if they ever knew, how voracious caterpillars of an obscure moth from the American tropics saved Australia's pastureland from the overgrowth of cactus; how a Madagascar "weed," the rosy periwinkle,

provided the alkaloids that cure most cases of Hodgkin's disease and acute childhood leukemia; how another substance from an obscure Norwegian fungus made possible the organ transplant industry; [and] how a chemical from the saliva of leeches yielded a solvent that prevents blood clots during and after surgery.

This treasury of life is in peril. Wilson says that human activity has led the earth into "the largest spasm of mass extinction since the end of the Cretaceous period, 65 million years ago" and that this may result by century's end in the loss of a substantial fraction of existing species.

Not all the news is bad; some species have been brought back from the brink of extinction. He tells the story of the Chatham Island black robin, and the breeding of "Old Blue," the last surviving female, with "Old Yellow," the last surviving male. Such bright spots are the exception, however, and the picture he paints is not one to invite complacency. Yet Wilson is not an environmental absolutist or extremist. He calls himself a humanist, and much of his argument is couched in terms of the value of living nature to man—economically, aesthetically, psychologically, and even spiritually. Nor is he an enemy of technological progress and economic growth, or a crier of inevitable doom. With a one-time investment of $30 billion, he says, the world can come through the most critical period (the next hundred years) tolerably well as far as land creatures are concerned. (Preserving sea creatures will be more costly.)

The Creation has as its subtitle A Meeting of Science and Religion. Wilson has rightly been seen as an antagonist of religion, although he is not a fanatical hater of religion like Richard Dawkins. Wilson has an appreciation of the depth and complexity of human nature that leads him to what he calls "existential conservatism." This shows, for instance, in his healthy skepticism toward the "giddily futuristic" fantasies of genetic engineering. "It is far better to work with human nature as it is . . . than it would be to tinker with something that it took eons of trial and error to create." Consequently, Wilson does not have Dawkins's puritanical impulse to extirpate deeply rooted aspects of human nature.

Nonetheless, at a philosophical level, Wilson remains a proponent of a worldview that cannot share intellectual space with religious belief, which makes it interesting that in The Creation, he proposes a truce. He suggests, in spite of what he sees as a deep and irreconcilable contradiction between science and religion, that they form an alliance to save the world of living things. Such cooperation is useful because science and religion are "the two most powerful forces in the world today," and such cooperation is possible because the preservation of living nature is a "universal value."

The book is written in the form of a letter to an imaginary Southern Baptist pastor, whom he addresses as "my respected friend." Wilson notes his own Southern Baptist upbringing in Alabama and how he once "answered the altar call" and "went under the water." Nevertheless, there is a jarring inconsistency of tone throughout the book. The most unctuous professions of respect alternate with the most disdainful references to the Baptist's beliefs in end-time prophecies, the torment of the damned (that will last for "trillions and trillions of years . . . all for a mistake they made in choice of religion"), and "the sacred scripture of Iron Age desert kingdoms." Wilson speaks on one page of the "religious qualities that make us ineffably human" and on another of religion as the ignorant worship of "tribal deities." The "respect" he has for his Baptist friend seems at times to be of the kind that a naturalist might have for an orangutan. It is a respect for biodiversity; no intellectual equality is implied. The pastor has nothing to teach Wilson except as a specimen.

There is also a deep incoherence in the premise of the book. Wilson proclaims conservation a "moral precept shared by people of all beliefs" and yet avers that "the fate of ten million other [species] does not matter" for the "millions [of Americans who] think the End of Time" is imminent, a group he suspects includes his Baptist friend ("Pastor, tell me I am wrong!"). This idea of a causal link between end-time prophecy and the Religious Right's supposed indifference to the environment has been popularized by the likes of Bill Moyers, who simply proclaim it as a fact without adducing genuine evidence and despite the vigorous denials of actual evangelicals.

There is also some blame shifting in Wilson's account. Even the unpleasant by-products of scientific progress (which, Wilson claims, has been "often opposed by the followers of Holy Scripture") are somehow the fault of religion. After accurately describing how secular ideologies of progress have contributed to the neglect of the environment, Wilson, to lay equal blame on religion, implausibly conjures up the image of a hypothetical "religious scholar" who "might" argue for the unimportance of the "immense array of creatures discovered by science" on the grounds that they "are not even mentioned in Holy Scripture."

If Wilson knew more of the history of science, he would know that from Copernicus in the sixteenth century to Maxwell in the nineteenth, science was not "often opposed by followers of Holy Scripture" but was, in fact, largely built by them. Indeed, most great scientists in that period were such followers. But for Wilson, "science and religion do not easily mix," and his model scientist is Charles Darwin, who "abandoned Christian dogma, and then with his newfound intellectual freedom" made his great advances. Far more typical among the founders of modern science, however, was Kepler, who announced his greatest discovery with the prayer, "I thank thee, Lord God our Creator, that thou hast allowed me to see the beauty in thy work of creation."

Despite his low opinion of religious thought, Wilson makes liberal use of religious language and imagery. He speaks of "the Creation" (meaning for him the world of living things), "the planetary ark," the "redemption" of the environment, "Lazarus projects" to rescue endangered species, human life as the "mystery of mysteries," and pristine nature as "Eden." The word *spiritual* is sprinkled throughout his book. This is not just rhetoric, I think, meant to give a patina of religiosity to his ideas to make them more attractive to his imagined Baptist friend. He is up to something else, and what takes shape in the pages of *The Creation*, though never avowed explicitly as such, is a new religion, or a new form of a very old religion. It is naturalism writ large.

Here are the tenets of this Naturalist creed: Nature is all in all. It is an "ancient, autonomous creative force," the beneficent provider and source of life. Man is but a part of nature, and thus when we understand nature more fully we will learn "the meaning of human life" and "the origin and hence meaning of the aesthetic and religious qualities that make us ineffably human." Indeed, human beings find their proper fulfillment in nature, since "the human species . . . adapted physically and mentally to life on Earth and no place else." That is why we feel most at home and most serene in natural environments, especially those that most resemble the African savannah in which our species evolved.

For that matter, humans have a natural "biophilia," a love for and attraction to the rest of "living Nature." The human race did fall, indeed more than once, and each fall involved a "betrayal of Nature." We attempted to "ascend from Nature," whereas what we really need is to "ascend to Nature." In restoring and preserving living nature, we will restore Eden and experience nature's "deeply fulfilling beneficence." This fulfillment will be achieved in two ways: by "primal experience" of nature and scientific understanding of nature. The science of biology is the path to both: "Biology now leads in reconstructing the human self-image. It has become the paramount science. . . . It is the key to human health and to the management of the living environment. It has become foremost in relevance to the central questions of philosophy, aiming to explain the nature of mind and reality and the meaning of life."

Thus, biological science is nature understanding itself. It is a way of life. Even laymen can partake in it through scientific education, nature excursions, field trips, "bioblitzes" (in which "citizen scientists" descend upon a locale to inventory its biodiversity), and other activities that will combine recreation, education, primal experience, scientific research, and saving the planet. By serving nature, we will also bring abundant material blessings upon ourselves in agriculture and medicine.

How did Wilson end up pitting science against biblical religion and erecting nature into a god? It begins with an ignorance of Western religious tradition. This reveals itself in little gaffes, as when he misuses the word magisterium, and when he innocently quotes a badly translated passage from a sixteenth-century chronicler that refers to the saints in heaven as our "lawyers" instead of "advocates." But his theological ignorance runs deeper. He plays with the word creation, even choosing it as the title of his book, while evincing no grasp of what it means. In its traditional and profounder meaning, creation is that timeless act whereby God holds all things in existence. It is not an alternative to natural theories of origin or natural explanations of change.

Just as the events of a play unfold according to an internal logic and have among themselves causal relationships, and nevertheless the whole play with all its parts has its being from the mind of the playwright, so too in the universe there are natural causes, processes, and laws, and yet the whole depends for its reality upon God. Did this insect evolve or is it created by God? To ask that is as silly as to ask whether Polonius died because Hamlet stabbed him or because Shakespeare wrote the play that way. For Wilson, nature is a play that somehow wrote itself, and, since he cannot find the author among its *dramatis personae*, he concludes that he must not exist.

The blindness that afflicts scientists like Wilson was accurately diagnosed twenty-two centuries ago by the author of the Book of Wisdom, speaking of the *physikoi* of ancient Greece. "They were unable from the good things that are seen to know him who exists; nor did they recognize the craftsman while paying heed to his works. . . . Yet these men are little to be blamed, for perhaps they go astray while seeking God and desiring to find him. For, as they live among his works, they keep searching; and they trust in what they see, because the things that are seen are beautiful. Yet again, not even they are to be excused; for if they had the power to know so much that they could investigate the world, how did they fail to find sooner the Lord of these things?" In the love of nature and the preservation of nature, the Christian can join, but not in the worship of Nature. The Naturalism of Wilson is idolatry.

22

PROPHET OF POINTLESSNESS

In reading Richard Dawkins I am reminded of an anecdote told by Werner Heisenberg. Heisenberg and several other great physicists were sitting around one evening talking about God and religion. The discussion ended up being dominated by Paul Dirac, who went into a long diatribe declaring religion to be the opiate of the masses. At the end of the evening someone turned to the brilliant Wolfgang Pauli and said, "You have been very quiet tonight, Pauli. What do you think of what Dirac has been telling us?" Pauli responded, "If I understand Dirac correctly, his meaning is this: there is no God, and Dirac is his Prophet."

Richard Dawkins was not always a prophet. In his early days he wrote well-regarded papers on the rules for grooming in flies and the nesting strategies of digger wasps. It was while toiling in the vineyards of zoological science that he apparently heard the call to preach. His pulpit is an endowed chair in "the Public Understanding of Science" at Oxford, and the message he proclaims in his elegantly written, if somewhat waspish, books and articles is that the universe and life have no meaning. "The universe we observe," he says, "has precisely the properties we should expect if there is at bottom no design, no purpose, no evil, no good, nothing but blind, pitiless indifference."

The root of Dawkins's philosophy is the insight, derived from neo-Darwinian theory, that life has no ulterior purpose, biologically speaking. Mosquitoes exist to replicate mosquito DNA and dung beetles to replicate dung beetle DNA. The whole drama of life is a meaningless genetic competition. Not surprisingly, many people find Dawkins's vision of a pointless universe rather repellant. He has been accused of spreading a cold and joyless message, a pessimistic nihilism. The present book seems to have been written to respond to these charges. Its preface begins thus:

> A foreign publisher of my first book confessed that he could not sleep for three nights after reading it, so troubled was he by what he saw as its cold, bleak message. Others have asked me how I can bear to get up in the mornings. A teacher from a distant country wrote to me reproachfully that a pupil had come to him in tears after reading the same book, because it had persuaded her that life was empty and purposeless.

This preface filled me with the keenest anticipation. I had always wondered what consolations could be found in a philosophy like Dawkins's. What would he have to say to that sleepless publisher or that desperate girl? Not what you might have expected. Here is a passage from chapter one, in which he is describing the time-line of life on earth:

> Fling your arms wide in an expansive gesture to span all of evolution from its origin at your left fingertip to today at your right fingertip. All across your midline to well past your right shoulder, life consists of nothing but bacteria. Many-celled, invertebrate life flowers somewhere around your right elbow. The dinosaurs originate in the middle of your right palm, and go extinct around your last finger joint. The whole history of Homo sapiens and our predecessor Homo erectus is contained in the thickness of one nail clipping. As for recorded history; as for the Sumerians, the Babylonians, the Jewish patriarchs, the dynasties of Pharaohs, the legions of Rome, the Christian Fathers, the Laws of the Medes and Persians which never change; as for Troy and the Greeks, Helen and Achilles and Agamemnon dead; as for Napoleon and Hitler, the Beatles and Bill Clinton, they and everyone that knew them are blown away in the dust of one light stroke of a nail file.

Vivid, striking, accurate, but hardly consoling.

Indeed, what Dawkins has to say to troubled souls is, basically, to grow up and stop snivelling: "The adult world may seem a cold and empty place," he writes, "with no fairies and no Father Christmas, no Toyland or Narnia, no Happy Hunting Ground where mourned pets go, and no angels—guardian or garden variety. . . . Yes, Teddy and Dolly turn out not to be really alive."

Dawkins believes that the charge of nihilism and coldness leveled against his philosophy stems from a certain view of science that sees it ridding the world of poetry and romance by explaining things previously steeped in wonder. The title of his book is taken from Keats's poem "Lamia": "Do not all charms fly / At the mere touch of cold philosophy? / . . . / Philosophy will clip an angel's wings, / Conquer all mysteries by rule and line, / Empty the haunted air, and gnomed mine— / Unweave a rainbow . . ." The word "philosophy" here refers to "natural philosophy," i.e., science, and the "unweaving" to Isaac Newton's explanation of the rainbow as being due to the prismatic effect of raindrops.

The greater part of Dawkins's book is devoted to answering Keats. Dawkins points out—and here he is quite right—that an increased understanding of nature should heighten rather than diminish our sense of wonder at it. He uses Keats's own example of the rainbow to make his point. The rainbow is a spectrum of light, and Dawkins explains how understanding this spectrum has enabled scientists to make remarkable discoveries. For example, decoding the spectra of light from stars allows astrophysicists to infer what stars are made of, a feat that one might have thought utterly impossible. And decoding the spectra from distant galaxies is what revealed to Edwin Hubble in 1929 the astonishing fact that the universe is expanding.

Dawkins develops this theme through many variations. Not only light but sound has a spectrum. He describes how the human brain is able to "unweave" the exceedingly complex patterns of sound vibrations that impinge upon our ears and interpret or "reweave" them. He goes on to describe the amazing ability of bats to see with sound, and the way that crickets' song is "cunningly pitched and timed to be hard for vertebrate ears to locate, but easy for female crickets, with their weathervane ears, to home in upon." Dawkins is at his best when describing the wonders that science has learned about living things. In his view, far from ridding the world of poetry, science reveals to us fit subjects for the great poetry of the future.

Dawkins contrasts this with a sense of wonder that feeds on the irrational and the inexplicable. He describes an audience at a magic show that grew angry when the magician's tricks were explained to them. It is this kind of degraded hankering after mystification that lies behind superstitions of all kinds, he alleges, including, of course, religion. What science has done is take the natural appetite for wonder and satisfy it with something true and worthy. Much of the book is taken up with the debunking of superstition in the manner of *The Skeptical Inquirer*.

In contrasting the two senses of wonder, the scientific and the obscurantist (which includes for him the religious), Dawkins directs his scorn at those "who are content to bask in the wonder and revel in a mystery we were not 'meant' to understand." This is a strange reproach, since it is the heart of Dawkins's own creed that we were not "meant" to do anything, let alone to understand. This is but one instance of a curious disjunction that exists between the tenets of Dawkins's philosophy and the values he wishes to base on them.

One sees this also in his discussion of astrology, which he attacks not only as false, but as fraught with "sad human consequences." But one of the problems with materialism is that it is little different from astrology in its human consequences. What is the difference between believing that one's actions are dictated by the orbits of the planets and believing that they are dictated by the orbits of the electrons in one's brain?

This book is based in its entirety on a simple mistake. It is not often that one can find exactly the point where an author goes off the track, but here one can. It is in the fifth sentence of the preface of the book, which begins, "Similar accusations of barren desolation, of promoting an arid and joyless message, are frequently flung at science in general." However, what people object to in Dawkins is not the science but the atheism. Because he cannot see the difference, he writes a book that is a 300-page non sequitur. In answering the charge that his atheism is a joyless creed, he says, in essence, that his atheism allows him to derive pleasure from the beauty and magnificence of nature as revealed by science. He may as well have said that his atheism allows him to enjoy a good steak or a game of baseball, or that his atheism gives him the great advantage of having a nose, two eyes, and ten fingers.

Those who believe in God, including the very substantial proportion of scientists who do, are every bit as able to thrill to scientific discovery as Dawkins is. They embrace scientific understanding and rejoice in it, as he does. But they have as well the joy of their faith, which tells them that the beauty of nature points to something higher, to a Wisdom greater than their own. For Dawkins it points to nothing. He is welcome to that conclusion, but there is not the slightest reason why any scientist or scientifically minded person should share it.

FINDING GOD THROUGH SCIENCE

23

THE (SCIENTIFIC) CASE FOR GOD

Patrick Glynn, a political journalist and former Reagan Administration official, has given us an elegantly written and absorbing account of his return to religious faith and the reasons for it. A major reason was the "significant body of evidence" that has emerged from "a series of dramatic developments in science, medicine, and other fields" in the last twenty years that "has radically changed the existence-of-God debate."

Gerald Schroeder, an Israeli physicist, has followed a similar path. He writes: "As a scientist trained at the Massachusetts Institute of Technology, I was convinced I had the evidence to exclude [God] from the grand scheme of life." But "with each step forward" he took in his understanding of science, "something kept shining through."

One may be tempted to object that "The Evidence," as the title of Glynn's book calls it, goes back a lot longer than twenty years. St. Paul knew nothing of modern science and yet felt justified in asserting in his Epistle to the Romans that God's "eternal power and deity," though invisible, are "manifest in the things that He has made." Faith does not need to wait upon the latest research. Nevertheless, Glynn and Schroeder are right that something important has happened in the world of science.

What has happened is that the great scientific discoveries that seemed to many thoughtful people to provide reasons for skepticism and even atheism have been shown to be either misleading or mistaken. To borrow a phrase from Ben Wattenberg, the good news is that the bad news is wrong.

The bad news is old and well known. Copernicus showed that we humans are not at the center of the universe—though, as Schroeder points out, the Bible never actually said we were. And Darwin—supposedly—showed that we are merely the products of chance mutations. Glynn quotes Bertrand Russell's dismal conclusion: the human race is just "a curious accident in a backwater." Galileo, besides embarrassing the Roman Catholic Church, helped bring about the triumph of mechanism over teleology, which, as Glynn notes, "went hand in hand with the decline of religious faith among the intellectual elite." It was no longer scientifically respectable to look for purpose in nature.

What has put these discoveries in a different light are more recent developments in the very same branches of science. From physics and cosmology have come the "anthropic coincidences." This term refers to the fact, now widely appreciated by physicists, that many features of the laws of nature seem arranged so as to make possible the emergence of life. For example, if certain parameters of the "Standard Model" of particle physics were even slightly different from what they are measured to be, either stars would never have formed or biochemistry would not be possible. Many of these anthropic coincidences are striking indeed, and have led at least a few scientists to reconsider their atheistic prejudices.

Glynn discusses anthropic coincidences at much greater length than does Schroeder. He observes that there are two ways out for the faithful atheist. One of them is to argue that the features of nature's laws that the deist and theist think were arranged may actually be inflexibly determined by some deep underlying principles. While this is very likely to be true, it hardly resolves the issue, since the structure of physical law did not have to be based upon those particular principles. The other way out is to posit the existence of an infinite number of universes (or domains of this universe) where the laws of physics assume a variety of forms. In this scenario one could argue that there was bound to be some universe or domain where the conditions would happen to be favorable for life. Though I think Glynn's response to this idea is not completely satisfactory, he is quite right to emphasize that these postulated universes or domains are almost certainly unobservable experimentally. They are, therefore, just as vulnerable to a positivist critique as any theological assertion ever was. The breathtakingly speculative character of these multiple-universe ideas provokes this telling observation from Glynn:

Praising science at the expense of religion in 1935, Bertrand Russell boasted: "The scientific temper of mind is cautious, tentative, and piecemeal. The way in which science arrives at its beliefs is quite different," [Russell] wrote, "from that of medieval theology. . . . Science starts, not from large assumptions, but from particular facts discovered by observation or experiment." Well, we've come a long way baby.

Developments in biology are likewise making it harder to believe that our existence is as "accidental" as Russell supposed. Glynn steers clear of evolutionary debates, but Schroeder has a great deal to say about them that is of interest. Schroeder argues that recent discoveries, relating in particular to the rapidity of certain evolutionary changes, make it appear doubtful that random mutations and natural selection are the whole story. He backs up his arguments with some interesting mathematics. He suggests, as others have done, that evolution is "channeled" in definite directions by the underlying principles of physics and chemistry. If so, evolution may be less a matter of randomness and more a matter of potentialities built into the laws of nature.

Before evolution in the ordinary sense can even begin, one needs a living thing. Schroeder recalls for us the great sensation created in 1953 by the experiments of Miller and Urey, which appeared to show that the origin of life from inorganic chemicals was a simple and almost solved problem. A frustrating half-century later it is generally admitted that the origin of life is a problem of surpassing difficulty.[1]

In cosmology, the bad news has also turned out to be wrong. Up through the nineteenth century, developments in physics suggested that the universe was infinitely old. Schroeder relates that as late as 1959, two-thirds of leading American astronomers and physicists surveyed still believed that the universe had no beginning. Only in the 1960s did science at last vindicate the reality of that "Beginning" of which the Book of Genesis spoke three thousand years ago.

One of the worst pieces of bad news for religion was the determinism of the laws of physics, for which evidence had been mounting for three centuries. If the state of the world at one time is determined by its state at a previous time, then our brains are not free. With the advent of quantum mechanics in the 1920s, however, physics was forced to abandon strict determinism.

Science has even had to backpedal on the very nature of religious belief itself. Freud diagnosed it as a neurosis. Yet, as Glynn recounts, numerous recent studies have shown that religious belief and practice correlate very strongly with overall happiness, psychological well-being, and marital satisfaction, and with markedly low rates of suicide, divorce, drug use, alcoholism, stress, depression, and a variety of related physical ailments.

Both of these books succeed brilliantly in building bridges between science and religion, but each, in its own way, goes a bridge too far. Glynn devotes a long section of his book to "near-death experiences," which he regards as direct evidence of the existence of the soul and of an afterlife. Although Glynn probably makes as good a case as can be made, it is possible, even for those of us who do not doubt the immortality of the soul, to remain unconvinced that the near-death phenomena are supernatural in origin.

The typical subject of an "autoscopic" near-death experience reports leaving his body, floating up into the air, and observing the medical procedures being performed upon him. "Observing with what?" one is bound to ask. The subjects of such experiences, if truly disembodied, have no retinas or other sensory apparatus with which to see the colors and shapes that they describe. (It is not reported whether the myopic among them are accompanied by their spectacles upon these excursions.) It would make more sense to suppose that such people are being granted a vision of what they would see could they look down upon the operation. However, it seems a funny kind of vision for God to grant, consisting of the knobs and dials on medical equipment. More plausibly supernatural are near-death experiences of the other kind, the "transcendental" ones, which involve visits to Heaven. Yet nothing precludes a purely naturalistic explanation—perhaps in psychoanalytic terms—of them either.

Schroeder's book is less about science and faith generally than about science and the Bible, and especially its first five books, the Torah. What he says about Scriptural interpretation is generally wise. He wittily suggests that we should "give unto Einstein what is Einstein's and unto the Bible what is the Bible's." Much of his exegesis, which often depends on the analysis of particular Hebrew words, is illuminating and profound. Even his less convincing efforts are quite ingenious. However, his determination to find a scientific explanation for every period of time mentioned in the Bible, from the Six Days of creation to antediluvian lifespans, leads to some rather curious results. He attempts to show that the Six Days are really the same as the 15 billion years of modern cosmology, using a strange blend of medieval cabala and the "time-dilation effect" of relativity theory.[2] He violates his own maxim here, giving unto Einstein what really belongs to the mystical numerology of the rabbi Nahmanides.

Not everything in these books is of equal value, but the story they tell, so personally, so learnedly, and in such fascinating detail, could hardly be more important. The modern mind was tragically rent by the scientific findings of an earlier era. These books show that science may help to join what once it put asunder.

24

THE FORM OF SPEAKING

Today we are learning the language in which God created life." With these words, President Clinton announced one of the great feats of modern science, the mapping of the human genome. Standing next to him in the East Room of the White House was the leader of the Human Genome Project, Francis S. Collins.

Collins has now written a book, *The Language of God*, but it is not the sort of book one might have expected him to write, for only a small part is devoted to the genome project. Rather, Collins has written the story of his other great discovery: the discovery not of new truths but of old truths. It is the story of how and why he came to believe in God.

As such, this book is almost unique. There are many conversion stories and many scientific autobiographies, but few books in which prominent scientists tell how they came to faith. If nothing else, Collins's book gives the lie, in most spectacular fashion, to the claim made by Richard Dawkins in an interview not long ago: "You won't find any intelligent person who feels the need for the supernatural," Dawkins declared, "unless [he was] brought up that way."

Francis Collins was not brought up that way; his family's view was that religion "just wasn't very important." Almost the only contact Collins had with religion as a child was singing in the choir at the local Episcopal church, where his parents had sent him to learn music with the admonition that he shouldn't take the theology too seriously. After discovering, in high-school science classes, "the intense satisfaction of the ordered nature of the universe," Collins entered the University of Virginia at the age of sixteen to major in chemistry. Up to then, he had given little thought to religion, though in his early teens he had had "occasional moments of . . . longing for something outside myself," most often associated with profound experiences of nature or of music. Exposed to the challenges of "one or two aggressive atheists" in his dorm, however, he quickly concluded that no religion had any "foundational truth."

The mathematical elegance of physics drew him into physical chemistry, where he was "immersed in quantum mechanics and second-order differential equations" and "gradually became convinced that everything in the universe could be explained on the basis of equations and physical principles." Discovering that Einstein, one of his heroes, had not believed in the God of the Jewish people, Collins concluded that "no thinking scientist" could take the idea of God seriously, and he "gradually shifted from agnosticism to atheism."

While working on his doctorate at Yale, Collins happened to take a course in biochemistry and was "astounded" by DNA and proteins "in all of their satisfying digital glory." It was a "revelation" to him that mathematics and "rigorous intellectual principles" could be applied to biology, a field he had previously disdained. Around this time, however, he began to wonder how he could "make a difference in the lives of real people" and whether he was cut out for a life of research. And so, just before completing his degree in chemistry, he switched to medical school.

It was in medical school that his atheism suffered a blow: "I found the relationships [I] developed with sick and dying patients almost overwhelming." The strength and solace so many of them derived from faith profoundly impressed him and left him thinking that "if faith was a psychological crutch . . . it must be a very powerful one." His "most awkward moment" came when an older woman, suffering from a severe and untreatable heart problem, asked him what he believed. "I felt my face flush as I stammered out the words 'I'm not really sure.'" Suddenly it was brought home to him that he had dismissed religion without ever really considering—or even knowing—the arguments in its favor. How could someone who prided himself on his scientific rationality do that? He was deeply shaken and felt impelled to carry out an honest and unprejudiced examination of religion. Attempts to read the sacred scriptures of various world religions left him baffled, however, so he sought out a local Methodist minister and asked him point-blank "whether faith made any logical sense." The minister took a book down from his shelf and handed it to him. It was C. S. Lewis's *Mere Christianity*.

Lewis gave Collins a simple, though crucial, insight: God is not a part of the physical universe and therefore cannot be perceived by the methods of science. Yet God speaks to us in our hearts and minds, both in such "longings" for the transcendent as Collins had himself experienced and in the sense of objective right and wrong, "the Moral Law." A key aspect of this moral sense is "the altruistic impulse, the voice of conscience calling us to help others even if nothing is received in return." Such altruism, says Collins, "is quite frankly a scandal for reductionist reasoning," for it goes directly contrary to the selfishness of the "selfish gene."

Collins reviews some of the attempts to explain altruism in evolutionary terms. One theory is that our primate ancestors rated altruism a positive attribute in potential mates. Another is that altruism provided survival advantages to its practitioners through "indirect reciprocal benefits." A third is that altruism benefited the whole group in which it was prevalent rather than the individuals who practiced it. Collins explains why none of these theories works. He then goes on to discuss several common objections to belief in God that troubled him at first but to which he was able to find satisfactory answers with the help of Lewis and other Christian writers. Collins presents these answers in clear, simple, and appealing language. Their power lies not only in strength of argument but also in their personal character, as when he discusses the problem of evil in the context of a tragedy that befell his own daughter.

Collins also examines what science has to say about the origins of the universe, life, and human beings. As he traces the history of the universe, he points to three discoveries that bolster the case for a creator. One is the "existence of mathematical principles and order in creation," laws whose "mathematical representation invariably turns out to be elegant, surprisingly simple, and even beautiful."

Another is the Big Bang, the putative beginning of the universe about fourteen billion years ago. And a third is the remarkable concatenation of "anthropic" coincidences and fine-tunings in the laws of physics that made possible the evolution of life.

It is interesting that Collins, a biologist, should take most of his "evidence for belief" from physics. As someone who came to biology through the physical sciences, he is obviously keenly aware of what Pope Benedict has called "the mathematical structure of matter, its intrinsic rationality, . . . the Platonic element in the modern understanding of nature." One notes, by contrast, that some of the biologists who are most outspoken in their atheism have come from a background in zoology rather than the physical sciences. It may be that the scientists most susceptible to crude materialism are those who know the least about matter.

The physics and cosmology in the book are well done, but Collins's discussion of the Big Bang is open to several criticisms. It is not quite accurate to say that the Big Bang "forces the conclusion that nature had a defined beginning." Most physicists and cosmologists think it possible that the Big Bang was only the beginning of one phase of the universe's history; the conclusion that the universe had a beginning at some point (whether at the Big Bang or earlier) is not yet forced by the physics alone. Collins also too simply equates the creation of the universe with the fact that it had a beginning in time. Even a universe that had no beginning in time would still require its existence to be explained. And finally, there are points at which Collins seems to speak of the Big Bang as miraculous in the sense that the laws of physics broke down there, which is very doubtful. To be fair, these are issues that may be too subtle for a satisfactory treatment in a book aimed at such a wide audience. And Collins's main point is certainly valid: nature could not have created itself, and the Big Bang, by underlining the contingency of the world's existence, supports the idea of creation.

As Collins moves from discussing the origin and development of the physical universe to the origin and development of life, he must enter on the battle-scarred terrain of evolution, a subject that takes up most of the latter half of the book. Here his message and his primary audience change. Up to this point he has been speaking on behalf of religious belief. He now turns around and speaks to his fellow Christians, especially his fellow evangelicals, on behalf of evolution. His fundamental purpose, however, remains the same: "to call a truce in the escalating war between science and spirit," a war that "was never really necessary" but "was initiated and intensified by extremists on both sides."

Collins is appalled that "Young Earth Creationism is the view held by approximately 45 percent of Americans" and that "many evangelical Christian churches are aligned" with it. The persistence of this view, which is at once so theologically simplistic and scientifically indefensible, is "one of the great puzzles and tragedies of our time." The danger is not to science but to faith: "Young people brought up in homes and churches that insist on Creationism sooner or later encounter the overwhelming scientific evidence in favor of an ancient universe and the relatedness of all living things through the process of evolution and natural selection. What a terrible and unnecessary choice they then face!"

In his appeal to Young Earth Creationists, Collins deploys both scientific and theological arguments. Though the evidence for evolution comes from many directions, he naturally focuses on the recent, powerful evidence that comes from studying the genomes of different species, evidence that, he says, "could fill hundreds of books of this length." One of the examples he gives is the existence of "pseudogenes." These are genes that have suffered mutations that "turn their script into gibberish" and render them defunct. "The human gene known as caspase-12, for instance, has sustained several knockout blows, though it is found in the identical relative location in the [genome of the] chimp. The chimp caspase-12 works just fine, as does the similar gene in nearly all mammals." If the body of man did not evolve, but was formed as the Young Earth Creationists believe, then "why would God have gone to the trouble of inserting such a non-functional gene in this precise location?"

In Collins's view, the Intelligent Design movement, unlike Young Earth Creationism, "deserves serious consideration" scientifically. Nonetheless, he sees it as a misguided and doomed effort that is, ironically, "on a path toward doing considerable damage to faith." It is driven by a fear that Darwinism is incompatible with biblical belief and is an attempt "to find a scientifically respectable alternative."

Collins argues forcefully that Darwinian evolution is, in fact, perfectly compatible with biblical faith. He avoids the trap into which so many liberal theologians have fallen: thinking that the lesson of evolution is that everything evolves, including God. Collins sees clearly that the key to harmonizing Darwinian evolution with Jewish and Christian faith is through the traditional teaching, so profoundly elaborated by St. Augustine, that God is outside time: "If God is outside of nature, then He is outside of space and time. In that context, God could in the moment of creation of the universe also know every detail of the future. That could include the formation of the stars, planets, and galaxies, all of the chemistry, physics, geology, and biology that led to the formation of life on earth, and the evolution of humans. . . . In that context, evolution could appear to us to be driven by chance, but from God's perspective the outcome would be entirely specified. Thus, God could be completely and intimately involved in the creation of all species, while from our perspective, limited as it is by the tyranny of linear time, this would appear a random and undirected process." With the aid of St. Augustine and

C. S. Lewis, Collins knocks down one theological objection to Darwinian evolution after another.

For reasons that are unclear, Collins chooses to end his book with a lengthy appendix on medical-ethics issues, in which he defends certain positions that are necessitated neither by science nor religion. Not only does this run counter to the aims of the rest of the book, but the level of argument by which he attempts to justify "somatic cell nuclear transfer," a form of cloning, hardly does him credit.

Still, *The Language of God* is a book of enormous value. At a time when so many people on both sides are trying to foment a conflict between science and religion, Collins is a sorely needed voice of reason. His book may do more to promote better understanding between the worlds of faith and science than any other so far written. I suspect that Collins himself would regard that as an achievement no less important than the one for which he was honored six years ago in the East Room of the White House.

MISCHIEVOUS MYTHS ABOUT SCIENTIFIC REVOLUTIONARIES

25

FROM MYTH TO HISTORY AND BACK

For centuries the trial of Galileo was the stuff of myth: Galileo tortured by the Inquisition; his defiant words after recanting ("e pur si muove," "but it does move"); the infallible Church proclaiming the dogma that the Sun goes round the Earth. None of these details is true, but that did not seem to matter much to those who exalted Galileo as a martyr to truth.

Fortunately, the twentieth century saw a movement away from such polemical accounts. Anticlerical prejudice is still evident in Giorgio de Santillana's *The Crime of Galileo* (1955). However, through the work of such scholars as Alexandre Koyré, Stillman Drake, Jerome Langford, and Richard Blackwell, a more accurate understanding of the case began to emerge and take hold. Langford's *Galileo, Science, and the Church* (1966) is still the best introduction to the subject, especially in explaining the scientific and theological issues, and its main conclusions have held up well.

The new book by William R. Shea and Mariano Artigas, *Galileo in Rome*, represents the finest in modern Galileo scholarship. Shea holds the "Galileo Chair" of the History of Science at the University of Padua, where Galileo was once professor of mathematics. Artigas, a Catholic priest with doctorates in physics and philosophy, is professor of the philosophy of science at the University of Navarra. Their book tells the story of the great founder of modern science from the viewpoint of his six visits to Rome, the first as a 23-year-old job seeker, the last as an old and fearful man summoned to appear before the Inquisition. Shea and Artigas offer no strikingly new theories, but that is to their credit. Their aim rather is to let us walk in the footsteps of Galileo and see afresh and in vivid context the events of his rise and fall.

Galileo became a celebrity in 1610 when he turned his telescope to the heavens and made a series of remarkable discoveries. These were quickly confirmed by the leading astronomers of the day, including the Jesuits of the Roman College. Galileo's most critical telescopic discovery was that Venus had phases like the Moon. These phases revealed that Venus and Earth were sometimes on opposite sides of the Sun, a configuration impossible in the Ptolemaic theory.

While proving Ptolemy wrong, these discoveries did not prove Copernicus completely right, for there existed a compromise idea due to Tycho Brahe. Tycho's theory agreed with Copernicus as far as the *relative* movements of the celestial bodies were concerned, but assumed, like Ptolemy, that the Earth was at rest. The Jesuit astronomers embraced Tycho's theory because it reproduced all existing observations just as well as Copernicus, while not raising sticky scriptural issues.

Galileo, on the other hand, was convinced of the full truth of Copernicanism, and became increasingly outspoken for it. When accused of contradicting Scripture, he penned the famous *Letter to Castelli,* in which he argued that Scripture in describing nature spoke according to appearances, not literally. It was this exegetical foray that spurred the Holy Office into action. While many factors were involved in the opposition to Galileo, not least an entrenched Aristotelianism, it is clear that the critical issue for Cardinal Bellarmine and the Roman Inquisition, which he headed[1], was the interpretation of Scripture.

Bellarmine laid out his views with great lucidity in a letter to Paolo Foscarini, a friend of Galileo. The Council of Trent, he noted, prohibited interpreting Scripture in matters of faith and morals contrary to the Fathers. While the motions of the Sun and Earth are not of the *substance* of the faith, he admitted, they are matters of faith incidentally, since Scripture makes assertions about them. Therefore the strictures of Trent apply, and one must follow the Fathers, who understood the relevant passages literally.

Logically speaking, Galileo's position was not inconsistent with Trent: if astronomical matters do *not* pertain to the faith, then the Father's interpretations do not necessarily have to be followed, according to Trent. And if the Fathers' naïve literalism on these matters is *not* followed, there is simply no reason to assume they pertain to the faith. However, the Holy Office failed to see this. On February 26, 1616, Galileo was secretly enjoined[2] from defending "in any way" the motion of the Earth or immobility of the Sun. Eight days later, the Congregation of the Index prohibited books that maintained the truth of Copernicanism.

Bellarmine was reasonably well informed about astronomy. He knew that heliocentrism had advantages *as a calculational method* for predicting the appearances of the heavens, but he sharply distinguished this from the claim that the Earth actually moved. He conceded to the latter only a bare possibility. "If there were a true demonstration [that the Earth is moving]," he wrote to Foscarini, "it would be necessary to proceed with great caution in explaining the passages of Scripture which seemed contrary, and we would have to say that we did not understand them rather than declare something false which had been demonstrated to be true." However, he had "grave doubts" that such a demonstration was possible, and "in a case of doubt, one may not depart from the holy Fathers."

Galileo had a friend, admirer, and protector in Maffeo Cardinal Barberini; and when Barberini ascended the papal throne as Urban VIII in 1624, Galileo saw a chance to rehabilitate Copernicanism. Galileo had developed a brilliant theory of the tides, which he believed was the needed "demonstration" of the Earth's motion. Urban, unaware of the secret injunction that bound Galileo (Bellarmine had since died), encouraged him to write, thinking that Galileo would discuss Copernicanism "hypothetically" rather than maintaining its truth. Galileo, badly misjudging the situation, published his great *Dialog on the Two Chief World Systems*, in which he not only vigorously argued for Copernicanism, but also lampooned one of Urban's own pet arguments. (Urban's argument was that no matter how well a theory explains effects, one cannot know that the theory is true, since an omnipotent God has the power to produce the effects in some other way. Taken to the limit, of course, this line of reasoning would strike at the root of all empirical knowledge.) Urban, thinking himself betrayed and held up to public ridicule by a man he had protected, was enraged. The long-forgotten injunction against Galileo was discovered at this point in the files of the Inquisition. Galileo was forced to abjure and sentenced to house arrest for life. He lived in reasonable comfort[3], was allowed to receive visitors, and continued to publish on scientific matters until his death.[4]

It is one of the great ironies of scientific history that Galileo's proofs of the Earth's motion were invalid, and his theory of the tides mistaken. Many of the issues involved in the question of the Earth's motion could not be resolved without the theoretical breakthroughs of Newton, who was born the year Galileo died. The first real observational evidence that the Earth moved did not come until 1728, when the phenomenon of aberration of light was seen.[5]

Wade Rowland, author of another new book on the Galileo case, holds a chair of Ethics in Communications at Ryerson University in Toronto. He is not a historian, philosopher, theologian, or scientist, at least to judge from the rather gross errors he makes in all those fields. It is remarkable that one so ill equipped should undertake a reinterpretation of so complex an episode in history. What is most remarkable about the book, however, is its thesis, which is essentially that Galileo had it coming.

It required decades of patient scholarship to advance from Galileo myth to Galileo history, but in one long stride Wade Rowland takes us back again. The new myth that he proposes is just the old one turned on its head. He accepts the discredited notion that the Catholic Church was hostile to scientific truth; however, rather than blaming the Church for this he praises her, for he is pretty hostile to scientific truth himself.

In Rowland's view, science has not made life happier or better; it has merely turned men into materialists and consumers. While it has cured diseases and produced abundance, it has also created pollution and nuclear weapons. The knowledge it gives does not make men wiser, but probably more foolish. Its arrogant reductionism seeks to abolish all meaning, purpose, and transcendence from the world. Of course, one can answer such complaints by distinguishing truth from the uses to which it is put. However, what Rowland objects to in science most of all is precisely its claim to tell us the truth about the physical world:

> Here in concise form is . . . "Galileo's mistake." . . . It is simply not correct to assert, as Galileo did, that there is a single and unique explanation to natural phenomena, which may be understood through observation and reason, and which makes all other explanations wrong.

Of course, a sane man would not say that because one explanation of a thing is correct all other explanations are wrong. He would say, however, that all *contrary* explanations are wrong. And that is certainly what Bellarmine, Urban, and Galileo all said. They all agreed that, since Scripture is right, anything contrary to it must be wrong, just as they agreed that anything contrary to what has been demonstrated by reason and observation must be wrong. When it came to the Earth's motion, they all believed that there was a fact of the matter, they just disagreed on what it was.

Rowland, however, employs all the standard postmodernist stratagems to attack the notions of scientific truth and fact. "All scientific knowledge," he says, "is culturally conditioned. None of its laws or facts [is], strictly speaking, objective." Science is "rooted in consensus" and "socially constructed." "Scientists do not discover laws of nature, they invent them." Indeed, "reason is a human invention, . . . a process that takes place according to rules of logic that we make up . . ."

Experiments cannot provide objective verification of theories, he claims, because experiments are interpreted using those same theories. "[T]heory and experiment are inextricably tied up together in a kind of recursive loop." Science's "basic method is in this way circular . . ." The subjectivity of science explains "why, from time to time, there are 'revolutions' in science that overthrow one complete set of assumptions in favor of another." Physics does not give us truth about the world, but only yields mathematical "models" that more or less "work" or are "useful."

Is there anything to this critique? Very little. It is true that scientific knowledge is "socially constructed" in the sense that it is acquired through the cooperative efforts of a community of scholars, but this in no way implies that the reality thus known is *constituted* by those efforts. (Some reality, of course, is socially constructed in the postmodernist's sense, namely *social* reality, or aspects of it.) And science does, of course, depend a great deal on consensus, but it is the apprehension of truth that brings about such consensus (if scientists are objective), not consensus that makes things true.

The widely discussed dependence of experiment upon theory does lead to a kind of circularity, but only the harmless kind that was involved in, say, the making of maps. Maps were made by explorers; and explorers had to rely on existing maps. That circularity obviously did not prevent better and better maps from being made. Nor does it prevent better and better theories of the physical world.

The "revolutions" that occur in science hardly ever involve the overthrow of a "complete set of assumptions" as Rowland asserts. To use his example, Newtonian mechanics was *not* entirely overthrown by relativity; it is, indeed, the one and only correct limit of relativity theory when velocities are small. Moreover, most of the fundamental insights and concepts of Newtonian physics remain valid in relativity theory, including Newton's three laws of motion. What Einstein did was supply crucial insights about the structure of space-time that were missing from the Newtonian picture. Newtonian physics was not annulled, but sublated in a higher viewpoint. So it is with almost every great scientific advance.

All the postmodern tomfoolery in which Rowland indulges has nothing to do with the Galileo case. All the principals in that case believed in "the natural light of human reason." It is true that Galileo's contemporaries failed to appreciate what the physicist Eugene Wigner famously called "the unreasonable effectiveness of mathematics" in understanding the physical world. With few exceptions, they did tend to think of mathematical theories in merely instrumental terms, as convenient calculational tools that worked but could not be of much help in getting at the essence of things. However, theirs was an excusable ignorance; they lived before Newton.

Galileo made mistakes, both political and scientific, but the fact remains that he was the one forced to abjure the truth. Why did the Church authorities rush to judgment? Ironically, it was from a desire to be cautious. They observed all around them the dreadful consequences to which novel interpretations of Scripture could lead: Christendom lay shattered, the Thirty Years War raged. Their mistake was in thinking it cautious to condemn, when true caution in the case of Galileo lay in forbearance. They were blindsided by the Scientific Revolution, but at least, unlike the postmodernists, they were not willfully blind.

26

CRACKPOTS AND THE EINSTEIN MYTH

I got an e-mail Monday from a friend who is a philosophy professor asking what I thought of the new "theory of everything" ("TOE") developed by one Garrett Lisi, who apparently is being talked up on the Internet and in some newspapers as a "new Einstein." Lisi does not have a job at a university or research lab (although he obtained a Ph.D. in physics from UC San Diego in 1999), and is portrayed in some accounts as a "surfer dude" who does physics in his spare time.

My friend's e-mail caused me a momentary twinge of embarrassment, as I had never even heard of Lisi or his theory. I did a quick search and found the paper that was causing all the ruckus. It is called "A Surprisingly Simple Theory of Everything." My own impression (based on a cursory reading) was that the paper does not propose a consistent theory of *anything*, let alone everything. Investigating further, I found that people who have looked more closely at the paper than I am inclined to do have come to the same conclusion. The physicist and indefatigable physics blogger Luboš Motl goes so far as to use the word *crackpot* to describe this work.

Anyone who works in cosmology or particle physics—fields where sexy things like quarks, grand unified theories, and expanding universes are discussed—will, over the course of his career, get approached by people claiming to have revolutionary new theories. Some of them are merely Walter Mitty types, whose dreams of scientific glory are undisturbed by any real knowledge of the nitty-gritty realities of science or research. Others are probably nuts in some clinically recognized sense. One always wonders, when visited by such people, whether they will become violent if one is too honest with them. Recently, a rather hulking fellow in a leather jacket came to my office to explain his "unified field theory" to me. He began by asking politely if I would mind if he closed the door of my office behind him. I replied, "I'd rather the door remained open, actually" (adding to myself, "so they'll be able to hear my screams"). Between the crazies and the dreamers lies a broad spectrum of crackpots. I don't know whether there is a technical term in psychiatry for crackpots, or whether psychologists even study the phenomenon of crackpottery; but if they don't they should, because it is real and not at all rare.

Some of these crackpots are amusing characters. When I was at the University of Washington in the early 1980s, a fellow who styled himself Rheo H. Star came breezing into the Physics Department claiming to have a theory that explained everything from the interactions of quarks to the propulsion systems of flying saucers. He had a gift for impressive terminology. One of his equations he called the "Tri-gon Tensor Equation." And he had invented a device (it looked like an electric chair) called the "psycho-dynamometer." I sure hope he never used it on anyone. Over the years, I suppose I have talked to or been sent material by dozens of would-be scientific revolutionaries. Much of the blame for this kind of thing lies with the Einstein myth. We have all heard that Einstein flunked math in school. We have all heard that Einstein was a nobody, an outsider working alone in a patent office, who was able by the force of his untutored genius to sweep away all that went before. All nonsense, of course. Einstein did very well in subjects like math and physics in school. (He did poorly in French, though, because he hated it and didn't study.) Einstein obtained a doctorate in physics. He had a profound and detailed knowledge of the cutting-edge physics of his day. His theory of relativity did not sweep away all that went before, but was an entirely logical outgrowth of earlier physics.

It is not just the crackpots who are victims of the Einstein myth. Some graduate students suffer from Einstein complexes too. They don't want to work on anything that does not have the possibility of radically revising our view of the universe. Anything less than that is too pedestrian. Not for them the patient step-by-step progress of science. That was not Einstein's attitude. One of his most important contributions—the one for which he won the Nobel Prize, in fact—came from thinking carefully about a rather dry, technical, and mundane-seeming phenomenon called the photo-electric effect.

The Einstein myth is part of the larger Romantic myth of the genius as rebel: Beethoven shaking his fist at the heavens. Nothing is great unless it's "transgressive." Fortunately, science is not much affected by this idiocy. Partly, this is because experimental data serves as a reality principle. Partly it is because science is so technical that the b.s. artist is simply weeded out when he proves unable to acquire the necessary technical skills. It seems that the humanities are not in so fortunate a condition.

In the final analysis it is the experts who must police things. Generally, in the natural sciences this works. The kooks are kept out and largely ignored. Of course the kooks bitterly complain that "the establishment" is out to get them, as it was out to get all the other great rebel-geniuses they imagine scientific history to be full of. The problem in so many other fields is that not a few of the experts give every appearance of being kooks themselves. Architectural experts destroy beautiful old Catholic churches. Liturgical experts give us liturgies that are painful and embarrassing ordeals. Literary theorists write impenetrable prose. Psychologists give us twinky defenses. The question arises: When is one to trust the experts and when is one to trust one's own instincts? It may be the central problem of our times.

My own guiding principle is to trust the experts (generally speaking) on anything purely technical, but to rely more on my own judgment as far as human realities go. I trust the architect on what will keep the building up, but not on what is beautiful. I trust the pediatrician, but not always the child psychologist. When we had our first child, my wife read a number of books on how to raise one's kids. I never wanted to hear what they had to say, much to her annoyance. She noted that they had degrees in the subject and I didn't. My own feeling was that if it took a degree to raise a child properly, the human race would have died out 100,000 years ago. I'd rather trust my parents' advice and example and my own instincts in such matters than some egghead of dubious sanity.

But physics is a technical field, and so if you want to know whether a theory of physics makes any sense, it is a pretty safe bet to trust the professional physics community. Trust me on that; I am an expert.

NOTES AND SOURCES

Ch. 1 is the 2002 Erasmus Lecture of the Institute for Religion and Public Life, delivered at the Union League Club, New York City, November 15, 2002, and published in *First Things*, March 2003.

1. For a thorough and rigorous analysis of statements by Catholic theologians and Church authorities up through the early part of the twentieth century and their bearing on biological evolution, see Ernest C. Messenger, *Evolution and Theology: The Problem of Man's Origin* (New York, Macmillan, 1932). See also the article "Catholics and Evolution" (written by E. Wasmann) in *The Catholic Encyclopedia* (New York: Robert Appleton Company, 1909).
2. Encyclical letter *Humani generis*, Pope Pius XII, 1950.
3. One finds this concept, for example, in the *Summa Theologiae* of St. Thomas Aquinas: "God's act of intellect is His substance." (*Summa Theologiae*, Part I, Question 14, Article 4).
4. Pope St. John Paul II used this expression many times, but it was used first by the Second Vatican Council, *Gaudium et spes* (par. 22).
5. The term "Weak Anthropic Principle" is used here to refer to what is now more commonly referred to as the "multiverse hypothesis."
6. Of course, Brighton is not in South Wales. The mixing of geographical metaphors is due to Chesterton himself.

Ch. 2 is a review of *The Evolution Controversy: A Survey of Competing The-*

ories by Thomas B. Fowler and Daniel Kuebler, published in *Modern Age*, Winter 2009.

1. While the ID movement has never taken an official position against common descent, most of its leading theorists do not believe in common descent, a fact that I was not aware of when I wrote this book review.
2. A simpler explanation is the fact that most of the "ID theorists" actually do not believe in common descent.
3. William Dembski, in particular, claims that there are "no-go theorems" (having to do with what he calls "conservation of information") that demonstrate this.

Ch. 3 is a review of *A Devil's Chaplain: Reflections on Hope, Lies, Science, and Love* by Richard Dawkins, *First Things*, August/September 2004, altered slightly.

1. Richard Dawkins, *A Devil's Chaplain: Reflections on Hope, Lies, Science, and Love*, 46.
2. Dawkins, *A Devil's Chaplain*, 84.
3. Dawkins, *A Devil's Chaplain*, 39.
4. Dawkins, *A Devil's Chaplain*, 18.
5. Richard Dawkins, *Unweaving the Rainbow: Science, Delusion, and the Appetite for Wonder* (New York: Houghton Mifflin, 1998), 53.
6. As argued elsewhere in this volume, Darwinism in itself is simply a biological idea (the evolution of species by natural selection) that is theologically harmless. But Dawkins and many others read into Darwinism sweeping philosophical implications, which include a thoroughgoing materialism and crude reductionism. Their view would be better called "hyper-Darwinism."
7. One can certainly have a coherent account of objective morality that is in some sense naturalistic and does not posit the existence of a creator God. Aristotle's moral philosophy is an example. However, it is hard to ground objective morality without positing the existence of objective ends, purposes, duties, or values. For materialists such as Dawkins, however, one of the main lessons of evolution is that there are no such things.
8. This was not mere hyperbole, but based on the following calculation. Modern scholarship, following the work of Henry Kamen, estimates

the total number of people executed by the Spanish Inquisition to be roughly of the order of 10,000, the vast majority being in the first century of its existence. That is about 1,000 executions *per decade* in its most active period. Stalin ruled for 30 years. Estimates of the number killed under his rule vary widely between several million to tens of millions. That works out to roughly of order 1,000 *per day*. Estimates for Mao Zedong or Pol Pot would result in even higher rates of killing.

Ch. 4 is a review of *Full House: The Spread of Excellence from Plato to Darwin* by Stephen Jay Gould, published in *Public Interest*, Spring 1997, available online at www.nationalaffairs.com/archive/public_interest/.

Ch. 5 was published in *First Things*, October 2005.

1. It was actually not a letter, but an address delivered in person by the pope.
2. The word "immediately" here does not mean "right away" or "suddenly." It means "directly" rather than through some intermediate means, such as a natural process.
3. Ryland's views have evolved since this article was written.
4. On the other hand, Dembski has often seemed to argue that the question is in effect already settled. For example, he has written of "no go theorems" (which involve what he calls "conservation of information") that make it impossible for evolution to produce all of the complexity seen in living things.

Ch. 6 was published in *First Things*, November 2012.

1. Though St. Augustine was born in 354 AD, the quotation comes from his *City of God*, which was composed in the early fifth century.
2. The so-called Cosmic Background Radiation tells us directly about conditions at the time that this radiation "last scattered" from ordinary matter, which is called the "recombination" time. The present best estimates place this as about 380,000 years after the Big Bang.
3. Only 33 of the 38 Nobel prizes were for science (physics, chemistry, and medicine). Four were for peace and one for economics.

Ch. 7 is a review of *Darwin's Black Box: The Biochemical Challenge to Evolu-

tion by Michael J. Behe published in *The Public Interest*, Winter 1997, available online at www.nationalaffairs.com/archive/public_interest/.

1. Behe is a biochemist, not a molecular biologist. The fields overlap.
2. This may have been true when this review was written, but is no longer so.

Ch. 8 was published in "On the Square," the blog of *First Things*, February 9, 2010.

1. What I had in mind here was the fact that many scientists portrayed the ID movement as simply "Creation Science" (a pseudo-science based on Young Earth Creationism) dressed up with more sophisticated arguments. That certainly is unfair, since the main "ID theorists," William Dembski, Michael Behe, and Stephen Meyer, are not Young Earth Creationists. On the other hand, a large proportion of the grassroots supporters of the ID movement are Young Earth Creationists, as became clear in the famous 2005 trial *Kitzmiller v. Dover Area School District*.
2. While it is true that the ID movement has no official position on common descent, several of the leaders of the movement do not believe in it (Michael Behe being a notable exception).

Ch. 9 was published in *Commonweal*, November 20, 2009.

Ch. 10 is an invited essay for *Big Questions Online*, July 10, 2012, sponsored by The John Templeton Foundation, and selected by *Arts and Letters Daily*.

1. A more thorough discussion can be found in Stephen M. Barr, *Modern Physics and Ancient Faith* (South Bend IN: University of Notre Dame Press, 2003), chs. 24-25.

Ch. 11 was published in *First Things*, March 2007, and reprinted in *The Best American Spiritual Writing 2008*, ed. Philip Zaleski (New York: Houghton Mifflin Harcourt Publishing Co., 2008).

1. Planck did a calculation that involved the assumption that the energy in the oscillators that emit light (namely, atoms and molecules)

comes in discrete units, i.e., is quantized. However, he did not think of light itself as made up of particles. That step was taken by Einstein.

2. It is questionable whether the Bohmian idea can reproduce all the successes of "relativistic quantum field theory." This would be a fatal difficulty, because relativistic quantum field provides a fantastically accurate description of a vast range of phenomena all the way down to distances of about a thousandth the size of an atomic nucleus. However, recent progress has been made in constructing Bohmian relativistic field theories.

3. I somewhat mischaracterized Hodgson's view here. He was not an advocate of Bohmian mechanics specifically, though he did think that both the Copenhagen interpretation and the Many Worlds interpretation were wrong and that the correct approach would turn out to be one that restored the philosophical "realism" of classical physics, even at the price of restoring determinism.

Ch. 12 is a review of *The Conscious Mind: In Search of a Fundamental Theory* by David Chalmers published in *First Things*, November 1997.

1. This is too sweeping a statement.

2. In ordinary speech we tend to distinguish thought and behavior, the former being internal and the latter external. But Chalmers is using a technical philosophical language, according to which even things that we "do" internally, such as willing, understanding, and believing, are "behavior." Moreover, in this terminology such mental activities do not necessarily presuppose consciousness, so that even a completely unconscious machine could be said to have "beliefs." For example, a chess-playing program might be said to "believe" that its king is in check or that its position is superior.

3. In the traditional Christian view, the "spiritual" pertains to rationality and freedom, which human beings possess, but subhuman animals lack.

Ch. 13 is a review of *Mind and Cosmos: Why the Materialist Neo-Darwinian Conception of Nature Is Almost Certainly False* by Thomas Nagel published in *Commonweal*, May 17, 2013.

Ch. 14 is a review of *Neuroscience, Psychology and Religion: Illusions, Delu-*

sions, and Realities about Human Nature by Malcolm Jeeves and Warren S. Brown published in *First Things*, January 2010.

Ch. 15 is a review of *What Remains to Be Discovered: Mapping the Secrets of the Universe, the Origins of Life, and the Future of the Human Race* by John Maddox published in *First Things*, April 1999.

1. An exception is dark matter, which is now known to make up about a quarter of the mass in the observable universe. One can also cite such phenomena as neutrino mass and baryogenesis as requiring non-Standard Model physics.

Ch. 16 is a lecture given at the first "Atom and Eve" conference, sponsored by The John Templeton Foundation, Washington Theological Union, November 12, 2011.

Ch. 17 is a lecture given at Conference on Science and Faith, Franciscan University of Steubenville, December 2, 2011.

1. One school of thought allowed by the Church says that a person's body in the next life will be the "same" as the one he has in this life, not because it has the same physical composition, but because it is animated by and appropriate to the same spiritual soul. In any event, the question of what makes the body the "same one" has never been settled by a definitive judgment of the magisterium of the Catholic Church.
2. The "evangelical Protestant gentleman" was Charles W. Colson.

Ch. 18 was written for "On the Square," the blog of *First Things*, September 10, 2010.

1. By "system of universes" I am not referring to the "multiverse" idea. There are various versions of the multiverse idea. Some of them are based on universes coming into and passing out of existence as discussed here. Others involve the "Many Worlds Interpretation" of quantum mechanics. But the multiverse scenarios most often considered by physicists are those in which the different "sub-universes" within the multiverse are just widely separated regions within a single very large universe.

Ch. 19 was published in *First Things*, October 2010, and reprinted in *The Best Spiritual Writing* 2012, ed. Philip Zaleski (New York: Penguin Group USA, 2011).

Ch. 20 was published in *First Things*, November 2000.

Ch. 21 is a review of *The Creation: A Meeting of Science and Religion* by Edward O. Wilson published in *First Things*, October 2006.

Ch. 22 is a review of *Unweaving the Rainbow: Science, Delusion, and the Appetite for Wonder* by Richard Dawkins published in *First Things*, August/September 1999.

Ch. 23 is a review of *God the Evidence: The Reconciliation of Faith and Reason in a Postsecular World* by Patrick Glynn and *The Science of God: The Convergence of Scientific and Biblical Wisdom* by Gerald L. Schroeder published in the *National Review*, January 26, 1998, © 1988 by National Review, Inc. Reprinted by permission.

1. On the other hand, many interesting and plausible ideas have been proposed for prebiotic evolution, including the "RNA world" hypothesis, and the idea that life may have begun near thermal vents in the ocean. Moreover, there is evidence that the first life on earth made its appearance quite quickly (within about 100 million years) after the planet became habitable, which suggests that the beginning of life may not be as improbable or difficult as one might have supposed.
2. To be more blunt than I wished to be when I wrote this review, Schroeder's use of the time dilation effect of relativity is completely nonsensical.

Ch. 24 is a review of *The Language of God: A Scientist Presents Evidence for Belief* by Francis S. Collins published in *First Things*, December 2006.

Ch. 25 is a review of *Galileo in Rome, The Rise and Fall of a Troublesome Genius* by William R. Shea and Mariano Artigas and *Galileo's Mistake: A New Look at the Epic Confrontation between Galileo and the Church* by Wade Rowland published in *First Things*, January 2004.

1. This is misleadingly phrased. Robert Bellarmine was a Cardinal Inquisitor and also the pope's chief advisor on matters of doctrine. He took the leading role in the Roman Inquisition's dealings with Galileo in 1616.

2. It is still debated by scholars whether this injunction, an unsigned copy of which survived in the files of the Roman Inquisition, was ever actually served on Galileo, or whether he was given a weaker command that still allowed him to discuss the Copernican theory as a mere "hypothesis."

3. Galileo was permitted to serve his house arrest at his villa in Arcetri, near Florence.

4. Galileo was forbidden to write about Copernicanism, but was allowed to publish on any other scientific questions, and it was during his last years, while under house arrest, that he published his great work on motion and the law of falling bodies, which was to physics what Copernicus's book was to astronomy.

5. In observations that began in 1725 and continued for several years, James Bradley established the phenomenon of the aberration of light and developed the correct theory of it in 1728, which he reported to the Royal Society in 1729.

Ch. 26 is an entry written for "Firstthoughts," a blog of *First Things*, March 5, 2008.

DIRECT QUOTATIONS

(Not included here are quotations taken from the books under review.)

Aquinas, Thomas, Saint

— on contingency: *Summa theologiae*, I, 22,4 ad 1

Arrhenius, Svante, quoted in "The Proofs for the Existence of God in the Light of Modern Natural Science" (Address of Pope Pius XII to the Pontifical Academy of Sciences, November 22, 1951), par. 47. (http://www .papalencyclicals.net/Pius12/P12EXIST.HTM)

Augustine, Saint

— *credo ut intelligam*: This was a maxim of St. Anselm of Canterbury, based on St. Augustine's saying *"crede ut intelligas"* (believe so that you may understand), *Tract. Ev. Jo.*, 29.6.

— on the nature of time: St. Augustine, *Confessions*, tr. John K. Ryan (New York: Doubleday and Co., Inc., 1960), bk. 11, chs. 13, 30.

— on the past as "present memory": St. Augustine, *Confessions*, tr. John K. Ryan, (New York: Doubleday and Co., Inc., 1960), bk. 11, ch 20.

Benedict XVI, Pope (Joseph Ratzinger)

— on the platonic element in modern physics: "Faith, Reason and the University: Memories and Reflections," Lecture of Pope Benedict XVI at the University of Regensburg, September 12, 2006. (http://www.vatican .va/holy_father/benedict_xvi/speeches/2006/september/documents/ hf_ben-xvi_spe_20060912_university-regensburg_en.html)

— on resurrection of the body: Joseph Ratzinger, *Introduction to Christianity*, tr. J. R. Foster (New York: Herder and Herder, 1970), 277.

Bohr, Niels

— on consciousness of machines: quoted by John A. Wheeler in "Not consciousness but the distinction between the probe and the probed as central to the elemental quantum act of observation," in *The Role of Consciousness in the Physical World*, ed. R. G. Jahn (Boulder, CO: Westview Press, 1981), 94.

— on quantum mechanics boggling the mind: Bohr is widely quoted as making the following statement or some variant of it: "Anyone who is not shocked by quantum theory has not understood a single word."

Botvinnik, Mikhail, quoted in Garry Kasparov, *On My Great Predecessors*, Vol. 1 (New York: Everyman, 2003), 339.

Cabanis, Pierre, quoted in Frederick Copleston, *The History of Philosophy* (Garden City, NJ: Doubleday, Image Books, 1963), vol. 4, p. 50.

Calvin, John, *Institutes of the Christian Religion* (Presbyterian Board of Publications, 1928), bk. I, ch. VIII.

Catechism of the Catholic Church

— on the spiritual soul: *Catechism of the Catholic Church*, sec. 33.

Catholic Encyclopedia

— on evolution: "Catholics and Evolution" in *Catholic Encyclopedia* (Robert Appleton Company, 1909).

— on hell: "Hell" in *Catholic Encyclopedia* (Robert Appleton Company, 1910).

Chesterton, Gilbert K.

— on observation and deduction: *Orthodoxy* (New York: Doubleday, 1959), 33.

Clement of Rome, "The First Epistle of Clement to the Corinthians," in *Early Christian Writings: The Apostolic Fathers*, tr. Maxwell Staniforth (New York: Penguin, 1968), 33-34.

Collins, Francis S., *The Language of God: A Scientist Presents Evidence of Belief* (New York: Free Press, 2006), 205.

Colson, Charles W., Letter to the editor, *First Things*, May 2007.

Communion and Stewardship: Human Persons Created in the Image of God, par. 69. (http://www.vatican.va/roman_curia/congregations/cfaith/cti_documents/rc_con_cfaith_doc_20040723_communion-stewardship_en.html)

Crick, Francis

— on free will: quoted in John Horgan, *The Undiscovered Mind: How the Human Brain Defies Replication, Understanding, and Medication* (New York: Touchstone, 1999), 247.

— on man as "a pack of neurons": Francis Crick, *The Astonishing Hypothesis: The Scientific Search for the Soul* (New York: Charles Scribner's Sons, 1994), 3.

Dawkins, Richard

— on being "a fulfilled atheist": Richard Dawkins, *The Blind Watchmaker, Why the Evidence of Evolution Reveals a Universe without Design* (New York: W. W. Norton, 1996), 6.

— on belief in the supernatural: "The Problem with God: Interview with Richard Dawkins," interview by Laura Sheahen.

Democritus, quoted in Frederick Copleston, *A History of Philosophy* (New York: Doubleday, 1963), 1, I, 144-47.

Dirac, Paul Adrian Maurice

— on "beauty in one's equations": P. A. M. Dirac, "The Evolution of the Physicist's Picture of Nature," *Scientific American* 208 (5) (1963).

— on "pretty" mathematics: quoted in Abraham Pais, *Inward Bound: Of Matter and Forces in the Physics World* (Oxford: Oxford University Press, 1986), 290-91.

Disraeli, Benjamin, *Coningsby, or The New Generation*, bk.IV, ch.xiii, The

Works of Benjamin Disraeli, the Earl of Beaconsfield (New York: AMS Press, 1976), vol. 13, p. 319.

Elitzur, Avshalom, "Consciousness and the Incompleteness of the Physical Explanation of Behavior," *The Journal of Mind and Behavior*, vol. 10 (1989): 1-20.

Felix, Menucius, "Octavius" 18, 4, in *The Faith of the Early Fathers*, tr. William A. Jurgens (Collegeville, MN.: Liturgical Press, 1970) vol. I, 109.

Feynman, Richard P.

— on mysteriousness of quantum mechanics: Richard P. Feynman, Robert B. Leighton, and Alan Sands, *The Feynman Lectures on Physics* (Addison-Wesley, 1964), vol. I, ch. 37, 1-2.

Giorelli, Giulio, quoted in Daniel Dennett, *Freedom Evolves* (New York: Viking, 2003), 1.

Gould, Steven Jay

— on dethronement of man: Stephen Jay Gould, *Full House, The Spread of Excellence from Plato to Darwin* (New York: Harmony Books, 1996), 17.

Haldane, J. B. S., *The Inequality of Man* (London: Chatto and Windus, 1932).

Hawking, Stephen

— on "fire" in the equations: Stephen Hawking, *A Brief History of Time: From the Big Bang to Black Holes* (London: Bantam, 1988), 174.

— on God as "blue touch paper": Stephen Hawking and Leonard Mlodinow, *The Grand Design* (New York: Random House, Inc., 2010), 180.

Heisenberg, Werner

— on beauty: Werner Heisenberg, "The Meaning of Beauty in the Exact Sciences" in *Across the Frontiers* (New York: Harper and Row Publishers, Inc., 1974), 183.

Irenaeus of Lyons, Saint, *Adversus Haeresis*, 4,4,3.

Jeans, Sir James

— on "waves" of knowledge: Sir James Jeans, *Physics and Philosophy* (New York: MacMillan, 1943), 136-39.

— on universe as a "great thought": Sir James Jeans, *The Mysterious Universe* (London: Penguin Books, 1937), 137.

John Paul II, Pope, Message to the Pontifical Academy of Sciences on Evolution, delivered on October 22, 1996. (https://www.ewtn.com/library/PAPALDOC/JP961022.HTM)

Kepler, Johannes, quoted in Werner Heisenberg, "The Meaning of Beauty in the Exact Sciences" in *Across the Frontiers* (New York: Harper and Row Publishers, Inc., 1974), 173.

Knox, Ronald A., *The Hidden Stream* (Garden City, New York: Doubleday, Image Books, 1964), 145.

Laplace, Pierre Simon Marquis de

— on determinism: Pierre Laplace, *A Philosophical Essay on Probabilities* (New York: Dover, 1951), 4-5.

— on God "hypothesis": quoted in James R. Newman, "Laplace," in *Lives in Science, a Scientific American Book* (New York: Simon and Schuster, 1957), 51.

Lasker, Emanuel, quoted in Garry Kasparov, *On My Great Predecessors*, Vol. 1 (New York: Everyman, 2003), 275.

Lonergan, Bernard J. F., *Insight: A Study in Human Understanding* (New York: The Philosophical Press, 1967), 639-77.

Lucas, John R., "Minds, Machines and Gödel," in *The Modeling of Mind*, ed. K. M. Sayre and F. J. Crossen (Notre Dame Ind.: University of Notre Dame Press, 1963), 255.

Macaulay, Thomas Babington, Lord, *Critical and Historical Essays* (London: Longman, Green and Co., 1898), 2:280.

Mayr, Ernst, quoted in Alvin Plantinga, *Where the Conflict Really Lies: Science, Religion and Naturalism* (Oxford: Oxford University Press, 2011), 11.

Minsky, Marvin. Minsky's statement about human beings being "machines made of meat" is widely quoted.

National Academy of Sciences, statement on religion and evolution. /http://www.nas.edu/evolution/Compatibility.html

Nernst, Walther, quoted in Robert Jastrow, *God and the Astronomers* (New York: Norton, 1992), 104.

Newton, Sir Isaac, *The Mathematical Principles of Natural Philosophy*, tr. Andrew Motte (New York: Daniel Adee, 1848), 507.

Pagels, Heinz R., *The Cosmic Code: Quantum Mechanics as the Language of Nature* (New York: Simon & Schuster, 1982), 160.

Pascal, Blaise, *Pensées*, no. 162, tr. W. F. Trotter (New York: E.P Dutton & Co., Inc., 1958), 48.

Pauli, Wolfgang, quoted in Werner Heisenberg, "Science and Religion" in *Physics and Beyond: Encounters and Conversations* (New York: Harper and Row Publishers, Inc., 1971), 85-7.

Peierls, Rudolf

— on consciousness: quoted in P. C. W. Davies and J. R. Brown, *The Ghost and the Atom* (Cambridge: Cambridge University Press, 1986), 75.

Putnam, Hilary, in *Minds and Machines*, ed. A. R. Anderson (Englewood, NJ: Prentice-Hall, 1964), 97.

Rabbinical commentary on creation, Genesis Rabbah Parashiyyot I.I.2, quoted in Jacob Neusner, *Confronting Creation: How Judaism Reads Genesis: An Anthology of Genesis Rabbah* (Columbia, SC: University of South Carolina Press, 1991), 15, 26.

Rey, Georges, *Contemporary Philosophy of Mind* (Oxford: Blackwell, 1997), 21.

Russell, Bertrand, *Religion and Science* (Oxford: Oxford University Press, 1961), 222.

Schrödinger, Erwin, *Mind and Matter* (Cambridge: Cambridge University Press, 1958), 103.

Sober, Elliott, quoted in Alvin Plantinga, *Where the Conflict Really Lies: Science, Religion and Naturalism* (Oxford: Oxford University Press, 2011), 11-12.

Weinberg, Steven

— on pointlessness of the universe: Steven Weinberg, *The First Three*

Minutes: A Modern View of the Origin of the Universe (Glasgow: William Collins, 1977), 148.

Weyl, Hermann

— on the spiritual element of the human mind: Hermann Weyl, *The Open World: Three Lectures on the Metaphysical Implications of Science* (New Haven, Conn.: Yale University Press, 1932), 31-32.

— on determinism: Weyl, *The Open World*, 28-29.

— on "sublime Reason": Weyl, *The Open World* , 54-55.

Wigner, Eugene P.

— on materialism: Eugene P. Wigner, "Remarks on the Mind-Body Question," in *A Scientist Speculates*, ed. I. J. Good (London: William Heinemann Ltd., 1961), reprinted in Eugene P. Wigner, *Symmetries and Reflections: Scientific Essays* (Woodbridge Conn.: Oxbow Press, 1979), 176.

— on thoughts as not material: Eugene P. Wigner, *Symmetries and Reflections*, 171.

Wilczek, Frank, *The Lightness of Being: Mass, Ether, and the Unification of Forces* (New York: Basic Books, 2008), 136.

Wilson, Edward O., *Consilience: The Unity of Knowledge* (New York: Alfred A. Knopf, 1998), 119.

Witten, Edward, quoted in John Horgan, *The End of Science* (New York: Addison-Wesley, 1996), 69.

Zuker, Charles, quoted in Maggie Fox, "Fly Gene Map May Have Many Uses, Scientists Say," *Reuters*, March 23, 2000.